Carlo Maria Gallimberti
Antonio Marra
Annalisa Prencipe

Consolidation

Preparing and understanding consolidated financial statements under IFRS

Updated to the new IFRS 10 and 11

Preface by Giovanni Andrea Toselli

In Collaboration with: 

McGraw-Hill Education

Milano • New York • Bogotá • Lisbon • London
Madrid • Mexico City • Montreal • New Delhi
Santiago • Seoul • Singapore • Sydney • Toronto

Publisher: Paolo Roncoroni
Acquisition Editor: Daniele Bonanno, Marta Colnago
Production: Donatella Giuliani
Cover graphic: Feel Italia, Milano
Cover image: © agsandrew
Printed and bound by CPI Group (UK) Ltd, Croydon, CR0 4YY

Contents

Preface

Financial Statements are produced by corporations and other economic entities for a variety of reasons. In today's sophisticated capital markets, the financial information provided by entities is one of the most important factors used by investors to build up rational expectations on the risks and returns of each investment opportunity, decide on their current and potential investments, assess the profitability of their invested capital. It is then clear that the quality of the financial information provided and its intelligibility by market participants all over the globe are of vital importance for capital markets to function properly.

Being a competitive and successful player in a globalized world requires complex business models and the use of different legal entities to operate in different countries or to facilitate the management of the different sectors in which a business is engaged. When a business is conducted via a number of different entities, the financial statements at the single-entity level does not give a comprehensive view of the performance of the overall business. In these cases it is more sensible to look at the performance of the economic subject behind the legal entity. In most instances, groups are made up by one parent entity and by various subsidiaries. The parent is the ultimate owner of the underlying business and the subject that coordinates all the activities of the other entities within the group (the subsidiaries). As for any other entity, the financial statements of the parent company only represent the activities of the parent, where the subsidiaries appear in a condensed way among parent's financial investments. The operations and activities of each subsidiary are not reported in the parent-only financial statements and, as a consequence, they do not convey information on the overall performance of the entire group.

In order to provide a more comprehensive set of information, to those interested in understanding the overall group results, it is then necessary to prepare "Consolidated Financial Statements". Consolidated Financial Statements are the instrument that best represents the overall performance of the economic subject depicted as if it were an individual entity, irrespective of the legal boundaries that separate the legal entities within the group. The practical application of this - apparently simple - concept of considering the group as a single entity hides many technical difficulties due to the complexity of the economic reality in which the individual entities carry out their businesses, and the transactions, individually performed with third parties, and with other group entities.

Of crucial relevance are also potential cross country differences which make comparability a key matter for the overall financial reporting quality. The issue of comparability of financial reporting, and transparency of the data available to the international stakeholders has, in fact, become increasingly important and relevant to both the academic discussion and the day-to-day life of financial markets. The potential heterogeneity, often laying on "accounting asymmetries", of information provided by different businesses might hamper investors' ability to assess their options and to best match their risk preferences. Thus, in the continuous attempt of increasing comparability, the search for a common ground in financial reporting has been an important goal on the agenda of several different jurisdictions which have developed various reporting platforms that have been utilized by companies to report their financial information both to comply with local regulations, and to serve the need of financial markets.

In the wake of this pressing need, the two main Standard Setters, responsible for establishing the accounting principles used in the major international financial markets, the USA-based FASB and the IASB (International Accounting Standards Board), whose standards are in use in the 27 countries of the EU, as well as, in many other jurisdictions, reached a common understanding for developing a platform of financial reporting criteria that would be broadly based on the same conceptual models. After several years of side by side work and discussion, FASB and IASB have reached a common, although not identical, ground in setting the principles for the preparation and presentation of Consolidated Financial Statements.

In broad terms the discussions which have taken place at the international level on the conceptual basis of consolidation can be grouped in two main aspects: *(i)* the definition of what needs to be included in the perimeter of the group; and *(ii)* the manner in which the financial information is to be adjusted in order to give a relevant view to the information's users.

The first concept is defined as the "*control principle*" which is the benchmark which defines the relationship between two entities as a parent/subsidiary one, hence leading to the need to group their individual accounts. This is a very sensitive topic since, in the past, a number of financial scandals and frauds have been perpetrated by abusing of certain requirements of the accounting rules excluding entities from a group and leading to a misrepresentation of the business performance. To ensure reliability of financial information it is necessary that the accounting guidance captures, all and only, assets owned and liabilities and risks assumed by the group. With this in mind, both Standard Setters concluded that a clear and precise definition of control was needed. The IASB, in this framework, added over time to the traditional control view various nuances aimed at giving more weight to the factual situation considering the actual ability to exercise the power to govern the financial and operating policies, the enjoyment of economic benefits, and the exposure to risks of an entity.

The second conceptual topic deals with the *relationship between the group and its shareholders* those that, in turn, carry controlling rights as well as those who participate in the investment in the subsidiaries, which are defined Non-Controlling Interests (or NCI). The approach followed by the IASB's literature is the one that suggests that the financial information should be presented as if all current owners are in the same relationship with the entity irrespective of whether they control it or own a minimal portion of one of the subsidiaries thus neutralizing ownership structure impact and, therefore, increasing comparability. In fact, a business owned by a number of investors both in the parent entity and in the subsidiaries would report its performance following the same criteria that it would if it were owned by a single investor. This allows the performance of different businesses to be presented solely on the basis of the transactions with third parties without the influence of transactions with owners.

Based on my professional experience as Technical Partner in PwC, the consolidation area constitutes a significant challenge for practitioners. Consolidation techniques have their "magic and tricks" for accountants and auditors. I welcome then this text book, which, despite its robust theoretical basis, provides a fresh eye to the current practices.

The book aims at providing a guide through the complex mechanism of consolidation by showing how to understand and prepare Consolidated Financial Statements under International Financial Reporting Standards (IFRS), nowadays the most widespread, set of accounting principles, all over the globe.

After a brief overview of IFRS, their environment and relevance this work, on a step by step approach, introduces students and professionals to the meaning of consolidated accounts and it guides them into the consolidation process.

This work has been written bringing together many years of teaching and research in the area, supported by the pragmatic input of the professional experience and, I especially appreciate the fact that it has been updated to the new requirements and relevant changes introduced by IFRS 10 and 11. In their writing authors clearly made an effort to make consolidation more approachable combining theory with illustrative examples and a battery of exercises, with solutions, for self-study practice. The continuous switch from the conceptual and theoretical discussion to practical examples and worked exercises will allow the reader to grasp the basic conceptual pillars of consolidation. Its practical approach makes this book a comprehensive guide precious for those that firstly approach this topic to obtain the necessary initial understating.

Giovanni Andrea Toselli

About the Authors

Carlo Maria Gallimberti is a Ph.D. candidate in Economics and Finance at Bocconi University, with major in Financial Accounting. Certified Public Accountant, before starting his Ph.D. he spent few years in consulting on finance and accounting related issues, gaining first-hand exposure on group and company valuations, mergers and acquisitions, debt restructuring, impairment of financial and intangible assets. His research interests focus on international accounting standards, group structure and debt contracting. He has been involved in both accounting and finance courses at undergraduate, graduate and MBA level. He is currently visiting research scholar at the Wharton School, University of Pennsylvania.

Antonio Marra holds a Ph.D. in Business Administration (Pavia University, 2009). He is Assistant Professor of Analysis and Interpretation of Financial Statements at Bocconi University and Professor at SDA Bocconi School of Management, where he teaches IFRS, Auditing, Financial Statement Analysis and Consolidation Accounting at Undergraduate, Graduate and Executive level. Antonio is Visiting Professor at Zicklin School of Business (New York, USA), Baruch College (New York, USA), and Tippie College of Management, University of IOWA (Iowa, USA). He is currently Coordinator of the Master of Science in Business Administration and Law, member of the Accounting Department Executive Committee and Official Teacher at the MISB Boconi Graduate Program in Mumbai, India. His research has been published on leading international academic and professional journals. Certified Public Accountant.

Annalisa Prencipe holds a Ph.D. in Business Administration and Management (Bocconi University, 2000). She is Associate Professor of Financial Accounting at Bocconi University and Professor at SDA Bocconi School of Management, where she teaches IFRS, Consolidation Accounting and Financial Reporting and Analysis at graduate and executive level. She is currently the Director of the Master of Science in Business Administration and Law and member of the Accounting Department Executive Committee. She is the author of several books and articles. Her research has been published on leading international academic and professional journals.

***

Giovanni Andrea Toselli is the National Technical Partner of PwC Italy. He is a member of EFRAG TEG, the body responsible for issuing the endorsement advice for IFRS in the European Union. He is clinical professor at Bocconi University and University of Pavia where he teaches Financial Accounting and Transparency in Financial Reporting and International Accounting. Speaker at several International IFRS events he is author of several articles and manuals on IFRS and Financial Reporting.

Acknowledgments

This book comes after several years of teaching in the area and from the crucial contribution of other people, besides the authors, that let this work become publishable. We would like to thank first Marta Colnago from McGraw-Hill for her tireless help and continuous support. Moreover, several research assistants of the accounting department at Bocconi University gave us their tremendous support and thus a special thank goes to: Mauro Coviello, Laura D'oria, Elia Ferracuti, and Maria Laura Ricchetti. Finally, besides thanking Giovanni Andrea Toselli from PwC for his incredibly nice preface, we are grateful to PwC Italy for its assistance and technical help. We mention, among others, Antonella Portalupi whose great support over all these months allowed us to better focus and prepare the book.

All mistakes are, in any case, our own responsibility.

In Collaboration with:

1

INTRODUCTION

1.1 Scope and overview of the book

This book provides a gradual approach to understanding and preparing consolidated financial statements in accordance with international accounting standards (IAS-IFRS).

Financial statements, both individual and consolidated, must be prepared in compliance with a specific and usually country-specific set of rules, the so-called generally accepted accounting principles ("GAAP"). We chose international financial reporting standards ("IFRS" or "IAS/IFRS") as the reference GAAP based on two main considerations. First, IFRS have been gaining considerable relevance in the international accounting framework, especially in relation to consolidated financial statements, and they are currently the most popular standards around the world. Secondly, IFRS are quite similar to another very influential set of standards, namely US GAAP.

It is important to stress here that in order to benefit at most from this book readers should preferably not be completely unfamiliar with accounting principles, since the consolidation process itself is not a basic-standard topic. However, specific knowledge is not required, since the topic is well-delimited, and we shall address the main related accounting issues while discussing the different issues.

Chapter two of this work provides a general introduction to IFRS and their environment , and Appendix A contains a brief overview of the main accounting standards. However, readers who do not feel comfortable enough or who have never been exposed to IFRS may refer to the following manuals for further reference:

(i) Alexander David, Anne Britton, Ann Jorissen, and David Alexander. 2011. *International financial reporting and Analysis*. Andover: Cengage Learning.

(ii) PricewaterhouseCoopers. *PwC Manual of Accounting IFRS 2013*. Bloomsbury Professional, 2012.

(iii) Bruce Mackenzie, Danie Coetsee, Tapiwa Njikizana and Raymond Chamboko. *Wiley IFRS 2013: Interpretation and Application of International Financial Reporting Standards*. Wiley, 2013.

(iv) Jerry J Weygandt, Paul D Kimmel, and Donald E Kieso. *Financial Accounting , IFRS Edition*. Wiley, 2 edition, 2012.

This book is structured as follows. Chapter two introduces IFRS, their main features, the reasons and expected benefits that led to their adoption, and the IFRS conceptual framework. We seek to outline, in a concise manner, the main aspects that have resulted in IFRS being the most widely used set of accounting standards worldwide, and the future steps towards global convergence. Once readers have been provided with a sufficient understanding of the overall accounting framework, we move to the real focus of the text: how to prepare and interpret consolidated financial statements. In Chapter three we try to make readers understand why it is not always enough to have "individual" (meaning "non-consolidated") financial statements to measure and report the performance of an economic entity.[1] Then, in Chapter four we define the concept of

[1] We always refer to "*individual* financial statements" as opposite to "*consolidated* financial statement". Advance readers may know that the world *individual* has a

"group" (i.e. we define what we can simply call the "consolidation area").

Starting from the notion of 'control' provided by IFRS, we draw a line between legal entities which indeed form the group and other entities which represent mere investments in other companies. Finally, after clarifying when we actually need to prepare consolidated financial statements, we learn how to prepare them through consolidation accounting, first at a more intuitive level (Chapter five), and then by studying in more depth the consolidation techniques for subsidiaries (Chapter six) and for associates and joint ventures (Chapter seven).

For ease of exposition, and to prevent readers from feeling like 'losing their grip on reality', throughout the book we use a number of practical cases - some of which are real-world extracts - and we make constant reference to the specific requirements contained in IFRS. In addition, we include several examples throughout the text, and a final chapter devoted to exercises, which translates all the issues addressed in the book into practice (Chapter eight).

1.2 How to use this book

To make the book as intelligible as the subject allows, we have paid particular attention to its structure and layout .

The book is organised into chapters which can be combined to form different stand-alone units, so that it may be flexibly used according to the level of learning you intend to achieve. If it is used as a textbook in basic accounting courses with the intent to provide

---

technical meaning and sometimes it should be used "*separate* financial statements" instead. We decided to be a little sloppy here in notation for the sake of simplicity.

a quick overview of consolidation accounting, we suggest to focus on chapters three to six, where students will learn the notion of 'group' under IFRS, the difference between individual and consolidated financial statements, and how to consolidate subsidiaries in simple circumstances. If the target audience is slightly more advanced, the instructor may want to include also chapter seven (consolidation accounting for associates and joint venture where we deal with the equity method). More advanced students will also benefit from reading the blue boxes inserted throughout the text.

We have tried to use a layout that helps readers to easily find their way through the text and to focus on each of the aspects treated. In particular, we make extensive use of icons, where each icon has a specific meaning.

The meaning of the icons is as follows:

Insights and more advanced issues which we decided not to treat in the main text to maintain a softer, yet rigorous, approach to consolidation. We strongly recommend to more advanced readers not to skip these boxes as they contain important aspects they may not want to miss.

Examples and cases taken from the real world, past teaching experience, case studies, and official accounting standards. We have tried to match each aspect of the consolidation process with one or more of such examples, in order to provide a more practical approach to the issues addressed.

The main definitions used in the text.

Moreover, in illustrating journal entries, we use a reporting scheme that should help readers to understand which element of the financial statements has been involved in the transaction which the journal entry refers to. The reporting scheme works as follows: the sign + (-) means increase (decrease) in the accounting item that follows and the items are the usual ones taken from the balance sheet or the income statement: e.g. "A" for Assets, "L" for Liabilities, "SE" for shareholders' Equity, etc. Note that the increase (decrease) in many income statement items is concisely reported as an increase (decrease) in "SE". Moreover, if the letter of the accounting item is preceded by a X this indicates that, in that transaction, the item is a contra entry. For further reference on the use of this reporting scheme, please refer to Libby, Robert, Patricia A Libby, and Daniel G Short. 2009. *Financial Accounting*. Boston: McGraw-Hill Irwin.

2

INTERNATIONAL FINANCIAL REPORTING STANDARDS (IFRS): AN OVERVIEW

Content of this chapter:

- The potential benefits of a global set of accounting standards
- IFRS Foundation and IASB duties and responsibilities
- IFRS dissemination around the world
- The accounting standards preparation process
- Rule- *versus* Principle-based accounting standards
- IFRS Conceptual Framework

2.1 Why do we need International Accounting Standards?

International Financial Reporting Standards (IFRS)[1], are the result of a "commitment to developing, in the public interest, a single set of high quality, global accounting standards that require transparent and comparable information in general purpose financial statements" [International Accounting Standards Board 2011, 5]. IFRS are the accounting standards which *have to* or *can* be used by organisations to prepare their - individual and consolidated - financial statements, as a consequence of a harmonisation and convergence plan across countries.[2] In a nutshell, then, IFRS are high quality accounting rules adopted by an increasing number of countries all over the world. However, since each country already has its own accounting principles,[3] and long and solid accounting tradition a natural question arises:

"Why do we need *another* set of standards?"

Globalisation has led to a progressive and growing integration between both markets for goods and services and capital markets, with the natural consequence that firms that previously had to rely almost exclusively on their domestic market can now trade, almost in the same way, also all over the world. This increased competitiveness in a worldwide dimension of the economic

---

[1] Usually IFRS is commonly used to identify the entire set of standards including both IAS (International Accounting Standards) and IFRS (International Financial Reporting Standards).

[2] Compulsory or discretionary adoption of IFRS, as well as the selected applying organizations, are a country-dependent choice which will be briefly examined further below in the text.

[3] We may refer further below in the text to such sets of accounting standards as "local GAAP", where GAAP stands for Generally Accepted Accounting Principles, as recalled in the introduction.

environment makes the efficiency of economic and financial communication a key factor in the proper functioning of financial markets better to protect market participants and allow a larger degree of transparency. This goal should be accomplished also through accounting standards, which can be defined as a set of concepts and techniques that are used with the aim of identifying, measuring and communicating financial information on a specific economic entity to different users.

Starting from that, we believe it is very important to examine all the reasons that encouraged and drove the development and subsequent spread of global accounting standards. The first aim when developing global standards is to improve the functioning of capital markets. The spreading of such accounting standards should in some way contribute to the removal of barriers and obstacles to cross-border acquisitions and divestitures and should improve the inflow of capital from international investors to a country because of its improved image and credibility. Last but not least, the spread of global accounting standards makes it easier to compare investment options from the vast array of investors acting in the markets, both as individuals or as companies or other types of organisations. Although partially connected to the first aim, a particular attention should be granted to the goal of improving the comparability of financial information across countries and, at the same time, increasing its quality. Moreover, using a single set of accounting standards removes the necessity to adjust financial statements prepared under different standards for comparability reasons, significantly simplifying the job of financial analysts. The promise of more accurate, more comprehensive and timely accounting information is an additional element that contributes to increasing the quality of a reporting system.

Furthermore, a single set of accounting standards would also lead to cost and risk reductions when looking at financial information itself. In fact, the development of international accounting standards would not only reduce the costs for reprocessing accounting information but would also decrease the costs of preparation of reconciliation accounts.

As can be seen, there are many potential expected benefits resulting from the adoption of international accounting standards. Their effective range, though, is yet to be demonstrated, especially for those effects which will materialise only in the medium-long term. So far existing findings have mixed results and seem to warn that the potential benefits of introduction of IFRS might be short-lived and have different impacts on different countries. This seems to show that contextual factors and incentives might prevail on the accounting standards per se. But this is a different story and in this book we will not investigate the gap, if any, between the expected benefits and those actually achieved thanks to the adoption of a single set of global standards.

Now, going back to our key focus we think a couple of easy examples might clarify what we theoretically developed above. A first practical answer about the need - and potential benefits - of a global set of standards may lie in the environment in which firms have being operating in the last few decades, i.e. an international setting where investors are spread around the world, and firms compete against each other independently of their country of origin. This, of course, drove the adoption of a common language to exchange information; if English was the natural choice in many aspects of the globalisation era, the choice was not obvious in the financial accounting context, where an *international, common* set of accounting standards able to cope with the rise in investors' demand for information was missing. Just think, for instance, of a German firm[4] operating in Italy. Several (costly) accounting-related issues may stem from this situation. First of all, should the German company prepare its financial statements according to Italian or German GAAP? When a firm is based in Italy, it usually needs to apply the GAAP required by the Italian law, and this translates in additional costs borne by the firm on a regular basis (e.g. learning Italian GAAP, producing multiple sets of financial statements - *(i)* one prepared using Italian GAAP to be compliant with the Italian regulation, and *(ii)* a second one applying German GAAP to report to their German investors - keeping up with any changes both in the Italian and in the German set of rules, etc...). But suppose that, due to some special circumstances, the firm is only obliged to prepare its financial statements according to German GAAP. In that case, there would be no extra accounting-related costs, since the difference in the accounting systems (the Italian and German ones) would not result in larger company expenses. Let us suppose now that the German company which operates in Italy is about to seek a loan from a local Italian bank due to more favourable loan conditions compared to German financial institutions[5]. If the firm was using German GAAP, the Italian bank may be reluctant to lend the money due to a lack of knowledge about how to read and interpret German financial reports.[6]

---

4 'German' in the sense that the firm's shareholders are German and are used to the German financial accounting system.

5 Given the turbulent economic context we face while we write this book, let us just be positive and imaginative: allow us to believe the example make sense.

6 Let us be, for the moment, rather superficial in claiming "how to read and interpret German financial reports" as a generic lack of correct interpretation of all the items classified in the company's reports; some examples might be a lack of knowledge concerning the accounting treatment of leases, whether reported values are

This may lead the bank to refuse the loan and force the firm to go back to a German bank to get a more expensive form of financing. Also in this case, then, the firm would experience an increase in costs due to accounting-related issues. While situations such as the one just depicted were not so frequent, let us say, 30 years ago, they are now widespread, given the globalisation trends in the last few decades (especially within Europe, where we have started to use the same currency, and have been constantly trying to build a common market). Another meaningful situation that can exemplify the need for and benefits of a common accounting language could be the investing activity of investment banks or mutual funds or any other investor (including private ones) which may be more willing to invest in foreign corporate bonds instead of local ones either because they are *ceteris paribus* more profitable or for hedging reasons; also in this case, if financial reports are not intelligible, the result may be a lost investment opportunity when the cost of understanding, interpreting and reclassifying financial reports outweighs the incremental investment opportunity's profits, or simply makes it in a way too time consuming and uncertain to potential investors. By the few and basic examples mentioned above, readers can easily see why the use of the same accounting principles is of critical importance. In a few words, we can say that a single set of higher quality rules should, across countries, decrease information asymmetry making investors' life easier in making informed investment decisions. These and many other reasons - left here unexplored - have urged several international organisations, such as the International Federation of Accountants ("IFAC") and the European Union ("EU"), to provide investors with reliable and

---

recognized at their current cash equivalents or at their face values, and other non-trivial issues concerning what forms the bank's pledgeable income.

high quality information independently of the firms' country of origin.

Once the need was clear, it was then necessary to appoint a competent entity to set up and coordinate, as stated by Christensen (2008), "the largest accounting change ever undertaken". Today, IFRS and ancillary activities are mainly developed by an international entity based in London, UK: the International Accounting Standard Board ("IASB"). The IASB is appointed by an independent foundation whose main duties, objectives and responsibilities are described in the box below (Box 2.1).[7]

Box 2.1 – IFRS Foundation and IASB

The IFRS Foundation, of which the IASB is the independent standard-setting body, defines itself as "an independent, not-for-profit private sector organisation working in the public interest". Its principal objectives are:

(i) to develop a single set of high quality, understandable, enforceable and globally accepted international financial reporting standards (IFRSs) through its standard-setting body, the IASB;

(ii) to promote the use and rigorous application of those standards;

[7] Further information on the IFRS foundation may be found in the introduction to the Official Guide to IFRS [International Accounting Standards Board 2011, page 5-13] and on the IFRS web page (www.ifrs.org).

(iii) to take account of the financial reporting needs of emerging economies and small and medium-sized entities (SMEs); and

(iv) to promote and facilitate adoption of International Financial Reporting Standards (IFRSs), being the standards and interpretations issued by the IASB, through the convergence of national accounting standards and IFRSs.

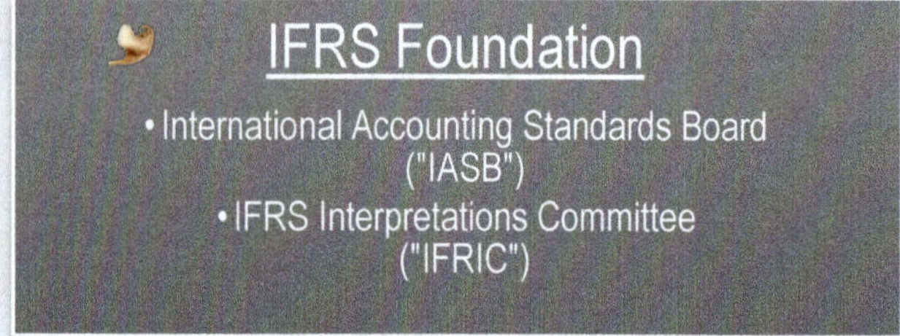

Source: http://www.ifrs.org/The-organisation/Pages/IFRS-Foundation-and-the-IASB.aspx.

As we have mentioned above, this book does not purport to provide an exhaustive collection of information about IFRS and the activities undertaken by IASB; however, it may be worthwhile to take a quick look at the history of this organisation, to get a clearer picture of the role of international accounting standards. For instance, it is possible to understand why we have two names for them: IAS and IFRS. As a matter of fact, up to 2000 international standards were issued by the International Accounting Standards Committee ("IASC"), whose members were professionals from some of the main developed countries worldwide[8]. The principles

[8] Specifically, Australia, Canada, France, Germany, Japan, Mexico, the Netherlands, United Kingdom and Ireland, and the United States

issued in that period are known as International Accounting Standards ("IAS"). Between 2000 and 2001, the IASC underwent a deep reorganisation process which gave rise to the present International Accounting Standards Board ("IASB") in 2001; we leave the details of the reorganisation aside;[9] we can only say that the new IASB is basically more independent and qualified to respond to increased duties and responsibilities. A chart of the IFRS Foundation and IASB is given below (Figure 2.1). Even though the IASB initially recognised (and partially still does) the old IAS, the new international accounting standards issued under its name are called International Financial Reporting Standards ("IFRS").

[9] Further information can be found on the IFRS official web page at http://www.ifrs.org

Figure 2.1 - IFRS Foundation and IASB structure

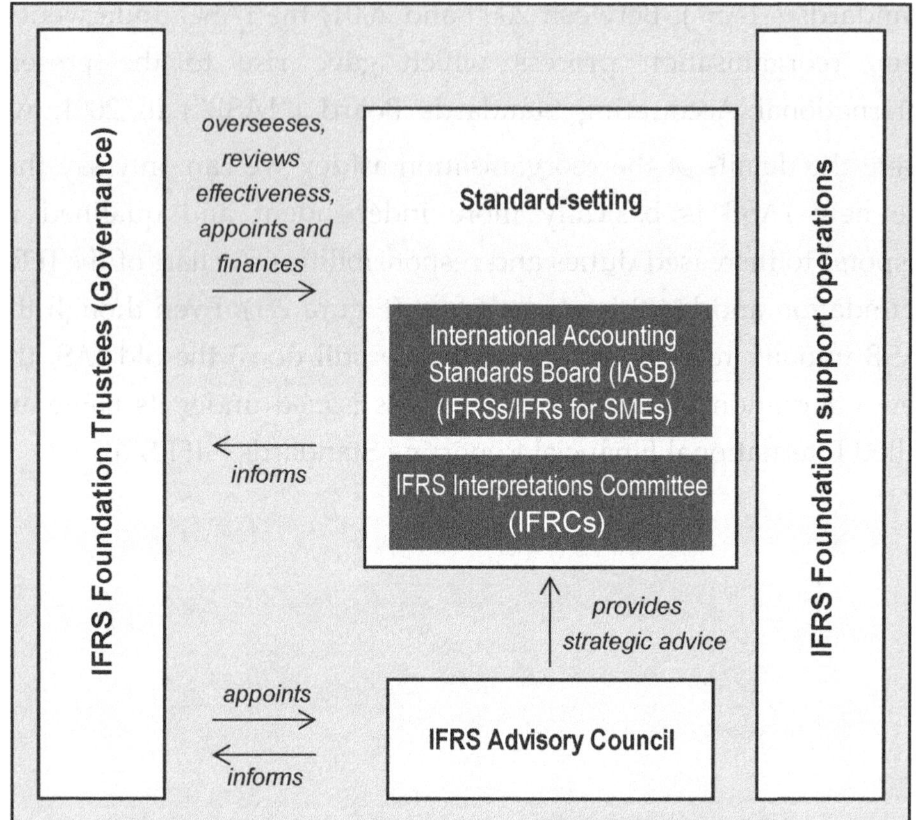

Adapted by the authors. Original source: IFRS Foundation, International Accounting Standards Board (IASB) "Who we are and what we do" brochure, Last revised: February 2012.

2.2 The relevance of IFRS

As mentioned earlier, sharing one and the same set of high quality standards may be important for companies in the current globalised and information-seeking scenario; in particular, when sharing the same set of accounting principles, capital, goods, and corporate markets seems to experience a functional increase (Landsman, Maydew, and Thornock 2012; Barth, Landsman, and Lang 2008; Armstrong et al. 2010; Li 2010; see the box below - Box 2.2 - for further information on research about the effects of IFRS). This should not be surprising, since by sharing the same rules we decrease the information asymmetry that may partially account for some frictions present in these markets.

Box 2.2 – IFRS and information asymmetry

Among other consequences, adopting one and the same set of accounting rules should affect the quality and quantity of information owned by investors and hence should help to:

(i) remove barriers to cross-border acquisition and divestitures;

(ii) increase the credibility of domestic capital markets among foreign capital providers;

(iii) increase the efficiency with which the stock market incorporates financial information in prices, by reducing the cost of processing it;

(iv) make it easier for investors to compare investment options.

Moreover, either directly or by decreasing information asymmetry, IFRS are typically deemed to affect other characteristics of earnings, such as their *value relevance*, i.e. how well earnings explain the variation of the company's underlying share price. Since IFRS are more market-oriented and typically make a wider use of fair values, they are assumed to be more value-relevant. Another earnings characteristic which is considered to be affected by the adoption of IFRS is the level of earnings management, i.e. the level of purposeful intervention in the external financial reporting process undertaken with the intent of obtaining some private gain (Schipper 1989).

Given that one of the aims of IASB is to provide *high quality* standards, IFRS should reduce such purposeful external interventions which do not reflect real-accounting information but only create noise. Finally, the cost of a firm's capital should be affected by the adoption of IFRS also indirectly, and is expected to decrease due to a lower amount of information asymmetry. The results of research in those areas, however, are not unambiguous, as reported in the next box.

At this point, readers may wonder whether, prior to the development of IFRS, investors engaged in cross-country investment activities at all, given the information barriers they faced. The answer is of course they did: the level of available information is just one of the (many) variables considered by investors in evaluating their investments; the truth is that, before the adoption of a common set of standards, those investments decisions were likely to be more costly and less accurate. By eliminating many international accounting differences, IFRS adoption has, on the one hand, made it possible to avoid many costly adjustments necessary to compare companies' financial statements; on the other hand, it has provided more accurate, comprehensive, and timely financial statement information, contributing to the improvement of the overall quality of financial reporting. The strength and breadth of these results are still a debated matter among scholars (see Box 2.3 for more info). Yet, it is not controversial that the adoption of a single set of accounting standards has been a fundamental milestone in creating a modern global market.

Box 2.3 – Research on IAS / IFRS

Since their adoption, vast accounting research has been devoting significant efforts to studying whether the EU's ambitions of greater comparability, enhanced efficiency, and lower information asymmetry have been, at least partially, satisfied through the adoption of the new body of international accounting standards. The results so far seem to support a positive outcome of IFRS application, even though the evidence is not unanimous. Barth, et al. (2008), for instance, comparing the economic environment before and after application of IAS/IFRS in more than 20 countries generally find an improvement in the quality of earnings. In a similar study, Daske et al. (2008) find that after the adoption of IAS/IFRS market liquidity increased, so that equity valuations and firms' cost of capital decreased; however, by looking within the cross-country sample, the authors find that such results only apply to countries where legal enforcement is strong and where firms have stronger incentives to be transparent. Other country-specific studies on the adoption of international accounting standards (e.g. Van Tendeloo and Vanstraelen 2005; Hung and Subramanyam 2007) find no significant differences brought by IAS/IFRS. The differences start to emerge when voluntary adoption is taken into account (e.g. Leuz and Verrecchia 2000). These results point to several implications: on the one hand, it seems that the improvement hoped for by the EU is country-dependent, demonstrating the crucial role played by legal and cultural factors in applying GAAP; on the other hand, it seems to suggest that further research is needed.

2.3 Global convergence of accounting standards

The process of developing and applying a single set of high quality accounting standards started a long time ago, back in the '70s. At that time[10], the IASC was created right after the International Federation of Accounting ("IFAC") formed, with the goal of coordinating worldwide accounting professionals with a set of harmonised standards. In the years that followed, the first international accounting standards were issued, with all the limitations and legal fragility due to the uncertain institutional status of the IASC at that time.[11] After some standards were issued, a second big shift in the international harmonisation occurred in 1995, when the IASC entered into an agreement with the International Organisation of Securities Commission ("IOSCO") and issued, towards the end of the '90s, the first core set of principles. In those years, after the rather unsatisfactory results following the application of the Fourth EU Directive,[12] the European Union

---

[10] Specifically, in 1973.

[11] The unclear and not-independent role exerted by the IASC was one of the main reasons that brought to the formation of the IASB, whose independence and authority are nowadays unquestioned.

[12] Fourth Council Directive 78/660/EEC of 25 July 1978, which aimed for the "coordination of Member States' provisions concerning the presentation and content of annual accounts and annual reports, the valuation methods used therein and their publication in respect of certain companies with limited liability".

started considering using IAS as the common accounting principles with which member states' companies could prepare their annual accounts. The next important step which allowed IAS to gain visibility was taken in 1999, when the EU formalised the goal to build a single capital market in the Financial Service Action Plan. After some consideration, the international accounting standards issued by the IASC were found to be the most appropriate set of accounting principles, so that the European Commission, in 2000, proposed that all listed companies use IAS/IFRS to prepare their financial reports. Notably, this obligation was for consolidated financial statements. The reason for such a choice will become clear in the next chapter, where we deal with the meaning of consolidation accounting. Formally the decision was adopted on 19 July 2002 through EU Regulation (EC) No. 1606/2002, by which the European Union agreed that from 1 January 2005 International Accounting Standards / International Financial Reporting Standards would apply for the consolidated accounts of the EU listed companies.[13] According to Regulation (EC) No. 1606/2002, International Accounting Standards include:

(i) all IAS and IFRS;

(ii) their Interpretations (SIC/IFRIC);

(iii) any modifications to the standards and interpretations issued, or to be issued, by the IASB.

So far we have seen that every EU listed company has to prepare its consolidated accounts applying IFRS. However, the European Commission considered that it was not safe irrevocably to transfer

---

[13] Regulation (EC) No. 1606/2002 and related materials are available at: http://ec.europa.eu/internal_market/accounting/legal_framework/ias_regulation_en.htm.

the responsibility for setting new accounting standards to a (private) organisation over which the EU has no formal authority (i.e. the IFRS Foundation and the IASB). This is the reason why in Regulation (EC) No. 1606/2002 the European Commission sets the rules for an *endorsement mechanism* through which it preserves the right of final decision on the applicability of individual IFRSs. The main subjects involved in the endorsement process are:

(i) The European Financial Reporting Advisory Group ("EFRAG"), a technical body made up of accounting experts;

(ii) The Accounting Regulatory Committee ("ARC"), a political body made up of representatives from member states;

(iii) Starting from 2006, a Standards Advice Review Group ("SARG"), an independent group of experts providing their opinion on each standard.[14]

Once the European Commission has listened to their opinion, IAS/IFRS are adopted as European regulations through specific rules published in the Official Journal of the European Union. Besides Regulation (EC) No. 1606/2002, the European Union also approved the accounting Directives 2001/65/EC and 2003/51/EC, which amended the IV and VII accounting Directives, in order to reduce the differences in financial statements between companies that are obliged to use IAS/IFRS and companies that are not. After EU endorsement, each member state can embrace IFRS in a variety of ways:

(i) adopting IFRS as national standards;

---

[14] The difference with the opinions released by ARC and EFRAG lies in the lack of conflicts of interest of SARG experts who are neither political appointees (ARC) nor other stakeholders such as audit firms, companies, users (EFRAG).

(ii) recasting them as national standards;

(iii) modifying national standards over time to converge towards IFRS;

(iv) basing national standards on IFRS;

(v) converging now, with expectation of adopting later.

Each country is then free to choose IFRS over its local GAAP or slowly converge towards IFRS; however, some entities are obliged to adopt the new international standards starting from 2005, e.g. any company listed in one of the EU stock markets. The list of the companies which have to apply IFRS is country dependent as well, so that it is not possible easily to separate them from other entities not required by law to adopt IFRS. However, we can briefly discuss the state of the art IFRS application. We will first do this from a worldwide perspective, focusing our discussion on the main economies, given the practical impossibility of a country-specific analysis; then we will focus on the European countries, trying to dig a little more into the specificities of the main EU member states.

In addition to Europe, convergence towards the use of IFRS involves other countries, being now a global phenomenon. In brief,[15] Canada has decided that, with a few exemptions, all Canadian publicly accountable entities[16] have to prepare their annual accounts in accordance with IFRS starting from 1 January 2011. Brazil has been converging towards IFRS starting from 2010

---

[15] The following taxonomy is just an approximation of the current situation, whose precise analysis is out of our scope. Therefore, we alert readers that some exemptions may apply to the general rules we are reporting (e.g. a certain subset of companies which are not required to use IFRS, or a slightly different adoption date).

[16] These include public companies and other entities with certain types of securities owned by the public.

and has required its listed companies to use IFRS as their standards; a similar situation is found in Argentina, with convergence starting from 2011, Chile in 2009 and Mexico in 2012. Figure 2.2 provides a summary picture of the current situation of countries which have approved the convergence process and will apply IFRS in the near future.[17]

Currently, companies in Japan can opt to choose IFRS voluntarily and in the near future a decision should be taken on their final mandatory application. In China IFRS are permitted for listed companies, with some relevant exception. India initially proposed a roadmap to converge towards IFRS, even though currently there are still a number of differences between Indian GAAP and IFRS which have to be settled.

In 2004 Australia issued Australian GAAP, which have been prepared to be equivalent to IFRS, and it is working to continue maintaining consistency; a similar situation is found in Hong Kong, Korea and New Zealand; Russia has developed and is implementing an endorsement process which should allow listed companies to prepare International Financial Reporting Standards compliant consolidated financial statements. South Africa has allowed its listed companies to apply IFRS, while other large companies may either apply IFRS or IFRS for SMEs18 and local GAAP are only used by residual categories of companies.

[17] Specifically, dates in the figure refer to the year in which countries chose to adopt IFRS, not to the first adoption year.

[18] IFRS for small and medium-sized enterprises.

Figure 2.2- Worldwide situation of IFRS adoption

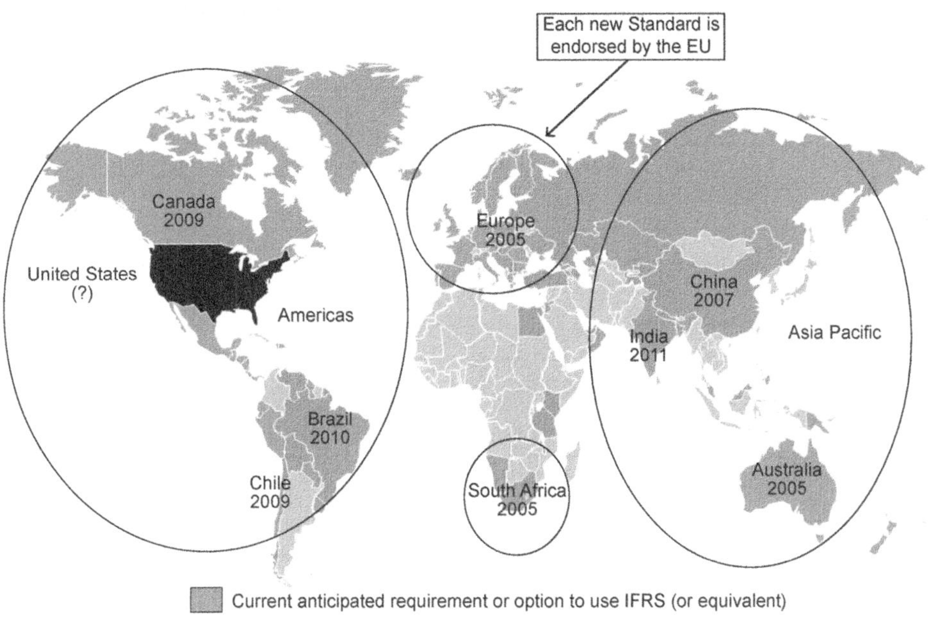

Source: prepared by Authors.

A summary of the updated state of the application of IFRS among listed companies in the Group of 20 (G20) countries is provided by the IFRS Foundation and reported below (see Table 1).[19] The US are purposely excluded from the table (see further below).

[19] The IFRS Foundation makes the following disclaimer "NOTE: The list refers to listed companies only. The table is not an authoritative assessment of the use of IFRS in those countries. In the majority of cases, the information has been provided by the relevant national authorities or is based on information that is publicly available. For definitive information on the use of IFRSs in any particular country or countries contact the relevant national authority or authorities directly."

Table 2.1 – Worldwide countries status

Country	Status for listed companies as of December 2011
Argentina	Required for fiscal years beginning on or after 1 January 2012
Australia	Required for all private sector reporting entities and as the basis for public sector reporting since 2005
Brazil	Required for consolidated financial statements of banks and listed companies from 31 December 2010 and for individual company accounts progressively since January 2008
Canada	Required from 1 January 2011 for all listed entities and permitted for private sector entities including not-for-profit organisations
China	Substantially converged national standards
EU	All member states of the EU are required to use IFRSs as adopted by the EU for listed companies since 2005
France	Required via EU adoption and implementation process since 2005
Germany	Required via EU adoption and implementation process since 2005
India	India is converging with IFRSs at a date to be confirmed.
Indonesia	Convergence process ongoing; a decision about a target date for full compliance with IFRSs is expected to be made in 2012
Italy	Required via EU adoption and implementation process since 2005
Japan	Permitted from 2010 for a number of international companies; decision about mandatory adoption by 2016 expected around 2012
Mexico	Required from 2012
Republic of Korea	Required from 2011
Russia	Required from 2012
Saudi Arabia	Required for banking and insurance companies; full convergence with

	IFRSs currently under consideration
South Africa	Required for listed entities since 2005
Turkey	Required for listed entities since 2008
United Kingdom	Required via EU adoption and implementation process since 2005

Source: Adapted from http://www.ifrs.org/Use-around-the-world/Pages/Use-around-the-world.aspx. Last revised: May 2013.

We did not include the US in the previous overview *because US GAAP arguably* represents, together with IFRS, the most influential set of accounting standards. The FASB (Financial Accounting Standards Board - responsible for developing US GAAP) and the IASB have long attempted to achieve convergence of their standards through:

(i) a formal liaison between FASB and IASB;

(ii) monitoring FASB and IASB major projects;

(iii) short-term convergence projects; and

(iv) joint and long-term convergence projects (e.g., revenue recognition, leases, liabilities and equity, consolidation, conceptual framework, financial statement presentation).

Both the IASB and the FASB are investing heavily in the convergence project and at the time of writing (May 2013) there is a tentative roadmap towards a single set of high quality accounting standards (for details see Box 2.4) and also a very positive signal given by the US Securities and Exchange Commission ("SEC"), which has eliminated the reconciliation requirements for foreign companies listed in the US that already prepare their financial statements in accordance with IFRS; however, some signals indicate that the effective beginning dates of adoption of the harmonised standards, originally estimated around 2015, may be further away.

At the moment, though, US based companies are not permitted to adopt IFRS.

Box 2.4 – Convergence between IFRS and US GAAP

Given the importance of the issue, the IASB and the FASB started working, in consultation with other national and regional bodies, on a convergence project long ago, back in 2002; this effort is embedded in an important memorandum of understanding known as the Norwalk Agreement, signed in September of that year. In the same convergence spirit, the SEC on the one hand allowed non-US companies that prepared their financial statements in accordance with IFRS to avoid reconciling their statements to US GAAP; on the other hand, it prepared a roadmap with instructions for US companies to adopt international accounting standards voluntarily.

In 2006 the IASB and the FASB set specific milestones to be reached by 2008 (A roadmap for convergence 2006 - 2008), and in 2008 the two boards issued an update to the Norwalk Agreement, emphasising the goal of joint projects to produce common, principle-based standards.

Not completely satisfied by the length of the process, in 2009 the G20 countries asked the standard setters to speed up the convergence project. In 2010, the SEC released a statement to provide an updated consideration on global accounting standards and its support for convergence of US GAAP and IFRS. This document includes a Work Plan to be executed by the SEC staff to provide more insightful analyses of the implications of a change to IFRS. The last version of the plan is dated 13 July 2012 and, as noted in the IFRS Foundation staff analysis of the SEC work plan document, highlights the following fundamental differences:

(a) Non-financial asset impairment requirements (in particular, IFRS permits the reversal of impairments, which could make earnings reported in accordance with IFRS more volatile than US GAAP) and recognition of non-financial liabilities (such as lawsuits or environmental cleanup obligations) in IFRS earlier than they would be recognised under US GAAP.

(b) The ability to re-measure property, plant and equipment and investment properties at fair value, which is permitted by IFRS but not US GAAP;

(c) The ability for US companies to use an inventory measurement method called LIFO, which is not permitted by IFRS;

(d) The requirement in IFRS for development expenditure to be capitalised, whereas US GAAP requires all development expenditure to be recognised as an expense as incurred;

(e) Specific requirements in US GAAP relating to uncertain

taxation positions, whereas IFRS has a more general contingency model; and

(f) A requirement in IFRS to depreciate components of an item of property, plant and equipment in some circumstances, which is not a requirement in US GAAP."

(IFRS Foundation staff analysis, October 2012, pp. 32-33)

From the researcher's side, a work examining the global status of convergence towards IFRS and the main differences between IFRS and US GAAP is offered by Barth et al. (2012). The authors find that IFRS firms have better? larger? accounting systems and value relevance comparability with US firms when they use IFRS - especially when mandatorily adopted in common law and high enforcement countries - instead of their local GAAP. This means that by only adopting IFRS, non-US firms are closer from an accounting perspective to US firms implying that the two sets of standards seem to converge. In spite of this positive result, the Authors point out that significant differences remain, which will have to be taken into consideration if the standards setters aim for effective global convergence.

As far as Europe is concerned, it is worth noting that the European Union (before enlargement) can be considered to be the "initiator" of the IFRS implementation process and that, as of today, International Financial Reporting Standards are applied in every European country. We have prepared a more detailed discussion of the current situation for the largest European economies in which we summarise the local requirements at each country level for listed companies, together with the current regulation for their statutory filings. To save some space and for readability reasons we inserted the discussion in a separate appendix (Appendix B), to which we refer interested readers.

Probably, Switzerland represents one of the most interesting situations among adopting countries in Europe. Switzerland has always been 'neutral' to many international decisions and this historical tradition has probably guided also the IFRS adoption choice: in Switzerland, as of today, registrants at the main board of the SIX[20] are required to use either IFRS or US GAAP for their consolidated financial statements. Other registrants may use IFRS, US GAAP or Swiss GAAP FER for their consolidated financial statements, providing companies with a lot of freedom in choosing their accounting standards. Also in this respect, Swiss neutrality is fully preserved.

2.4 The sparkling environment of IFRS

In the previous paragraphs, we pointed out that IFRS are rather new accounting standards issued by an even younger entity. This explains the lively environment and the richness in changes, amendments, and issuance of new principles and application guidelines. We think it is important to stress this point so that readers can understand that these principles constitute a rather dynamic, transforming and developing environment, where standards are adapting better to reflect underlying business transactions. Just to give you an idea of the number of amendments and the timing of IFRS issuance, we report here a brief history of a standard. Since this is a book on consolidation, we have decided to choose the recently released standard on consolidated financial statements (IFRS 10); for interested readers, the full history of the consolidation project can be found on the IASB's website.[21]

---

[20] The 20 Largest Swiss companies listed on the stock exchange.

[21] http://www.ifrs.org/Current-Projects/IASB-Projects/Consolidation/Pages/Consolidation.aspx

Example 2.1 – Short history of IFRS 10

In June 2003, the IASB decided to publish a single IFRS on consolidation to replace IAS 27 ("Consolidated and Separate Financial Statements and SIC-12 Consolidation - Special Purpose Entities").

In April 2008, in response to the global financial crisis and to the recommendation of the Financial Stability Forum, the Board decided to accelerate the consolidation project and proceeded directly to the publication of an exposure draft in December 2008. The comment deadline for the exposure draft ended on 20 March 2009. Round tables were held in conjunction with the derecognition project in North America, Asia and Europe in June 2009 and deliberations commenced in July.

In October 2009, the IASB and the FASB agreed to conduct their respective consolidation projects jointly, though with different timelines.

In January 2011, the FASB decided not to change the consolidation requirements relating to voting interest entities.

The IASB published the final consolidation and disclosure requirements on 12 May, 2011.

In December 2011, the IASB published for public comment an Exposure Draft of proposed amendments to IFRS 10 Consolidated Financial Statements.

In May 2012, the IASB discussed the proposed amendments to IFRS 10 Consolidated Financial Statements arising from the Exposure Draft published in December 2011.

In June 2012, the IASB issued Consolidated Financial Statements, Joint Arrangements and Disclosure of Interests in Other Entities:

Transition Guidance (Amendments to IFRS 10, IFRS 11 and IFRS 12).

In December 2012, IASB published for public comment an Exposure Draft of proposed narrow-scope amendments to IFRS 10 Consolidated Financial Statements. 23 April 2013 was set as the comments deadline for the standard.

As readers may understand, as we write the standard on consolidation is still changing. However, the proposed amendments are narrow-scoped and are mainly proposed for consistency reasons, so that potential changes will not affect the content of this book. Similar histories are found in each of the other standards forming IFRS. The number of changes ('amendments' is the technical word) and updates characterising the standards can be understood also by looking at the published IFRS. As readers already know, all standards named "IAS" were issued up to 2001 and those issued after that year fell under the umbrella of "IFRS". The official 2011 edition of the standards includes the following: IFRS 1 to 8; IAS 1, 2, 7, 8, 10-12, 16-21, 23, 24, 26-29, 31-34, 36-41.[22] The number of IFRS[23] standards (eight) and the number of IAS missing (twelve) is the result of the changes the IASB has made to the standards since it was created (i.e. more or less 10 years ago).

Both the history of IFRS 10 and the number of discarded IAS and issued IFRS shed some light on the dynamic and proactive environment in which international accounting standards are created. However, we may want to have a better look at how IASB actually develop IFRS and learn that the overall process (named "due process") is clustered around an international consultation

[22] International Accounting Standards Board 2012, Blue edition.

[23] This edition does not include the most recent standards IFRS 9 and IFRS 10.

process involving individuals and organisations from around the world.

Figure 2.3 – Stages of IASB Due Process

Source: Prepared by the Authors.

The due process comprises six stages, namely:

(i) Setting the agenda, where the Board seeks to address a demand for better-quality information;

(ii) Planning the project, where it decides whether to work alone or with other standard setters and establish a working group;

(iii) Developing and publishing the discussion paper, which is a non-mandatory step, to explain the issue and collect early comments from constituents;

(iv) Developing and publishing the exposure draft, which, unlike the discussion paper, outlines a specific proposal in the form of a tentative standard or an amendment to an existing one. After resolving issues at its meetings, the IASB publishes it for public comment;

(v) Developing and publishing the standard, after considering the comments received on the first exposure draft and after consideration of whether to publish a revised proposal for another round of comments. Before publishing the standard the IASB asks for an external review, normally undertaken by the IFRIC;

(vi) Holding regular meetings, after the standard is issued, with interested parties to help them understand any non-anticipated issues related to the practical implementation and potential impact of its proposals.

The presence of multiple subjects involved and the different steps in which every standard is issued allows the development process to be very democratic and dialectic, as one can see from the figure below.

Figure 2.4 – IFRS development process

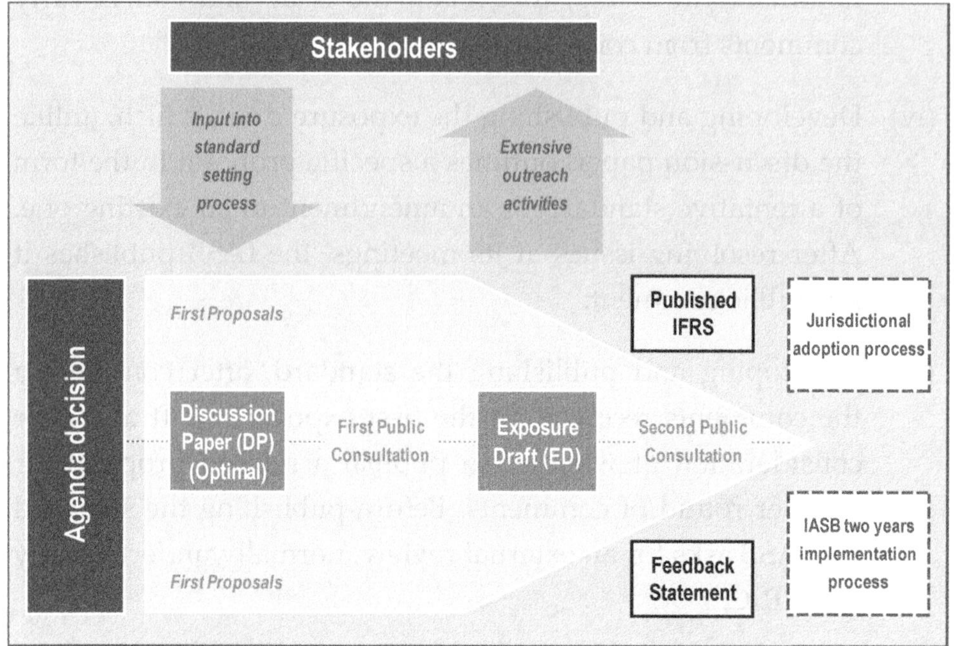

Adapted by the authors. Original source: IFRS Foundation, International Accounting Standards Board (IASB) "Who we are and what we do" brochure, Last revised: February 2012.

Now that we understand the nature, the scope, and the birth of the international standards together with their diffusion, we will start exploring the characteristics of IAS/IFRS in greater detail. We will do this in two steps. The first is to unveil a very general characteristic of IFRS, i.e. explain why they are 'principle-based' standards. The second step involves the illustration of the main principles inspiring IAS/IFRS, i.e. their theoretical framework. Let us begin with the first one.

2.5 Principle-based vs. rule-based standards

IAS/IFRS are principle-based standards (*see Box below*) since their primary role is to provide sensible principles to which all applying entities must conform, which aim to be as universal as possible and therefore independent of the actual contractual form chosen by applying entities for their business operations or transactions. A principle is a general statement which is intended to support the true and fair presentation of the economic consequences of business transactions and acts as a guide to action. Opposed to principle-based are rule-based standards, such as US GAAP, which attempt to rule all the actual situations that applying entities might face (see Box 2.5 for an example with leasing agreements).

Box 2.5 - Principles or rules oriented standards?

When going through the IFRS - especially the first times - readers may have the feeling of "missing part of the picture". This feeling becomes sharper if readers compare the international standards to US GAAP, where very precise indications with respect to many hypothetical situations are given. Let us just make an example (a very typical one) so that you can understand better what we mean: operating lease.

Under US GAAP there are four alternatives and sufficient criteria for recognising and measuring leasing agreements as being of an operating or finance nature ('capital' in the US GAAP wording), many of them with clear-cut rules (e.g. agreements with lease term equal to or greater than 75% of the asset's useful life are considered to be finance leases [SFAS13 par. 7 (C)]). IFRS do not provide any "fixed" rule, such as numbers or statistics, easily distinguishing the two types of agreements, providing readers with just a general classification ("A lease is classified as a finance lease if it transfers substantially all the risks and rewards incidental to ownership.", IAS 17, par. 8), some examples (IAS 17, par. 10) and potential indicators (IAS 17, par. 11); just to solve any residual doubt on the enforcement of such examples and indicators, the standard goes on specifying that "The examples and indicators in paragraphs 10 and 11 are not always conclusive." (IAS 17, par. 12). Readers may wonder why international standards wish to allow such great discretion instead of solving the matter easily as US GAAP do, limiting potentially opportunistic behaviours.

There are many answers for that, such as the impossibility of ruling out any future event, or the acknowledgment that, in some circumstances, the better judge for the right rule to apply is the one who is dealing with the actual situation; however there is a reason which appears to be rather straightforward: providing clear cut and "fixed" rules may be more dangerous than beneficial! Suppose a manager wants to recognise the lease as operating due to some personal advantage. Under US GAAP it would be enough to convince the lessor to set the lease term equal to 74% of the asset's useful life (given the other conditions are met). This may still not be enough under IAS/IFRS, since if the manager wants to treat the lease as operating, he or she has always the burden - independently from the percentage of the asset's useful life stated in the contract - of proving that there is no effective transfer of the risks and rewards incidental to ownership.

Of course it is difficult to affirm that principle-based standards are superior to rule-based ones or *vice versa*, since they both have advantages and disadvantages. For instance, generally rule-based principles are easier to apply since they are more detailed and imply less discretion. However, if the same person confronts a situation which is not exactly the one indicated in the rules, he or she may face a lack of indications on the correct accounting treatment to employ. This would not happen if a general principle, adaptable to different circumstances, was stated. Moreover, few general principles may be more intelligible, compared to trying to regulate all possible situations and exemptions. It is then safe to say that the IASB's choice of using principle-based standards is a consequence of the large number of potential applying entities, which form an extremely heterogeneous set, to the point that some flexibility in the standards may favour the adoption process. A short and purely illustrative indication of the main pros and cons of rule-*versus* principle-based standards is reported in the table below.

Table 2.2 – Pros and cons of rule-based standards

PROS	CONS
Provide detailed guidance and clarification and precise answers to questions	Reduce or eliminate the exercise of professional judgment
Provide greater comparability	Financial statement should be capable of comparison when the economic reality of similar transactions and events is understood in a similar way by the users of those financial statements
Are authoritative and enforceable	Do not prevent dishonest practice, but encourage interested parties to find loopholes

Their complexity is only a consequences of the complexity of the underlying business	Cause complexity and delay in keeping abreast of change. A well-defined set of principles provides the framework for dealing with complexity, retaining a strong focus on representing the economic reality
Deter creative accounting	Foster creative accounting by diverting judgment from economic reality to the detail of application
Set out greater detail which is especially important where translation is needed	Greater difficulties in translating details

Source: Prepared by the Authors.

To conclude, as readers may have started to understand, the difference between principles and rules is not always clear-cut and a combination of both approaches might lead to superior results; as specified in the box, this is one of the main differences between IFRS and US GAAP. The future convergence between the two sets of standards, if it is ever reached, may be revealing in terms of eventual hybrid solutions.

2.6 The theoretical framework of IFRS

IFRS are a set of dynamic, young principles prepared in a dialectic and open environment. Even the conceptual framework on which each standard is based is changing. In the official guide (International Accounting Standards Board 2011, 75), the IASB states that:

> *"The International Accounting Standards Board is currently in the process of updating its conceptual framework. This conceptual framework project is conducted in phases. As a chapter is finalised, the relevant paragraphs in the Framework for the Preparation and Presentation of Financial Statements that was published in 1989 will be replaced."*

However, while changing, the conceptual framework remains the basis on which the present and future statements are issued. Consequently, before starting to explore the main rules governing consolidation, we conclude our (brief) introduction to IFRS with an overview of the main principles which have been and still are inspiring the release of IFRS, i.e. their conceptual framework.

Financial statements are prepared and presented for external users by many entities around the world. Although such financial statements may appear similar from country to country, there are differences which have probably been caused by a variety of social, economic and legal circumstances and by different countries having in mind the needs of different users of financial statements when setting national requirements. These different circumstances have led to the use of a variety of definitions of the elements of financial statements: for example, assets, liabilities, equity, income and expenses.

They have also resulted in the use of different criteria for the recognition of items in the financial statements and in a preference for different bases of measurement. The International Accounting Standards Board is committed to narrowing these differences by seeking to harmonise regulations, accounting standards and procedures relating to the preparation and presentation of financial statements. It believes that further harmonisation can best be pursued by focusing on financial statements that are prepared for the purpose of providing information that is useful in making economic decisions.

The *Conceptual Framework* sets out the concepts that underlie the preparation and presentation of financial statements for external users. The purpose of the *Conceptual Framework* then is to assist the Board in the development of future IFRSs and in its review of existing IFRSs, promoting harmonisation of regulations, accounting standards, and procedures relating to the presentation of financial statements by providing a basis for reducing the number of alternative accounting treatments permitted by IFRSs.

Indeed, it should help national standard-setting bodies in developing national standards, preparers of financial statements in applying IFRSs properly and in dealing with topics that still have to form the subject of an IFRS, auditors in forming an opinion on whether financial statements comply with IFRSs, and users of financial statements in interpreting the information contained in financial statements prepared in compliance with IFRSs.

It is worth mentioning here that the *Conceptual Framework* is not an IFRS and, hence, does not define standards for any particular measurement or disclosure issue. Nothing in the *Conceptual Framework* overrides any specific IFRS. The Board recognises that in a limited number of cases there may be a conflict between the *Conceptual Framework* and an IFRS. In those cases where there is a conflict, the requirements of the IFRS prevail over those of the *Conceptual Framework,* which again provides only guidance to enhance the proper application of the accounting standard itself.

The *Conceptual Framework* is composed of three main parts:

i. ***Objective of financial statements***: to provide financial information about the reporting entity that is useful to existing and potential equity investors, lenders, and other creditors in making decisions in their capacity as capital providers.
ii. ***Qualitative characteristics and elements of financial statements***: fundamental qualities are relevance and faithful representation while enhancing qualities are comparability, verifiability, timeliness and understandability. The most important elements of financial statements are assets, liabilities, equity, revenues, and expenses.
iii. ***Recognition, measurement, and disclosure concepts***: where accounting principles, assumptions and constraints are described.

Each of these three main parts is carefully detailed in the framework with the idea of providing IFRS users with the larger guidance possible to maximise a proper application of the standards. For a deeper analysis of the conceptual framework as well as for any other issues concerning IFRS and their application, we kindly ask readers to refer to the *Conceptual Framework* itself and to the many IFRS specific manuals available[24] since this book is meant to discuss the consolidation process under IFRS, not IFRSs in general, and this is what we start discussing about from Chapter 3 on.

[24] Some of which are suggested in Chapter 1.1.

3

THE MEANING OF CONSOLIDATION

Content of this Chapter

- The economic meaning and relevance of consolidation
- Individual versus Consolidated Financial Statements

3.1 Meaning and relevance of consolidated statements

Before learning how to prepare consolidated financial statements under IFRS, it may be useful to take a step back to understand what consolidated financial statements are and what their role is in a company's accounting system and for the company's stakeholders.

First of all, let us ask a simple question: "What do we need consolidated financial statements for?" In order to have consolidated financial statements, first we need to have a group of companies. The controlling entity - i.e. the entity at the top of the group which controls all other companies ("Elia System Operator" in the example pictured in Figure 3.1) - is in charge of the preparation of consolidated statements. In a nutshell, the role of consolidated financial statements is to inform readers on how well the group as a whole (not just the controlling entity within the group), is performing in order to allow them to make sound financial decisions. However, as all other companies, the controlling entity already prepares a set of (individual) financial reports. The second question then becomes: "Aren't these financial statements enough to understand the group's financial performance?" The answer may be not trivial. In fact, as readers might recall, since the controlling entity controls the other companies belonging to the group, these will be recognised among the entity's financial or operating assets. As such, if those companies are performing well, the controlling company can maintain their book values and will recognise a gain in case of disposal; on the other hand, in case one or more controlled companies are performing poorly, in accordance with IFRS they will be impaired and the controlling entity will recognise an impairment loss and a decrease in their book values.

Figure 3.1 – Group structure example of a European listed company

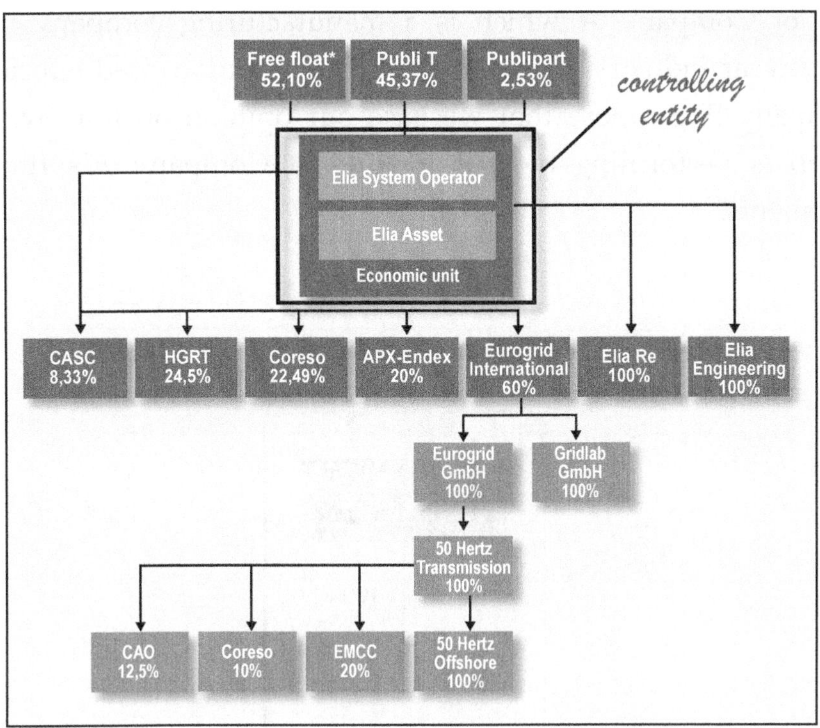

The picture represents a typical group structure of a listed company. In this case, this company is listed in the Belgium stock exchange and is mainly engaged in the electricity market.
Source: http://www.eliagroup.eu/en/~/media/images/EliaGroup/about-us/Shareholders.jpg.

So, why is this information not enough? Why is it not sufficient to look at the controlling entity's financial statements and base our financial decisions on them only? The aim of this (short) chapter is to convince readers that, although important, the information conveyed by the individual financial reports is not always enough and, even worse, could provide misleading information on the group's overall performance.

Let us start with an example to make our point. Consider the case of Company A which is a manufacturing company in the sportswear industry. Company A has one fully-owned subsidiary, Company B. Suppose that we base our opinion on how well the group is performing by just looking at Company A's financial statements.

Figure 3.2 - Company A controlling Company B

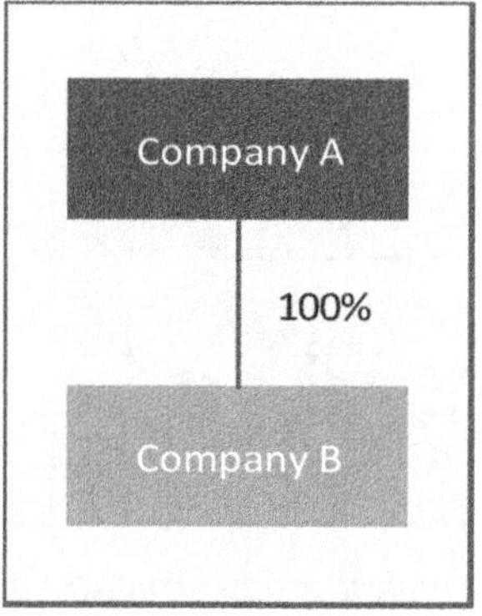

Below we report Company A's Statement of Financial Position ('SFP' or 'Balance Sheet – BS') and Income Statement ('IS' or 'Profit & Loss account – P&L') at the end of a given year.

Company A "Statement of Financial Position" (SFP)			
Cash & Cash Equivalents	350	Accounts Payable	120
Accounts Receivables	150	Current portion of Notes Pay.	120
Inventory	130	Accrued Expenses	100
PPE	100	Long Term Debt	340
Long Term Investments	400	Shareholders' Equity (SE)	450
TOTAL ASSETS	***1,130***	***LIABILITIES + SE***	***1,130***

Company A "Income Statement" (IS)	
Net Sales	1250
Cost of Goods Sold	450
Selling, General and Administrative Expenses	200
Depreciation and Amortisation	100
Operating Income (EBIT)	***500***
Financial Expenses / (Revenues)	(50)
Income before taxes	550
Taxes	275
Net income / (loss)	***275***

Let us suppose that we are considering whether to invest some money in Company A. It seems pretty much a robust company with: *(i)* a positive net income, *(ii)* good liquidity, and *(iii)* a quite balanced capital structure. What else can we ask? It sounds good! However, since we are deciding whether or not to invest our money in the company, we may prefer not just to 'have a look' at the SFP and IS. We may want, instead, to perform a more complete economic analysis (in particular a *ratio analysis*), computing some key financial indicators capable of providing us with additional insights on whether the company is really doing fine.

First, we reclassify its statement of financial position by looking at the structure of short- and long-term assets and liabilities. The reclassified SPF is the following:

Company A - SFP Reclassified	
Short-term Assets	630
Long-term Assets	500

Short-term Liabilities	340
Long-term Liabilities	340
Total Equity	450

Then, we compute some selected ratios to investigate liquidity, solvency, and profitability[1].

Liquidity Ratios		
Acid Test	Cash & Equivalents/Short-term Liabilities	1.03
Current Ratio	Short-term Assets/Short-term Liabilities	1.85
Solvency Ratios		
Debt Ratio	Total Liabilities / Total Assets	0.60
Debt-to-Equity	Total Liabilities / Shareholders' Equity	1.51
Profitability/Efficiency Ratios		
ROE	Net Income / Owners' Equity	61.1%
ROA	EBIT / Total Assets	44.2%
Asset Turnover	Sales / Total Assets	1.1
ROS	EBIT/ Sales	40.0%

The ratio analysis confirms our initial impression[2]: the company looks liquid (we have cash and equivalents exceeding short-term liabilities), quite efficient and profitable (good ROS, good ROE and ROA). After looking at this picture, the financial statements reader may feel comfortable enough to invest his or her money in

[1] Please forgive us for not giving more details on financial ratios but this is not the purpose of this book.

[2] For a better analysis we need to carry out an industry comparison and a trend analysis.

Company A. However, so far we have only focused on Company A's (i.e. the controlling entity) financial statements, relying on the assumption that as long as the "long-term investments" (where Company B is included) perform well, we do not need to worry too much about Company B's results.

Let us now have a look at the operations which led Company A to have such nice results. Suppose that, at the beginning of the year, Company A had some junk bonds[3] in its portfolio and, having heard rumours about our interest in investing in its shares, decided to get rid of them to look more appealing. But who may accept to buy such bonds paying a price for them? Maybe Company B... please remember that Company A controls Company B and can force its management to accept the deal![4]

---

[3] Junk bonds, also known as 'high-yield bonds' or 'speculative bonds', are those bonds issued by companies which are considered to be *very risky* and sometimes on the edge of defaulting. Companies (especially investment companies or hedge funds) usually buy these kind of bonds for speculative purposes, since their yield spread is substantially higher (3-4 per cent) vs. government bonds).

[4] Readers may wonder at this point what it means that Company A *controls* Company B. The notion of control will be clarified further on in the book; for the time being, just consider that company A owns Company B and thus is able to determine Company B's management decisions.

Figure 3.3 - Company A selling junk bonds to Company B

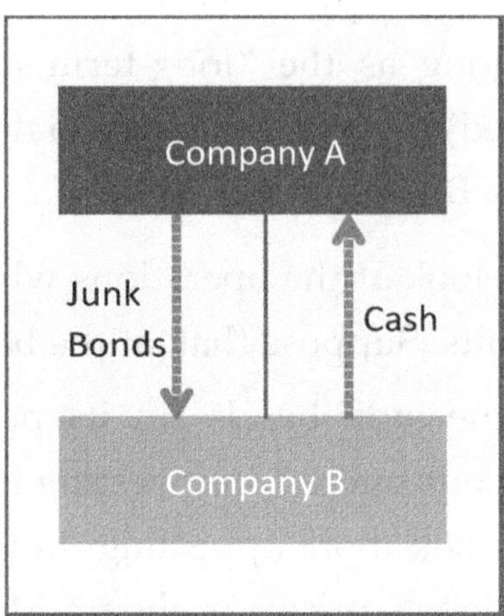

The situation is depicted in Figure 3.3. In relation to the sale, Company A will record the following journal entry (we assume no profit/loss on the sale):

	Debit	Credit
Cash (+A)	150	
Financial Investments (-A)		150

Furthermore, suppose that, in November, Company A's sales were not satisfactory at all. Since Company A's managers know that the reader is a sophisticated analyst and that he or she will look at Company A's profitability and efficiency ratios, it forced again Company B to buy a lot of sportswear[5], letting Company A to boost its sales revenues and financial resources.

[5] This implies in our example that the sale of sportswear is the business of, at least, Company A.

Figure 3.4 - Company A to Company B transaction

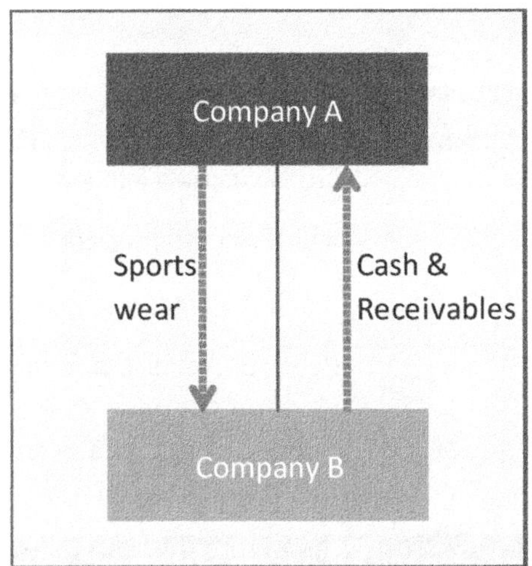

The situation is depicted in Figure 3.4. The related Company A's journal entries are:

	Debit	Credit
Cash (+A)	300	
Accounts Receivables (+A)	130	
Sales (+R, +SE)		430
Cost of goods sold (+E, -SE)	380	
Inventory (-A)		380

However, these impositions on Company B came at a price. First, Company B had to contract new (costly) short-term debt to get the necessary liquidity to fulfill the requests and pay the bonds and part of the sportswear in cash. Moreover, Company B, which is not strictly involved in the sale of sportswear, has now a substantial part of its inventory filled with it and will have to find a way to get rid of the accumulated merchandise. To be more specific, let us suppose that these are Company B's financial statements at year end:

Company B "Statement of Financial Position" (SFP)			
Cash & Cash Equivalents	10	Accrued Interest	50
Inventory (Sportswear)	430	Short-term Debt	500
Fin. Invest. (Junk Bonds)	50	Accounts Payable	130
Other LT assets	210	Shareholders' Equity	20
TOTAL ASSETS	700	LIAB + SE	700

Company B "Income Statement" (IS)	
Net Sales	100
Cost of Goods Sold	230
Selling, General and Administrative Expenses	250
Depreciation and Amortisation	100
Operating Income (EBIT)	***(480)***
Financial Expenses / (Revenues)	100
Income before taxes	(580)
Taxes	0
Net income / (loss)	***(580)***

Both the SFP and the IS of Company B do not look very promising after the transactions required by Company A.[6] Just to

[6] The junk bonds are reported at 50 due to the impairment that Company B had to recognise on them in accordance with IAS 39, par. 58 (the contra entry in the income statement is a loss, in accordance with IAS 39, par. 63, that we classified among financial expenses).

get an idea, let us briefly recalculate for Company B the same ratios used for the analysis of Company A:

Company B – SFP Reclassified	
Short-term Assets	440
Long-term Assets	260
Short-term Liabilities	680
Long-term Liabilities	0
Total Equity	20

Liquidity Ratios		
Acid Test	Cash & Equivalents/Short-term Liabilities	0.01
Current Ratio	Short-term Assets/Short-term Liabilities	0.65
Solvency Ratios		
Debt Ratio	Total Liabilities / Total Assets	0.97
Debt-to-Equity	Total Liabilities / Shareholders' Equity	34
Profitability/Efficiency Ratios		
ROE	Net Income / Owners' Equity	-2,900%
ROA	EBIT / Total Assets	-69%
Asset Turnover	Sales / Total Assets	0.14
ROS	EBIT/ Sales	-4,800%

Obviously, the last thing we want to do is to invest our money in this company. After the intra-group transactions mentioned above, Company B is in a very bad shape and cannot be considered a wise investment choice.

A careful reader might object that, since we want to invest our money in Company A, which is a separate legal entity from

Company B and is protected by limited liability, in the event of Company B's default, its creditors will not be able to seize Company A's assets. This may be true, but if you were asked again whether you want to invest money in Company A, would you still feel comfortable enough to answer 'yes'? Maybe not! Probably not all of you would feel comfortable with such an investment and, most probably, the wiser ones would choose differently since they fear limited liability might not be enough to protect their investment. As a matter of fact, considering that Company A's subsidiary (i.e. Company B) is likely to default, we might fear that Company A will spend money and effort in trying to rescue it, threatening our investment value. Moreover, after analysing the sources of Company A's results, we understand that they are not *sustainable* in the long run, and that Company B is being used to "sweep the dirt under the carpet". This awareness should ring a bell and let us foresee that sooner or later, this dirt will come out!

Better to figure out the relation between the companies within a group, the reader may think of Company A and Company B as a man and a woman. Before the wedding, it is fair to think at their wealth as different and independent from each other. But when the happy couple gets married, the overall wealth becomes the sum of the two, and consequently, we should consider both partners when judging the family's wealth. For example, even if one of the two partners is an ambitious attorney or a very successful entrepreneur earning several thousand euro per year, in case the other one is a *shopaholic* and spends twice the income earned by the former, then the family is heading for trouble! Looking only at the tax return of the former partner (the attorney) may be misleading.

The point is that, when it comes to families[7] (groups), the *individual* (a single company's) wealth is indeed different from the overall (*consolidated*) figure and, if we want to be able to judge the economic entity in its entirety (the family, in our previous example and the group of companies in the corporate world) it is then important to use the *consolidated* data in lieu of the individual ones.

"But again I don't understand why I should care about the group's overall performance when I'm just investing some money in one specific company, which seems profitable and solid" a reader may ask. Fair enough, the objection is not completely unsound, in the sense that the investor's aims should be considered: if the goal is, for instance, to grant a 6-month loan to Company A, we all agree that this may be a good idea since we are pretty sure that we are going to see our money plus interest in due time.

However, if the goal is to invest in the company for the long term, for instance by acquiring some shares, then we may want to think more carefully. In fact, even if we are investing our money in Company A for speculative reasons, we are anyway betting that the value of the company will increase in the future, so that we can get some dividends out of it and, when we sell our investment, we can get a profit out of its disposal (i.e. a capital gain). Now that you know that Company A's performance is not sustainable, the likelihood that its value will increase in the future is not very high. If Company A is profitable only thanks to Company B, it is reasonable to assume that at a certain point Company B will be so leveraged out that it will not be able to deal with debts any longer and will go bankrupt. From then on, Company A will no longer be able to replicate its performance and its profits will fall, together with its value.

What we have presented here is just an oversimplified example. Of course, things in reality are much more complex; for instance, it is unlikely that a bank will lend money to Company B to back up Company A in the situation that we depict. Nevertheless, through the example above, we have learnt two important facts. The first is that individual financial statements are an important, although not always sufficient, means of gathering information with respect to a specific company. The second is that, when it comes to groups, the information gathered from an entity's individual financial reports is far from being sufficient to have a clear picture of the current (and prospective) situation of that company or, even more evidently, of the overall group. In order to acquire the missing pieces of information, we need to rely on the financial situation of the entire group, which is condensed in the consolidated financial reports.

Let us continue our example of Company A and B looking at consolidated financial statements. Readers will have to take a leap of faith as we report the consolidated SFP and income statement without entering into the details of how such reports have been prepared (we will provide the tools and the knowledge for understanding the process of getting to those numbers in detail in the following chapters of the book).

"Consolidated Statement of financial position" (SFP)			
Cash & Cash Equivalents	360	Accounts Payable	120
Accounts Receivables	20	Accrued Interests	50
Inventory (Sportswear)	510	Accrued Expenses	100

Junk Bonds	50	Short-term Debt	620
PPE	100	Long-term Debt	340
Other LT investments	590	Shareholders' Equity	400
TOTAL ASSETS	1,630	LIAB + SE	1,630

"Consolidated Income Statement" (IS)	
Net Sales	920
Cost of Goods Sold	300
Selling, General and Administrative Expenses	450
Depreciation and Amortisation	200
Operating Income (EBIT)	***-30***
Financial Expenses / (Revenues)	50
Income before taxes	-80
Taxes	275
Net income / loss	***-355***

We can immediately see that the picture arising from these statements is not as bright as that for Company A taken alone. The reason for the difference is that the consolidated financial reports are not influenced by any intra-group transactions between the consolidating entities (i.e. the transactions between Company A and B). Let us now perform the ratio analysis again to understand how solid, liquid, profitable and efficient the group is.

SFP Reclassified	
Short-term Assets	890
Long-term Assets	740
Short-term Liabilities	890

Long-term Liabilities	340
Total Equity	400

Liquidity Ratios		
Acid Test	Cash & Equivalents/Short-term Liabilities	0.40
Current Ratio	Short-term Assets/Short-term Liabilities	1.00
Solvency Ratios		
Debt Ratio	Total Liabilities / Total Assets	0.75
Debt-to-Equity	Total Liabilities / Shareholders' Equity	3.07
Profitability/Efficiency Ratios		
ROE	Net Income / Owners Equity	-88%
ROA	EBIT / Total Assets	-1.8%
Asset Turnover	Sales / Total Assets	0.56
ROS	EBIT/ Sales	-3.3%

Had we invested our money in Company A (i.e. in the group!) at the beginning of the year, the investment would have not been profitable (negative net income and ROA) and we would have found ourselves with an overall unbalanced capital structure, at least in the long run. In this sense, the consolidated statements effectively summarise the situations of Company A and B as if they were a single entity and this is exactly the reason why we need to look at them when judging how an economic entity is performing.

We hope this brief example makes clear how important consolidated numbers are for understanding companies' wealth and make informed decisions.

3.2 Consolidated vs. individual financial statements: a case study

In order to provide readers with a touch closer to reality, we will apply the analyses we have just seen to a real company. The firm we have selected is Autogrill S.p.A., an international listed company, active in different countries worldwide with a reasonably complex group structure (just to make the case non-trivial).

Figure 3.5 – Autogrill's simplified group structure

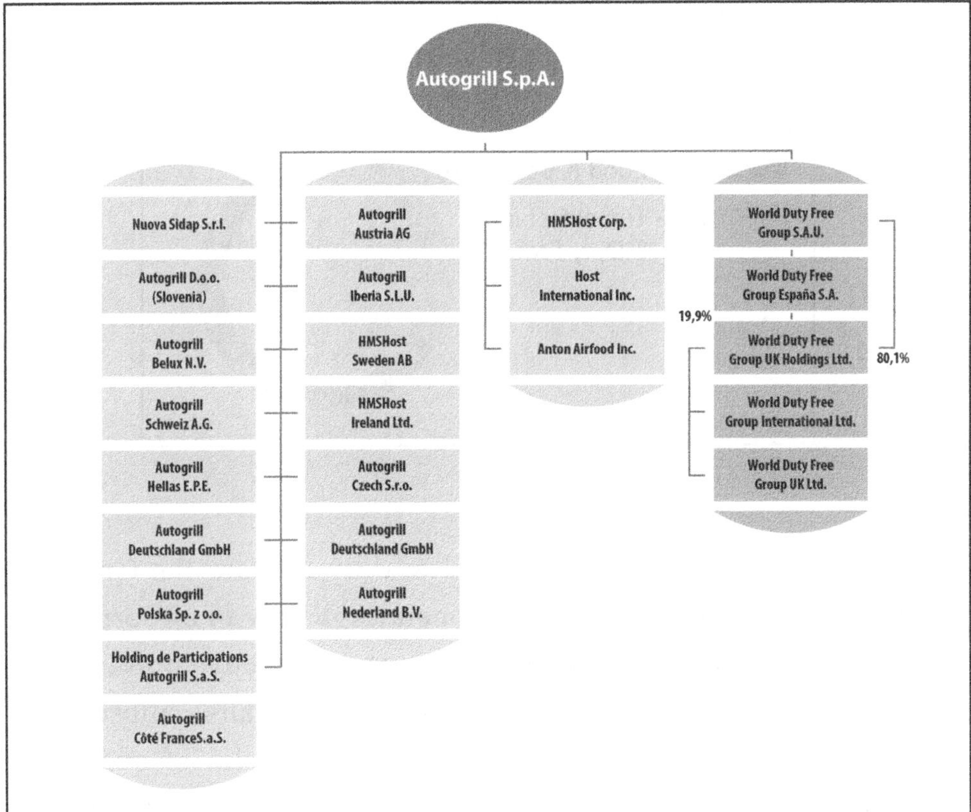

Source: Autogrill consolidated financial report 2011, available at http://www.autogrill.com/tools/GetFile.aspx?id=9084&archive=1

After briefly introducing the company's profile, we will report its individual and consolidated financial statements[8] and then comment its individual and consolidated figures in a similar fashion to what we have done in the Company A – Company B example.

Autogrill is the world's leading provider of food & beverage and retail services for travellers. The Group is present in 39 countries with about 63,000 employees and manages 5,300 points of sale in 1,200 locations.

Figure 3.6 – Autogrill's sales by business segment

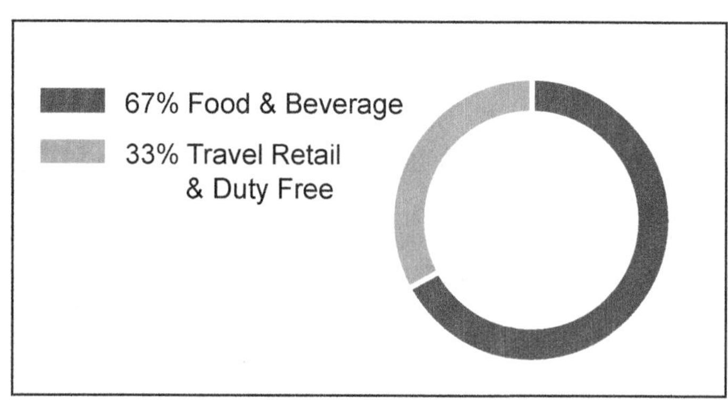

Source: Autogrill's webpage.

Food & beverage and travel retail & duty-free are the Group's two business segments. The Group operates mainly in airports and motorways, followed by railway stations and a selective presence in high street stores, shopping centres, trade fairs, museums, and cultural facilities). The Company has a portfolio of over 350 international and local brands, managed directly or under licence.

[32]Autogrill's financial statements are publicly available on the company's website www.autogrill.com

Figure 3.7 - Autogrill's brand portfolio

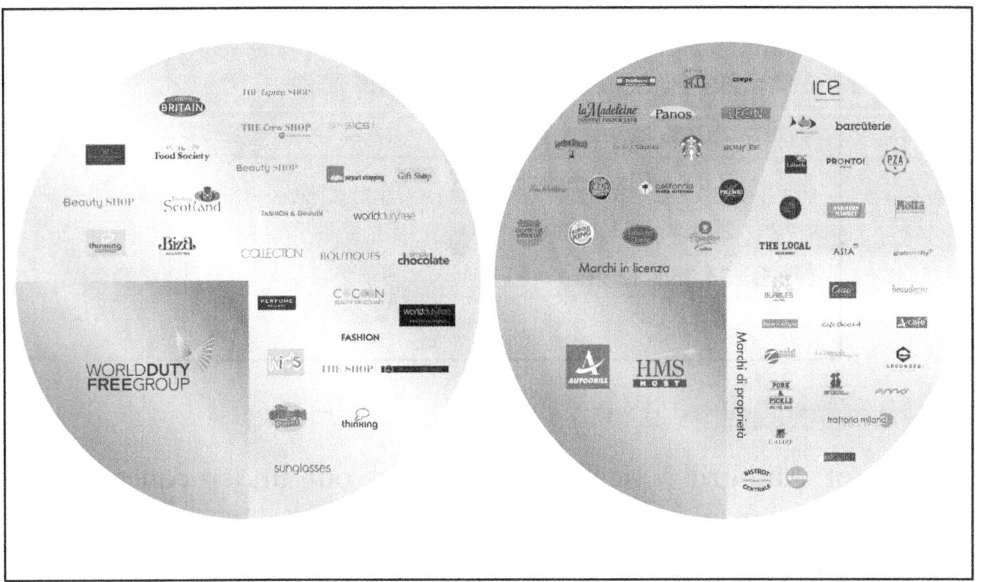

Source: Autogrill consolidated financial report 2011, available at http://www.autogrill.com/tools/GetFile.aspx?id=9084&archive=1

Autogrill S.p.A has been listed on the Italian stock exchange since 1997 and is included in the FTSE MIB index, which lists major enterprises in terms of market capitalisation. Its share capital amounts to € 132,288m and is made up of 254,4m ordinary shares with a par value of € 0.52. Autogrill is controlled by Schematrentaquattro S.r.l. (Schematrentaquattro S.r.l. is totally owned by Edizione S.r.l., the Benetton family's holding company), which holds 59.3% of the stock. The rest is held by institutional investors and other minority shareholders.

Figure 3.8 – Autogrill's ownership structure (May 2013)

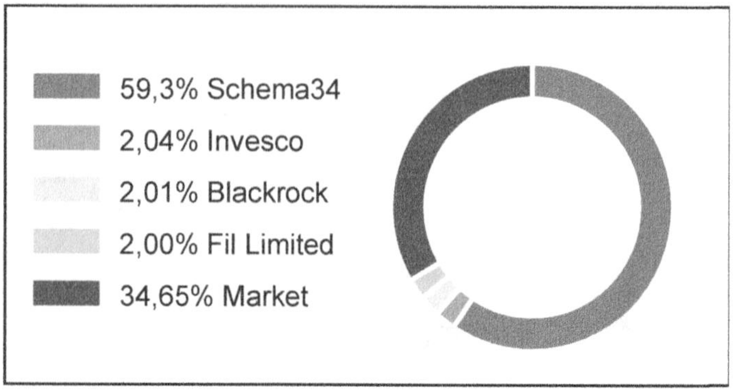

59,3% Schema34
2,04% Invesco
2,01% Blackrock
2,00% Fil Limited
34,65% Market

Source: Autogrill's webpage.

Most of Autogrill's business is carried out under concession, which is also reflected in its financial statements. Autogrill's growth strategy aims to increase cash generation by boosting sales per passenger, to expand operations in the areas and channels served, to ensure the constant innovation of products and concepts while improving customer service, and to enter new, high-growth markets in terms of demographic and traffic trends.

Now that we have a rough idea of the business and the group , let us focus now on the individual financial statements (i.e. only Autogrill S.p.A as controlling company, which includes the Italian business and Group Corporate functions) and the consolidated financial statements (Autogrill S.p.A. plus all the other controlled companies). First, we report the two balance sheets and income statements; then, we compute the main ratios to see how they change from one set of documents to the other.

Figure 3.9 – Consolidated and Individual Balance Sheet 2011 of Autogrill

figures in € mil

ASSETS	Consolidated	Individual	Change	LIABILITIES AND EQUITY	Consolidated	Individual	Change
Current assets	*755*	*258*	*496*	LIABILITIES	3,190	1,190	2,000
Cash and cash equivalents	212	32	181	*Current liabilities*	*1,253*	*467*	*786*
Other financial assets	18	56	-39	Trade payables	632	238	395
Tax assets	13	0	13	Tax liabilities	25	10	15
Other receivables	192	93	99	Other payables	369	85	284
Trade receivables	53	27	26	Due to banks	184	78	105
Inventories	266	50	216	Other financial liabilities	31	56	-25
Non-current assets	*3,235*	*1,701*	*1,534*	Bonds	0	0	0
Property, plant and equipment	923	217	706	Provisions for risks and charges	12	0	12
Goodwill	1,411	84	1,327	*Non-current liabilities*	*1,938*	*723*	*1,214*
Other intangible assets	744	37	707	Other payables	71	12	59
Investments	12	1,153	-1,140	Loans, net of current portion	1,239	613	626
Other financial assets	17	201	-184	Bonds	332	0	332
Deferred tax assets	95	0	95	Deferred tax liabilities	164	19	146
Other receivables	33	10	23	Post-employment benefits and other employe			
Assets held for sale	*0*	*0*	*0*	benefits	76	65	11
TOTAL ASSETS	3,990	1,960	2,030	Provisions for risks and charges	55	14	41
				Liabilities held for sale	*0*	*0*	*0*
				EQUITY	799	770	30
				– attributable to owners of the parent	780	n.a.	
				– attributable to non-controlling interests	20	n.a.	
				TOTAL LIABILITIES AND EQUITY	3,990	1,960	2,030

Source: Figures are taken from Autogrill's consolidated and individual financial report 2011, available at http://www.autogrill.com. The summarizing chart has been made by the Authors.

Figure 3.10 – Autogrill's Consolidated and Individual Income Statement

figures in € mil

	Consolidated	Individual	Change
Continuing operations			
Revenue	6,422	1,307	5,115
Other operating income	132	74	58
Total revenue and other operating income	6,554	1,381	5,173
Raw materials, supplies and goods	2,696	625	2,071
Personnel expense	1,473	323	1,150
Leases, rentals, concessions and royalties	1,194	183	1,011
Other operating cost	575	158	417
Depreciation and amortization	299	58	241
Impairment losses on plant, property and equipment and intangible assets	15	0	15
Operating profit	303	34	269
Financial income	2	185	-183
Financial expense	-85	-109	24
Adjustment to the value of financial assets	-1	-65	64
Pre-tax profit	219	45	174
Income tax	-80		-80
Profit from continuing operations	139	45	94
Discontinued operations			
Profit from discontinued operations (net of taxes)	–	-13	-25
Profit for the year	139	32	107
Profit for the year attributable to:			
– owners of the parent	126	n.a.	
– non-controlling interest	13	n.a.	

Source: Figures are taken from Autogrill's consolidated and individual financial report 2011, available at http://www.autogrill.com. The summarizing chart has been made by the Authors.

By comparing the financial statements of Autogrill, the most evident difference in Figure 3.9 and Figure 3.10 is the magnitude of the consolidated figures compared to the individual ones, especially in the balance sheet and in the upper part of the income statement. This difference becomes clear if we think that the consolidated financial figures include not only the assets, liabilities, and results of operations of the controlling entity but also those of the other companies of the group (after consolidation adjustments aimed at removing the effect of intra-group transactions, as we will see further below). This difference will become trivial once we understand how to prepare consolidated financial statements; for now, you can think of them as the sum of all the individual financial statements of the group entities, net of all the transactions undertaken within the group.

We now calculate the usual ratios to investigate the liquidity, solvency, and profitability dimensions and see how the usual indicators change if computed using the consolidated vs. the individual financial statement figures. Those ratios are computed just to let us compare what we did in the previous example with a real company but they are not intended to provide a faithful representation of Autogrill's actual situation (as a company and as a group), for which more detailed analyses would be required.[9]

[9] Please note that the ratios reported are the Authors' calculations and although the numbers used as a basis for the calculation are taken from the Autogrill S.p.A.'s official 2011 Financial Statements, the numbers might be different from the ones that Autogrill S.p.A. shows in its management report and financial statements. Differences might arise from different (both proper ones) formulas used for the analyses. These ratios are, indeed, calculated only for explanatory purposes and are not intended to provide a complete presentation of Autogrill's performance or financial situation (as a company and as a group), for which more detailed analyses would be required.

Figure 3.11 - Autogrill's Ratio analysis comparison: Consolidated vs. Individual

Liquidity Ratios		Consolidated	Individual
Acid Test	Cash & Equivalent / Current Liabilities	17.0%	6.8%
Current Ratio	Current Assets / Current Liabilities	60.2%	55.3%
Solvency Ratios			
Debt Ratio	Total Liabilities / Total Assets	80%	61%
Debt-to-Equity ratio	Total Liabilities / SH Equity	3.99x	1.55x
Profitability/Efficiency Ratios			
ROE	Net Income / Owners Equity	17.4%	4.1%
ROA	EBIT / Total Assets	7.6%	1.7%
Asset Turnover	Sales / Total Asset	1.61x	.67x
ROS	EBIT/ Sales	4.7%	2.6%

Looking at liquidity, we can notice that the group (i.e. consolidated financial statements) is in a better shape compared to Autogrill S.p.A. standing alone (controlling entity, i.e. individual financial statements). This is probably due to an excess of cash of some of the controlled companies, either because their business/segment requires higher levels of cash, and/or thanks to more favourable financing conditions, and/or because they have better cash management systems, etc. This would also explain why Autogrill S.p.A. is more leveraged than the whole group: 85% (i.e. 613/723) of long-term liabilities are loans compared to 64% (i.e. 1.239/1.938) for the group; a similar pattern is found in short-term loans (17% vs. 15%). Even though more dependent on bank loans, Autogrill S.p.A. looks however more solvent compared to the whole group, which presents a rather aggressive capital structure (the debt to equity (D/E) ratio is almost 4x), although we should be more specific here and divide between financial liabilities and operating ones better to assess the group's capital structure. Lastly, we can see that all the group's profitability and efficiency ratios are higher than the ones related to Autogrill S.p.A. If we look at the income statement, we can see that this difference is partially explained by the different source of the controlling company's revenues (Autogrill S.p.A. generates part of its profits as financial income), which naturally reflects the fact that Autogrill S.p.A. is a holding company and thus its operating activity generates only a part of its overall revenues.

All in all, if we only look at the individual financial statements of Autogrill we would probably underestimate its profitability and overestimate its capital structure, drawing potentially misleading conclusions about the opportunity of investing in the company. This is why it is important to prepare a different set of reports, capable of giving a general, more informative picture of the underlying economic unit, the group, which is where consolidated financial statements come into play.

The following chapters will deal now with the consolidation process and technicalities.

4

CONSOLIDATED FINANCIAL STATEMENTS

Contents of this Chapter

4.1 Introduction

In the previous chapter we explained that the information disclosed by a *single* company may be (substantially) different from the one disclosed by a *group* of companies. We also saw that, in order to overcome this difference and fill the gap between the two situations, we can use two different sets of accounting reports: the *individual financial statements*, when we are interested in the situation of each individual (legal) entity; the *consolidated financial statements*, when we are interested in the situation of the economic subject behind the individual legal entity, i.e. the group.

In this chapter we will take a closer look at consolidated financial reports and will learn how they are prepared. We will actually try to go beyond that and learn how to prepare consolidated financial reports on our own.

In particular, we first need to understand *when* we need to prepare consolidated financial statements. In other words: when are we dealing with a group of companies? In the previous chapters we saw that it is very common for a company to hold stakes in other entities, usually recorded under the item "investments in other companies" or "equity investments". But is this enough to have a *group* of companies? Moreover, once we have clarified that we are dealing with a group of companies, we need to learn *how* to proceed and prepare the consolidated accounts. Is the consolidated situation just the plain sum of the individual entities' reports? Careful readers may already have guessed, from the previous chapter, that the situation is not that simple (and this is the reason why we will spend time on it!). For example, we need to make sure that the individual financial reports we are "merging" are consistent and comparable; moreover, we need to watch out for those transactions within a group that may bias the group's real situation. Last but not least, in order to answer the preceding questions, we need to choose an accounting framework. Although the mechanisms of consolidation have a similar structure in different sets of accounting standards, there are a few specific issues (e.g. the definition of *control* we use to decide when we have to prepare consolidated financial statements, or the *recognition value* of the consolidated assets and liabilities) that do change according to the set of standards applied. As already mentioned, the accounting standards we use in this book are the IFRS. Throughout the text we report and refer to those standards in several passages in square brackets (e.g. [IFRS 10 par. 4] means IFRS number 10, paragraph 4).

A word of caution must be spent regarding the current applicable rules. Before 2011, there were basically four main standards dealing with the issue of consolidation:

a) IAS 27 - *Separate Financial Statements*

b) IAS 28 - *Investments in Associates*

c) IAS 31 - *Interests in Joint Ventures*

d) IFRS 3 - *Business Combinations*

and a main interpretation standard contained in SIC 12, *Consolidation - Special purpose entities*. Due to a number of unclear aspects, and in response to rising demand for additional information, in May 2011 the IASB issued a new standard that basically superseded IAS 27 (which now deals only with separate financial statements) and SIC 12, i.e. IFRS 10 - *Consolidated Financial Statements*. This new accounting standard is the major output of the

IASB's consolidation project,[1] which has led to a single and more comprehensive definition of control. Moreover, the IASB issued two other new standards (IFRS 11 - *Joint Arrangements* and IFRS 12 - *Disclosure of Interests in Other Entities*) and revised two existing standards (IAS 27 - *Separate Financial Statements* and IAS 28 - *Investments in Associates and Joint Ventures*). All the new standards are effective for annual periods beginning on or after 1 January 2013 or 2014,[2] even though their earlier application is allowed. This book is based on the new set of accounting standards, on which all the illustrated references are based. However, to give a sense of the major changes and to explain better, also in comparative terms, the new standards, we introduce some boxes which refer to the old principles.

The structure of the current chapter is as follows: first, we try to understand and define when we are dealing with a plurality of companies which can (*must*) be considered as a group; in pursuing that, we will provide readers with an overview of IFRS 10 and IFRS 3, which are the main references for consolidation accounting; here, descriptions of the concepts of *control, subsidiary,* and *consolidated financial statements* will be provided. Second, we illustrate the main steps of the consolidation process that lead the individual companies' financial statements to be included in the scope of consolidation. In the following chapter, we provide some details on the consolidation of two particular cases, i.e. associates and joint ventures. We will then make some examples and exercises to clarify

---

[1] For more information on the consolidation project, see http://www.ifrs.org/Pages/default.aspx.

[2] Depending on the applying country and on the specific accounting standard.

each of the main steps of the procedure and guide readers through the issue of consolidation.

4.2 The consolidation framework

As mentioned above, the main accounting standards within IFRS dealing with the issue of consolidation are:

a) IFRS 10 - *Consolidated Financial Statements*

b) IFRS 3 - *Business Combinations*

c) IAS 28 - *Investments in Associates*

d) IFRS 11 - *Joint arrangements*

e) IAS 27 - *Separate Financial Statements*

The above standards are the result of an important revision process, which went under the name of "consolidation project", undertaken by the IASB and regarding the issue of consolidated financial statements. We have listed the new standards following a "logical" criterion, rather than their chronological order of release: IFRS 10 establishes the principles for the preparation and presentation of consolidated financial statements when an entity controls one or more other entities; basically, it tells us *when* we need to prepare consolidated financial statements. IFRS 3 provides indications concerning *how* to prepare such consolidated statements, by establishing principles and requirements for how to recognise and measure assets, liabilities and other items involved in the consolidation process.[3] IAS 28 and IFRS 11 illustrate how to account

[3] To be precise, IFRS 10 already tells us something on *how* to prepare consolidated financial statements; however, the main operative indications are indeed contained in IFRS 3.

for investments in associates and joint ventures, and finally IAS 27 prescribes the accounting and disclosure requirements when an entity prepares separate financial statements. All these aspects, i.e. *when* to prepare group financial statements, and *how* to consolidate controlled entities (subsidiaries), joint ventures and associates, are addressed in this and in the following chapters.

4.3 Consolidation and the notion of control

We start our journey on consolidation by understanding *when* we are before a group of companies rather than a single company holding shares in a bunch of other entities. IFRS 10 helps us to answer this question. Suppose that Company A initially does not have any interest in other companies. Even if we did not study the consolidation principles, we are safe to say that in this case no consolidated report is required. Suppose now that Company A wants to expand its business abroad, let us say in Russia; to accomplish its goal better it acquires a smaller Russian-based company operating in the same industry. The acquisition involves 100% of the Russian company's existing shares. If we name the Russian company "Company B" we find ourselves in the same situation illustrated in the previous chapter. As a consequence, we already know that we need to consolidate the financial statements of Company A and Company B to let the underlying group's situation emerge. In this case - i.e. a zero investment and a 100%-owned investment - there is no particular problem in understanding whether we should or not prepare consolidated financial statements. What if Company A acquires a 60% stake in a third company (which with an incredibly imaginative effort we will call "Company C")? In this case, Company A only owns 60% of

Company C, so we may wonder whether the latter is part of Company A and B's group. However, the stake owned by Company A is sufficient to ensure control over all decisions taken in Company C's shareholders meetings. Hence, Company A is just using the minority shareholders (i.e. the shareholders who do not control Company C's decisions because they own too small a fraction of its equity) to leverage its investments. In other words, Company A has on Company C the same decision-making power it has on Company B, but it only had to pay for 60% of it. Therefore, also in this case, it seems correct to include Company C in the group. What if Company A has an additional 40% (i.e. less than 50%) stake in a fourth company which is a public company, meaning that Company A is *substantially* the ultimate owner of Company D? Or what if Company A holds just 10% of Company D but, thanks to some contractual agreement, has the power to govern all of Company D's relevant decisions? How many of these companies form a group together with Company A?

We can start grasping two facts from these examples. The first one is that understanding when we are dealing with a group of companies is not always straightforward, and deciding whether an entity belongs to a group requires a careful judgment based on all the possible evidence and information. As a matter of fact, for a variety of legal, fiscal and other reasons,[4] enterprises generally choose to conduct their activities not through a single legal entity, but through several entities which may end up in rather complex structures under the ultimate control of the parent company. This is

[4] These are mainly legitimate business-related reasons, but there are some noteworthy exceptions such as tax fraud or, as previously mentioned, intentional misrepresentations.

the reason why the individual financial statements of a parent company standing alone do not always present the true underlying financial situation of the overall economic group. Users of financial statements want information about the financial position of the group as a whole. In order to address this specific need, companies which are part of a group are required to prepare consolidated financial statements besides their separate ones.[5] Note that, as we pointed out earlier, providing investors with consolidated reports is not a matter of presenting "more" or "more precise" information regarding the group; it is the *only appropriate* way to illustrate the actual situation of the group as an economic subject. In this sense, the individual company's and consolidated situations may differ *substantially* and, if investors base their decisions on the individual company's situation, they may end up making the wrong choices (again, think of the example of Company A and B in Chapter 3).

Second, there is a close connection between the notion of 'control' and the notion of 'group'. At a preliminary stage (we will develop this further later on in this chapter) we can affirm that:

i. We can talk about a *group* of entities whenever an entity *controls* another one, normally - but not only - by acquiring its shares;

ii. In each group, the controlling entity has the obligation to prepare consolidated financial statements in accordance with IFRS;

---

[5] However, depending on the legal environment of the country applying IFRS and on the specific situation, not all companies are required to prepare their separate financial report together with their consolidated financial statementse.

iii. The controlled entity continues to exist as a separate entity with all its assets and liabilities.

IFRS 10 sets out when an entity is required to prepare consolidated financial statements, defines control, and explains how to apply the requirements to prepare consolidated financial statements.

***

Before proceeding with the illustration of the consolidation standards, we provide a formal definition of consolidated financial statements [IAS 27 par. 4].

Definitions 4.1 - Consolidated financial statements

Consolidated financial statements are the financial statements of a group in which the assets, liabilities, equity, income, expenses and cash flows of the parent and its subsidiaries are presented as those of a single economic entity.

Consolidated financial statements are the result of the consolidation of what we have called "individual financial statements", which are those related to a stand-alone company, this being either a parent or a subsidiary (or - as we will see later in this book - an associate or a joint-venture).[6] Therefore, as from now, we

[6] Note that IAS 27 [par. 4] uses the phrase ***separate financial statements*** to indicate those presented by a parent (i.e. an investor with control of a subsidiary) or an investor with joint control of, or significant influence over, an investee, in which investments are accounted for at cost or in accordance with IFRS 9 Financial Instruments. In this book, instead, we employ the more general definition of *individual*

will refer to the *individual financial statements* when considering the (non-consolidated) statements of an entity that has an equity interest in one or more other entities, and when considering statements of entities that do not have such interests.

Other definitions that we need to provide before moving to the illustration of IFRS 10 are the following [IAS 27 par. 4]:

Definitions 4.2 – Other relevant definitions dealing with consolidation

A ***group*** is a parent and all its subsidiaries.

A ***non-controlling*** [or ***minority***] ***interest*** is the equity in a subsidiary that is not attributable, directly or indirectly, to the parent.

A ***parent*** is an entity that has one or more subsidiaries

A ***subsidiary*** is an entity, including an unincorporated entity such as a partnership, that is controlled by another entity (known as the parent).

Now that we have provided readers with the main scope of IFRS 10 and the main definitions we are going to use throughout the work, we can go back to our first question: *when* do we need to prepare consolidated financial statements? As mentioned before,

financial statements to refer either to the separate financial statements (prepared by the parent company) or to the financial statements of individual subsidiaries, associates or joint-ventures.

consolidated financial reports are requested every time a company *controls* another entity. However, the notion of control is not easily defined, since one company can actually control another in different ways (e.g. by owning a majority of its shares, by contractual agreements, by other legitimate claims, etc.). This is why IFRS use a broad definition of control, i.e. the "power to govern the financial and operating policies of that entity so as to obtain benefits from its activities" [IFRS 10 par. 6 - 8]. In other words, any time a company can freely "use" another entity in order to gain something out of it, we can talk about control. Note that it is sufficient for the gain to be merely potential, therefore a company still controls another even if there is no favourable outcome (for instance due to a negative performance of the subsidiary). Better to frame the notion of control, paragraphs 6 – 8 of IFRS 10 expand the definition.

Definitions 4.3 – Control

An investor controls an investee when it is exposed, or has rights, to variable returns from its involvement with the investee and has the ability to affect those returns through its power over the investee.

Thus, an investor controls an investee if and only if the investor has all the following:

a) power over the investee;

b) exposure, or rights, to variable returns from its involvement with the investee; and

c) the ability to use its power over the investee to affect the amount of the investor's returns.

An investor shall consider all facts and circumstances when assessing whether it controls an investee. The investor shall reassess whether it controls an investee if facts and circumstances indicate that there are changes to one or more of the three elements of control listed in paragraph 7.

In other words, IFRS assume that control exists (and therefore consolidation is required) when the investor: (a) possesses power over the investee, (b) has exposure to variable returns from its involvement with the investee, and (c) has the ability to use its power over the investee to affect its returns. If all the three conditions are fulfilled *simultaneously*, we face a situation of control. Before exploring the meaning of each category, it is important to stress that the criterion used by IFRS in defining control is "principle-based", i.e. that it refuses to provide a fixed threshold (e.g. "we have control if the parent company has more than XXX% of shares in another entity"). Instead, it offers a general principle which aims effectively to identify all the situations in which any form of control is actually exerted, in compliance with the substance-over-form principle. In this sense, IFRS 10 prescribes considering all facts and circumstances when assessing control [IFRS 10 par. 8]. Moreover, in evaluating whether an entity controls another entity, there are other more complex issues that we will explore briefly in the last part of this chapter.[7]

Figure 4.1 contains a summary of the main topics concerning control that we are going to discuss in this chapter.

---

[7] We invite the interested reader to look directly at IFRS 10 or at more advanced IFRS handbooks for further reference.

Figure 4.1 - The concept of control: a summary

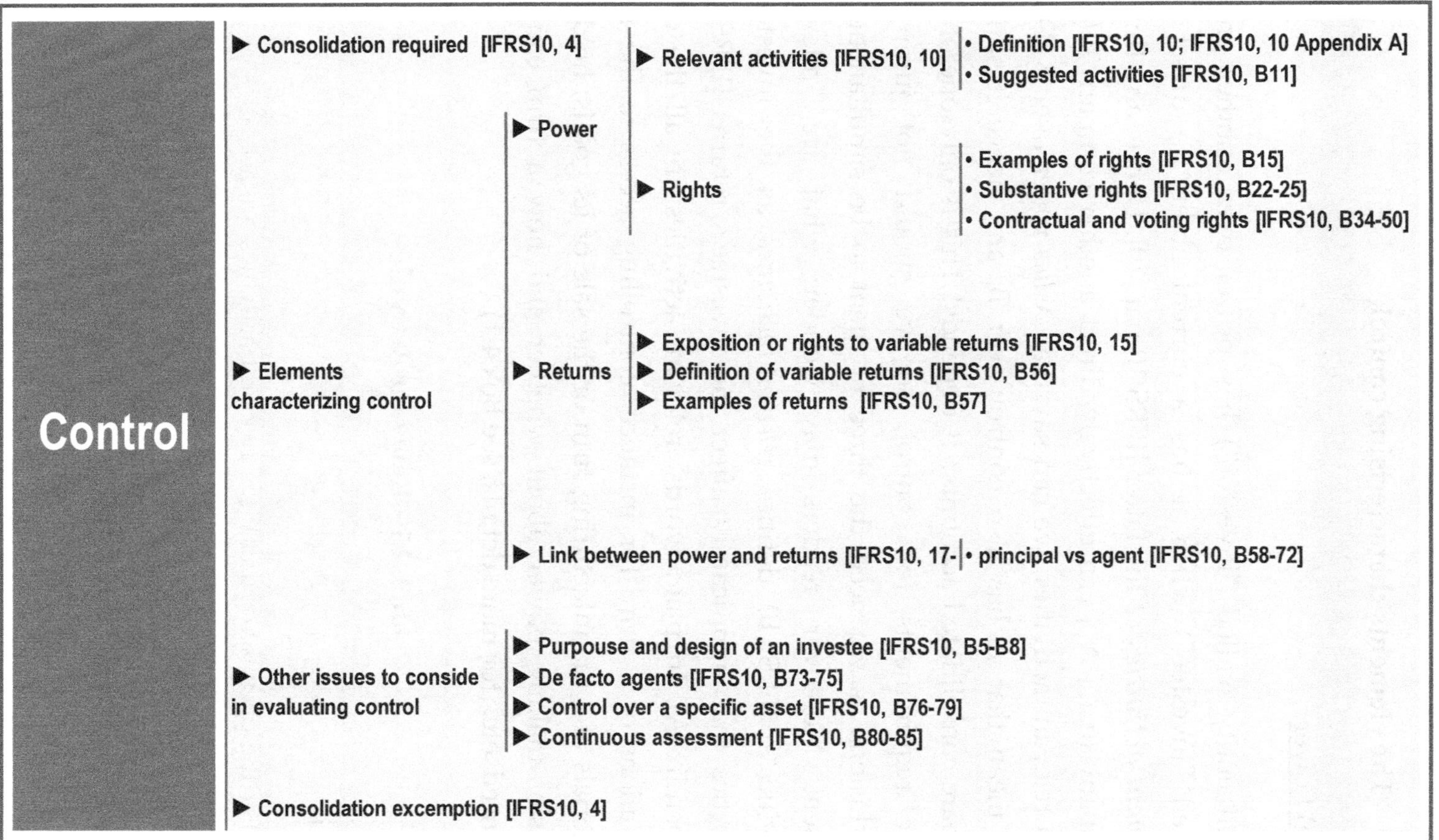

Source: Prepared by the Authors

4.3.1 The elements characterising control

(a) Power

An entity (called "investor") has power over another entity (called "investee") when it has a current ability to direct the ***relevant activities*** of the latter [IFRS 10 par. 10]. Hence, any time a company (e.g. "A") can effectively direct another company's (e.g. "B") relevant activities, we can say that A *has power* over B. Does this mean that A has also control over B, and hence it should prepare consolidated accounts? It depends! This is only one of the three requirements for control, so we should not jump to conclusions as we need the three of them to be simultaneously present. Moreover, readers may wonder: what are "relevant activities"? IFRS 10 defines *relevant activities* as the investee's activities that significantly affect the investee's returns [IFRS 10 Appendix A]. In plain words, relevant activities are all the core operations of a firm: for instance, controlling access to the raw materials of a manufacturing firm or the sale of its goods; holding decision-making power about whether and how a firm can be financed, etc. (for more details, see Box 4.1).

Box 4.1 - Relevant Activities

For the purpose of this IFRS, relevant activities are activities of the investee that significantly affect the investee's returns [IFRS 10 App A].

Examples of activities that, depending on the circumstances, can be relevant activities include (but are not limited to):

(a) selling and purchasing of goods or services;

(b) managing financial assets during their life (including upon default);

(c) selecting, acquiring or disposing of assets;

(d) researching and developing new products or processes; and

(e) determining a funding structure or obtaining funding. [IFRS 10 App B par. B11]

The ability to direct the relevant activities of the investee arises from legal ***rights*** the investor entity has over the investee, for instance voting rights coming from the ownership of shares, or contractual agreements between them (other rights are summarised in Box 4.2).

Box 4.2 - Rights that give an investor power over an investee

Examples of rights that, either individually or in combination, can give an investor power include (but are not limited to):

(a) rights in the form of voting rights (or potential voting rights) of an investee;

(b) rights to appoint, reassign or remove members of an investee's key management personnel who have the ability to direct the relevant activities;

(c) rights to appoint or remove another entity that directs the relevant activities;

(d) rights to direct the investee to enter into, or veto any changes to, transactions for the benefit of the investor; and

(e) other rights (such as decision-making rights specified in a management contract) that give the holder the ability to direct the relevant activities. [IFRS 10 App B par. B15]

Those rights may be easily identified, such as when they come directly from the voting rights carried by the shares owned: in these cases assessing power is not a big deal. In other circumstances, such as in the presence of contractual provisions contained in (usually long and complex) legal agreements, the assessment will be more difficult and will require considering more than one factor [IFRS 10 par. 11]. In such cases, even though the standard helps us by providing some indications (see Box 4.3), all the available evidence (again: contracts, agreements, financial instruments with administrative rights, etc.) must be used to understand who ultimately has power.

Box 4.3 - On assessing whether the investor has power

The following situations may provide evidence that the investor's rights are sufficient to give it power over the investee:

(a) The investor can, without having the contractual right to do so, appoint or approve the investee's key management personnel who have the ability to direct the relevant activities.

(b) The investor can, without having the contractual right to do so, direct the investee to enter into, or can veto any changes to, significant transactions for the benefit of the investor.

(c) The investor can dominate either the nominations process for electing members of the investee's governing body or the obtaining of proxies from other holders of voting rights.

(d) The investee's key management personnel are related parties of the investor (for example, the chief executive officer of the investee and the chief executive officer of the investor are the same person).

(e) The majority of the members of the investee's governing body are related parties of the investor. [IFRS 10 App. B par. B18]

When considering whether certain rights give the investor power over the investee, we should pay attention to whether those rights are 'substantive'. *Substantive rights* are those rights which the holder can *actually* exercise. Examples are the voting rights of ordinary shares, if the investor can legitimately vote; if for any reason the voting rights are not exercisable by the investor (e.g. if the investee went bankrupt and all the voting rights are legally exercised by an appointed external entity such as a bank), those rights are not substantive and shall not be considered in assessing control. Hence substantive rights are only those who are actually exercisable when decisions over the relevant activities need to be taken. For instance, a put option on the investee's shares that gives a majority of the voting rights to an investor, but is exercisable only in two years, does not confer power on the investor (at least not sooner than in two years). Determining whether rights are substantive requires judgment and the consideration of all useful information. Clearly this is an assessment that needs to be made case by case and for which IFRS 10 only provides some suggestions (see Box 4.4).

Box 4.4 - Substantial rights

Factors to consider in making that determination include but are not limited to:

(a) whether there are any barriers (economic or otherwise) that prevent the holder (or holders) from exercising the rights. Examples of such barriers include but are not limited to:

(i) financial penalties and incentives that would prevent (or deter) the holder from exercising its rights.

(ii) an exercise or conversion price that creates a financial barrier that would prevent (or deter) the holder from exercising its rights.

(iii) terms and conditions that make it unlikely that the rights would be exercised, for example, conditions that narrowly limit the timing of their exercise.

(iv) the absence of an explicit, reasonable mechanism in the founding documents of an investee or in applicable laws or regulations that would allow the holder to exercise its rights.

(v) the inability of the holder of the rights to obtain the information necessary to exercise its rights.

(vi) operational barriers or incentives that would prevent (or deter) the holder from exercising its rights (e.g. the absence of other managers willing or able to provide specialised services or provide the services and take on other interests held by the incumbent manager).

(vii) legal or regulatory requirements that prevent the holder from exercising its rights (e.g. where a foreign

> investor is prohibited from exercising its rights).
>
> (b) When the exercise of the rights requires the agreement of more than one party, or when the rights are held by more than one party, whether a mechanism is in place that provides those parties with the practical ability to exercise their rights collectively if they choose to do so. The lack of such a mechanism is an indicator that the rights may not be substantive. The more parties are required to agree to exercise the rights, the less likely it is that those rights are substantive. However, a board of directors whose members are independent of the decision maker may serve as a mechanism for numerous investors to act collectively in exercising their rights. Therefore, removal rights exercisable by an independent board of directors are more likely to be substantive than if the same rights were exercisable individually by a large number of investors.
>
> (c) Whether the party (or parties) holding the rights would benefit from the exercise of those rights. For example, the holder of potential voting rights in an investee (see paragraphs B47–B50) shall consider the exercise or conversion price of the instrument. The terms and conditions of potential voting rights are more likely to be substantive when the instrument is in the money or the investor would benefit for other reasons (e.g. by realising synergies between the investor and the investee) from the exercise or conversion of the instrument. [IFRS 10 App B par. B23]

Besides making sure that the rights on which the power of the investor is based are substantive, we want to make sure that its rights are not only 'protective'. *Protective rights* relate to fundamental changes to the activities of an investee or apply in exceptional circumstances. Examples may be the right of a bank to seize an asset of the investee if the latter fails to meet specified loan repayment conditions, or the right of another lender over the investee which prevents the latter from undertaking some specific transactions. It is easy to see that protective rights do not provide their owner with specific power over the investee but are some kind of defensive ('protective' indeed) mechanism. This is the reason why we *do not* observe power when the investor has only protective rights.

To clarify the matter we report some examples (for further reference see IFRS 10 Appendix B).

Example 4.1 - Substantial rights over relevant activities

The investee holds annual shareholder meetings where decisions about relevant activities are taken. The next scheduled shareholders' meeting is in eight months. However, a special meeting can be called by shareholders that individually or collectively hold at least 5% of the voting rights with at least 30 days' notice. Policies over the relevant activities can be changed only at special or scheduled shareholders' meetings.

Case A: An investor holds a majority of the voting rights in the investee. The investor's voting rights are substantive because the investor is able to make decisions about the direction of the relevant activities, when they need to be made. The fact that it takes 30 days before the investor can exercise its voting rights does not stop the investor from having the current ability to direct the relevant activities from the moment the investor acquires the shareholding.

Case B: An investor is party to a forward contract to acquire the majority of shares in the investee. The forward contract's settlement date is in 25 days. The existing shareholders are unable to change the existing policies over the relevant activities because a special meeting cannot be held for at least 30 days, at which point the forward contract will have been settled. Thus, the investor has rights that are essentially equivalent to the majority shareholder in the example A above (i.e. the investor holding the forward contract can make decisions about the direction of the relevant activities, when they need to be made). The investor's forward contract is a substantive right that gives the investor the current ability to direct the relevant activities even before the forward contract is settled.

Case C: An investor holds a substantive option to acquire the majority of shares in an investee that is exercisable in 25 days and is deep in the money. The same conclusion would be reached as in example B.

Another important issue to consider when assessing the rights of the investor over the investee's relevant activities is the mixture of voting and contractual rights. As we have mentioned several times, a right usually originates either from ownership of the investee, expressed through the ownership of a majority of its shares, or from one or more specific contracts, or from a combination of the two situations. Depending on how they combine, voting and contractual rights may give rise to four different situations, summarised in the table below.

Table 4.1 – Mixture of voting and contractual rights

	Contractual agreement	No contractual agreement
More than 50% votes	A	
Less than 50% votes	B	C

In situation A, the investor has power over the investee if the voting rights stemming from the shares owned give the investor the right to decide over the relevant activities or to appoint the majority of the members of the governing body that directs the relevant activities [IFRS 10 App B par. B35]. This is the most common situation and it is usually not difficult to evaluate. But is it always the case that a majority of votes implies power? Can you think of a situation in which, even though the investor owns more than 50 per cent of the voting rights, it still lacks power over the investee? Indeed, this is something we have just discussed a few lines above: non-substantive voting rights! For example, an investor that has more than half of the voting rights in an investee cannot have power if the relevant activities are subject to direction by a government, court, administrator, receiver, liquidator or regulator. If we are in situation B, the investor does not own a sufficient number of shares to have a majority of voting rights; however, by virtue of some contractual arrangement with other investors, it can obtain such a majority and hence exert power over the investee. Other contractual arrangements, not concerning the number of voting rights but the power to decide on other relevant activities (such as the manufacturing processes of an investee, or its financing activities), are included in this category [IFRS 10 App B par. B39-B40]. With regard to situation C, we need to make a further distinction. A first case may arise when the investor, even though holding less than 50 per cent of voting rights, still has the ability to control all the relevant activities because all other investors are too small and too dispersed actually to organise and effectively to contrast the investor [IFRS 10 App B par. B41-43]. Classic examples are the ownership structures of public companies, where the controlling subject rarely holds the majority of ordinary shares. In this case, we talk about "*de facto* control" (see Box 4.5 for more information).

Box 4.5 - *De facto* control

De facto control is one of the most significant changes introduced by IFRS 10. An investor with less than the majority of voting rights may hold the largest block of voting rights with the remaining voting rights widely dispersed. The investor may have the power unilaterally to direct the investee unless a sufficient number of the remaining dispersed investors act in concert to oppose the influential investor. However, such concerted action may be hard to organise if it requires the collective action of a large number of unrelated investors.

De facto control describes the situation where an entity owns less than 50 per cent of the voting shares in another entity, but is deemed to have control when it has the practical ability to direct the latter's relevant activities unilaterally. Judgment is required in applying the control concept to assess whether de facto control exists.

When an investor is required to consider whether it has de facto control over an investee, it must consider all the relevant facts and circumstances including the following:

(a) the size of the investor's holding of voting rights relative to the size and dispersion of holdings of the other vote holders, noting that:

(i) the more voting rights an investor holds, the more likely the investor is to have existing rights that give it the current ability to direct the relevant activities;

(ii) the more voting rights an investor holds relative to other vote holders, the more likely the investor is to have existing rights that

> give it the current ability to direct the relevant activities;
>
> (iii) the more parties that would need to act together to outvote the investor, the more likely the investor is to have existing rights that give it the current ability to direct the relevant activities;
>
> (b) potential voting rights held by the investor, other vote holders or other parties (see paragraphs B47–B50);
>
> (c) rights arising from other contractual arrangements (see paragraph B40); and
>
> (d) any additional facts and circumstances that indicate the investor has, or does not have, the current ability to direct the relevant activities at the time that decisions need to be made, including voting patterns at previous shareholders' meetings [IFRS 10 App B par. B42].

Another case arises when the investor owns not only ordinary shares, but also other instruments carrying *potential* voting rights, such as call options or warrants. In this case, if the stake owned by the investor is a minority one but after exercising the options rises to more than 50 per cent, this gives the investor power over the investee. However, attention must be paid to whether the potential rights are substantial: only if the investor can effectively and practically exercise its conversion rights will it obtain the majority of votes. If the call option, for instance, is only exercisable in two years, up to then the investor does not have power over the investee [IFRS 10 App B par. B47-B50].

Here are some examples on the topics just discussed (for further reference see IFRS 10 Appendix A).

Example 4.2 - Voting, contractual and potential rights

An investor acquires 48 per cent of the voting rights of an investee. The remaining voting rights are held by thousands of shareholders, none individually holding more than 1 per cent of the voting rights. There are no contractual agreements among them. In this case, on the basis of the absolute size of its holding and the relative size of the other shareholdings, the investor concludes that it has a sufficiently dominant voting interest to meet the power criterion without the need to consider any other evidence of power.

***

Investor A holds 40 per cent of the voting rights of an investee and twelve other investors each hold 5 per cent of the voting rights of the investee. A shareholder agreement grants investor A the right to appoint, remove, and set the remuneration of management responsible for directing the relevant activities. To change the agreement, a two-thirds majority vote of the shareholders is required. In this case, although there are a few other owners of the investee, investor A will always be able to appoint, remove and set the remuneration of management, independently from the other investors. Hence, investor A has power.

***

Investor A holds 45 per cent of the voting rights of an investee. Two other investors each hold 26 per cent of the voting rights. The remaining voting rights are held by three other shareholders, each holding 1 per cent. There are no other arrangements that affect decision-making. In this case, the size of investor A's voting interest and its size relative to the other shareholdings are sufficient to conclude that investor A does not have power. Only two other investors would need to co-operate to be able to prevent investor A from directing the relevant activities of the investee.

***

An investor holds 45 per cent of the voting rights of an investee. Eleven other shareholders each hold 5 per cent of the voting rights of the investee. None of the shareholders has contractual arrangements to consult any of the others or make collective decisions. In this case, the absolute size of the investor's holding and the relative size of the other shareholdings alone are not conclusive in determining whether the investor has rights sufficient to give it power over the investee. Additional facts and circumstances that may provide evidence that the investor has, or does not have, power should be considered.

***

An investor holds 35 per cent of the voting rights of an investee. Three other shareholders each hold 5 per cent of the voting rights of the investee. The remaining voting rights are held by numerous other shareholders, none individually holding more than 1 per cent of the voting rights. None of the shareholders has arrangements to consult any of the others or make collective decisions. Decisions about the relevant activities of the investee require the approval of a majority of votes at relevant shareholders' meetings – 75 per cent of the voting rights of the investee have been cast at recent relevant shareholders' meetings. In this case, the active participation of the other shareholders at recent shareholders' meetings indicates that the investor would not have the practical ability to direct the relevant activities unilaterally, regardless of whether the investor has directed the relevant activities because a sufficient number of other shareholders voted in the same way as the investor.

***

Investor A holds 70 per cent of the voting rights of an investee. Investor B has 30 per cent of the voting rights of the investee as well as an option to acquire half of investor A's voting rights. The option is exercisable for the next two years at a fixed price that is deeply out of the money (and is expected to remain so for that two-year period). Investor A has been exercising its votes and is actively directing the relevant activities of the investee. In such a case, investor A is likely to meet the power criterion because it appears to have the current ability to direct the relevant activities. Although investor B has currently exercisable options to purchase additional voting rights (that, if exercised, would give it a majority of the voting rights in the investee), the terms and conditions associated with those options are such that the options are not considered substantive.

***

Investor A and two other investors each hold a third of the voting rights of an investee. The investee's business activity is closely related to investor A. In addition to its equity instruments, investor A also holds debt instruments that are convertible into ordinary shares of the investee at any time for a fixed price that is out of the money (but not deeply out of the money). If the debt were converted, investor A would hold 60 per cent of the voting rights of the investee. Investor A would benefit from realising synergies if the debt instruments were converted into ordinary shares. Investor A has power over the investee because it holds voting rights of the investee together with substantive potential voting rights that give it the current ability to direct the relevant activities.

(b) Returns

The second element characterising control is the returns over the investment made by the investor. Specifically, in order to have control, the investor must be *exposed* to the investment, whose returns can be either negative or positive (this does not matter in assessing the control), and variable [IFRS 10, par. 15]. In defining *variable returns* the standards are quite flexible, including all the returns which can potentially vary depending on the investee's performance. In this sense, even if an investor holds a bond with *fixed* interest payments, such payments are nevertheless *variable* returns for the purpose of IFRS 10, since they are subject to default risk and they expose the investor to the credit risk of the issuer of the bond [IFRS 10 App B par. B56]. Returns over the investee are normally represented by dividends, interest, and changes in the value of the investor's investment, synergies, liquidity support, tax benefits and similar items (see Box 4.6 for more details).

Box 4.6 - Example of returns

Examples of returns include:

(a) dividends, other distributions of economic benefits from an investee (e.g. interest from debt securities issued by the investee) and changes in the value of the investor's investment in that investee.

(b) remuneration for servicing an investee's assets or liabilities, fees and exposure to loss from providing credit or liquidity support, residual interests in the investee's assets and liabilities on liquidation of that investee, tax benefits, and access to future liquidity that an investor has from its involvement with an investee.

(c) returns that are not available to other interest holders. For example, an investor might use its assets in combination with the assets of the investee, such as combining operating functions to achieve economies of scale, cost savings, sourcing scarce products, gaining access to proprietary knowledge or limiting some operations or assets, to enhance the value of the investor's other assets.[IFRS 10 App B par. B57]

(c) Link between power and returns

The last element characterising control is the investor's ability to use its power over the investee to affect the amount of the investor's returns [IFRS 10, par. 17]. In particular, the standard wants to make sure that power is held only by the ultimate effective controller of the investment. There may be situations, for instance, where the investor appears to have control over the investee, but the investor itself has to respond to some other entity. If an entity is primarily engaged to act on behalf and for the benefit of another entity, it is said to be an *agent*. In these cases of delegated authority, we want to make sure that control (and hence the consolidation) is attributed to the entity with the power to delegate, i.e. the *principal*, not to the agent which is exercising its decision-making authority on behalf of someone else. A typical example is an investment fund, i.e. a fund that provides investment opportunities to a number of investors. A fund manager must make decisions in the best interests of all investors and has wide decision-making discretion. To make sure he or she acts in the interests of the shareholders, compensation mechanisms are set up (for instance the fund manager is paid 1 per cent of the assets under management and 20 per cent of the fund's profits). Is the fund manager a principal or an agent? In other words, who controls the fund? The answer is: it depends! We cannot say straight away that the fund manager is always an agent (or a principal) since, in the spirit of IFRS 10, we need to check case by case if all the elements of control are present. Here are some examples that apply to fund managers.[8]

Example 4.3 – Delegated power

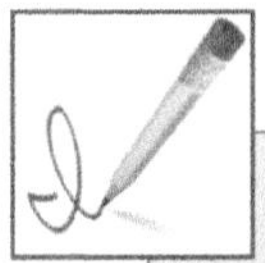

Case A

The fund manager has a 2 per cent investment in the fund that aligns its interests with those of the other investors. The fund manager does not have any obligation to fund losses beyond its 2 per cent investment.

The fund manager is an agent. In fact, although the fund manager's 2 per cent investment increases its exposure to variability of returns from the activities of the fund, such exposure is not significant.

Case B

The fund manager has a substantial pro rata investment in the fund, but does not have any obligation to fund losses beyond that investment. The investors can remove the fund manager by a simple majority vote, but only for breach of contract.

The fund manager is a principal. Although the fund manager is paid fixed and performance-related fees that are commensurate with

[8] For further reference, see IFRS 10, Appendix B.

the services provided, the combination of the fund manager's investment together with its remuneration could create exposure to variability of returns from the activities of the fund that is of such significance that it indicates that the fund manager is a principal. Moreover, the other investors' rights to remove the fund manager are considered to be protective rights, because they are exercisable only for breach of contract.

Case C

The fund manager has a 20 per cent pro rata investment in the fund, but does not have any obligation to fund losses beyond its 20 per cent investment. The fund has a board of directors, all of whose members are independent of the fund manager and are appointed by the other investors. The board appoints the fund manager annually. If the board decided not to renew the fund manager's contract, the services performed by the fund manager could be performed by other managers in the industry.

The fund manager is an agent. Although the fund manager is paid fixed and performance-related fees that are commensurate with the services provided, the combination of the fund manager's 20 per cent investment together with its remuneration creates exposure to variability of returns from the activities of the fund. However, the investors have substantive rights to remove the fund manager – the board of directors provides a mechanism to ensure that the investors can remove the fund manager if they decide to do so. Hence, although the fund manager has extensive decision-making authority and is exposed to variability of returns of the fund from its remuneration and investment, the substantive rights held by the other investors indicate that the fund manager is an agent.

4.3.2 Other issues to be considered in evaluating control

When the three elements of control - power, variable returns, and the link between power and returns - occur, we can conclude that an entity (investor) *controls* another entity (investee). In this case, we are looking at a group and the controlling entity (the parent) has to consolidate the controlled one (subsidiary).

Before going into the details of how the consolidation process works, we take a look at other issues that may be or have to be considered in assessing whether an investor owns control over an investee. First, we have seen that assessing control is not always straightforward. This is the reason why the IFRS tells us to look at the purpose and the design of an investee to determine whether the rights held by the investors over the investee's relevant activities are sufficient to determine control [IFRS 10 App B par. B5-B8]. This stresses again the importance of looking always for the *substance* of the situation, in accordance with the general spirit of IFRSs. The second issue we should evaluate in assessing control is whether there exist other parties which are actually acting on behalf of the investor. This situation closely recalls the principal-agent relationship we examined above, with the difference that the relationship between the investor (principal) and the other parties (agents) is not formally defined. In this case, we talk about '*de facto* agents' and the same considerations we made in the case of delegated power hold [IFRS 10 App B par. B73-B75]. The third issue is that an investor may have control not over the investee as a whole, but only over a portion of it. In these situations, if the portion controlled can be deemed to be an investee's separate entity in accordance with IFRS 10 App B par. B77, the investor shall consolidate only that portion of the investee. As a fourth issue, the investor shall assess again the control it has over an investee "if facts and circumstances indicate that there are changes to one or more of the three elements of control" [IFRS 10 App B par. B80]. Thus control must be continuously assessed and, if the parent loses control over one or more investees, it has to register the loss of control in accordance with IFRS 10 App B par. B97-B99.

Another relevant issue relates to the exemptions from consolidation. Even if the investor has control over one or more investees, there are situations in which the investor can avoid including those entities in the consolidated financial statements [IFRS 10 par. 4a]. In particular, the parent is exempted from presenting consolidated financial statements when:

- it is itself a fully-owned or partially owned subsidiary (in the latter case all its other owners need not to object to the parent not presenting consolidated financial statements), AND
- its debt or equity instruments are not traded in a public market nor is the parent about to apply for a public offering, AND
- its ultimate (or any intermediate) parent produces consolidated financial statements that are available for public use and comply with IFRSs.

Thus, a parent exempted from preparing consolidated financial statements has the option to: *(i)* present separate financial statements; or *(ii)* prepare consolidated ones.

Box 4.7 - Differences in consolidation exemptions

Other sets of accounting standards may contemplate different situations in which the parent company is exempted from preparing consolidated financial statements. For instance, Italian GAAP allow for the exclusion from consolidation of:

- entities that are held as subsidiaries on a temporary basis, for example, companies intended to be sold in the short term (consistently with IFRS 5);
- subsidiaries whose activities are dissimilar from those of other companies in the group;
- subsidiaries on which the parent exercises control in the presence of severe and sustained restrictions that significantly impair its ability to transfer funds to the parent.

Those exemptions are not contemplated by IFRS; hence all IFRS compliant Italian companies shall prepare consolidated financial statements in accordance with IFRSs even if one of the above (local) exemptions applies.

Figure 4.2 summarises the key issues to be taken into account when assessing control.

Figure 4.2 – The process of assessing control

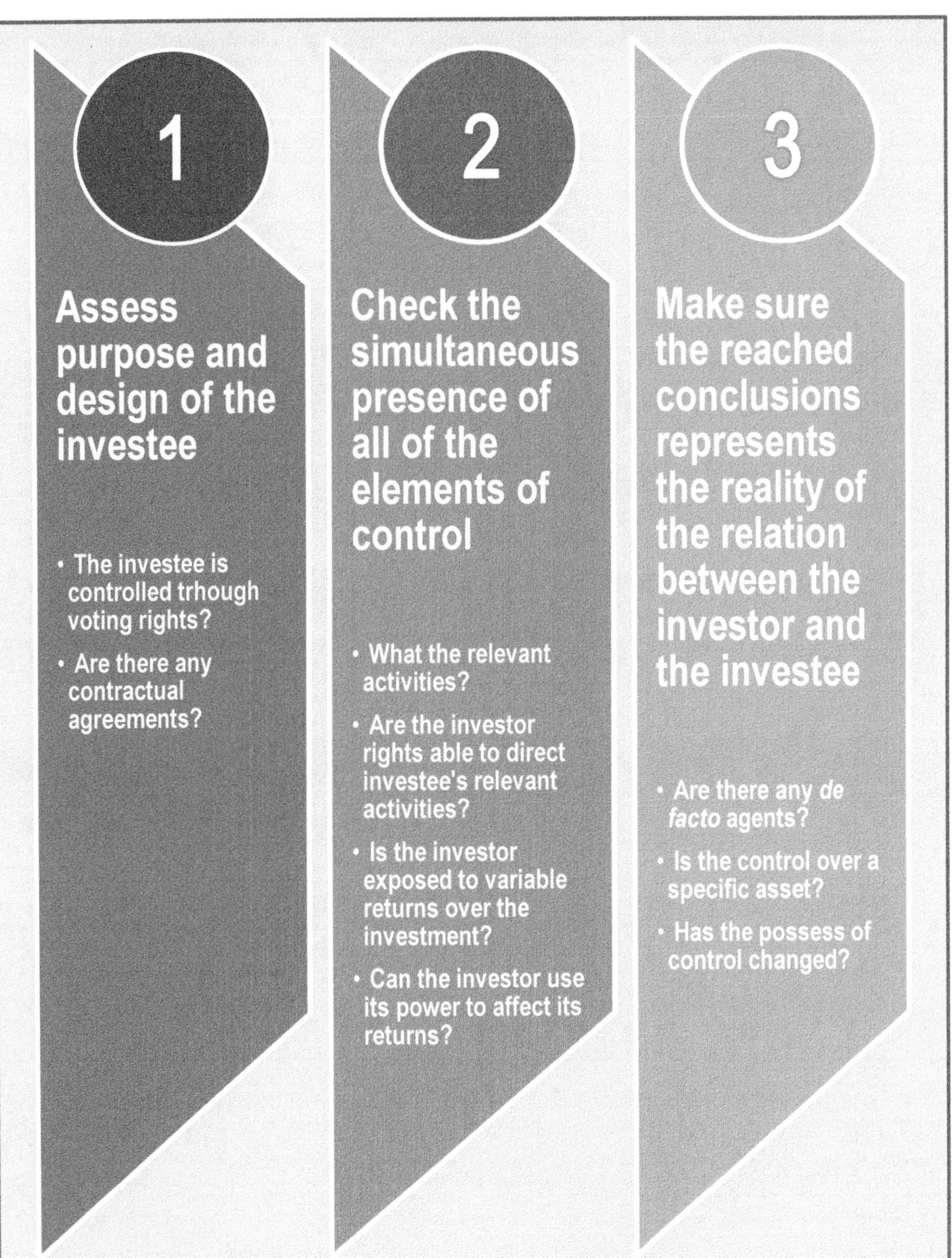

Source: Prepared by the Authors

5

COMBINING INDIVIDUAL FINANCIAL STATEMENTS: A PRIMER

Contents of this Chapter

- Consolidation and framework
- Accounting and market values
- The steps of the consolidation process

5.1 Introduction

In the previous chapter we learned *when* a parent entity needs to consolidate financial statements. Now we need to understand *how* this task can be accomplished, i.e. how to prepare consolidated financial statements through consolidation accounting.

Consolidation accounting is a method of combining the individual statement of financial position (or 'balance sheet'), the income statement (or 'profit and loss account') and other financial statements of the parent with those of its subsidiaries into an overall set of statements, *as if the parent and its subsidiaries were a single entity*.

In different words, the assets, liabilities, revenues and expenses, and other accounting items of each subsidiary are added to the parent's accounts as if the parent had acquired directly the assets and liabilities of the subsidiary instead of investing in its shares. The fact that the parent company has to add to its accounts all the assets and liabilities of the subsidiaries as if the parent had acquired them rather than invested in the subsidiaries' shares is crucial to consolidation accounting and needs to be properly understood. To help the reader, we provide the following example. Suppose ETA corp. wants to acquire your company and offers you two deals: deal#1 - buy all of your shares - or deal#2 - buy all of your assets, including unrecognised ones such as intangibles and goodwill, and take care of all your liabilities. Of course both deals have the same price. Would you prefer one deal over the other?[1] Your answer is probably going to be "no": as long as you give up the same thing (i.e. your company) and gain the same amount out of it the choice between the two deals is indifferent to you. This oversimplified

[1] For simplicity, we do not consider any fiscal impact or legal consequences such as transferability in contracts.

example helps us to clarify that the shares of a company represent in fact all of its assets and liability. This is true both for market values (as in the example just made, where we considered the selling price of all the assets and liabilities, independently from their accounting recognition) and for accounting values. This is nothing else than the 'old' well-known accounting identity: Asset - Liabilities = Shareholders Equity, and its valuation counterpart: Enterprise Value - Net Financial Position = Market Value of SE. The graphical representation of the two equations is provided in Figure 5.1.

Figure 5.1 - Accounting and Market Values

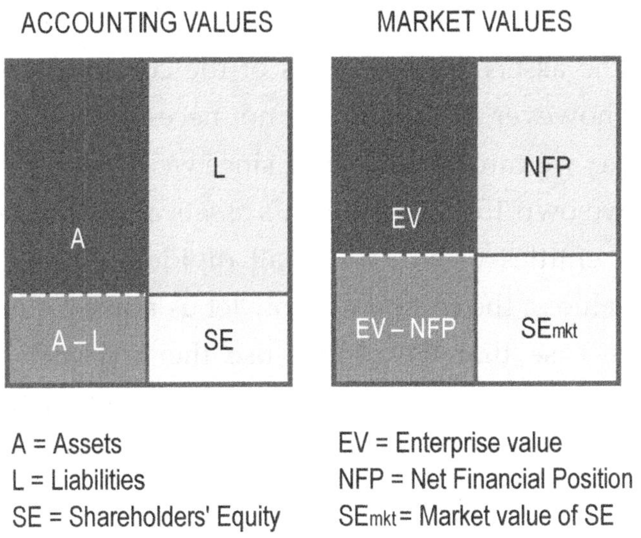

ACCOUNTING VALUES

A
L
A – L
SE

MARKET VALUES

EV
NFP
EV – NFP
SE_{mkt}

A = Assets
L = Liabilities
SE = Shareholders' Equity

EV = Enterprise value
NFP = Net Financial Position
SE_{mkt} = Market value of SE

EV	Market value of all net operating assets
NFP	Market value of all net financial liabilities
SE Mkt	Close to firm's selling price

Source: Prepared by the Authors

Although you, as an individual, are indifferent to the choice between the two deals, a company might not be, since the two deals have a different accounting impact on its financial statements: in the case of deal#1, the acquiring company (ETA in our case) should recognise the acquisition cost of each asset acquired separately, together with the amount of all liabilities; in case of deal#2, however, the acquiring company shall recognise only the price of the shares acquired among its assets in the individual financial statements.[2] Using a different perspective, through the possession of other companies' shares (which we find among the acquiring company's assets, usually among its long-term investments if the investment has a strategic purpose) we own a 'piece' of the underlying company. Indeed, there is a link between the shares owned and the assets and liabilities of the company to which the shares refer; however, this link does not necessarily translate into a 1:1 relation, i.e. we cannot think that, since we own 15% of company BETA, then we own 15% of all BETA's assets and liabilities: the 15% interest only entitles us to 15% of all dividends plus 15% of the liquidation value of the company. Now let us make a step further. Is it always the case that we cannot use the investee's assets and liabilities as if they were ours? In fact it is not! In the previous chapter we learned that if we have control over a company, we do have the power to make decisions over its relevant activities, such as the liquidation of its assets. Thus, if we have a controlling stake in another company, e.g. 70%, we can say that we have not only 70%, but substantially 100% of control on its assets and liabilities, hence the link between the investment recognised in the investor's

---

[2] According, of course, to the recognition and measurement rules of financial instruments set out in IAS 39.

financial statements and the assets and liabilities of the investee is even stronger.

Figure 5.2 – Link between the investment's carrying amount and the investee

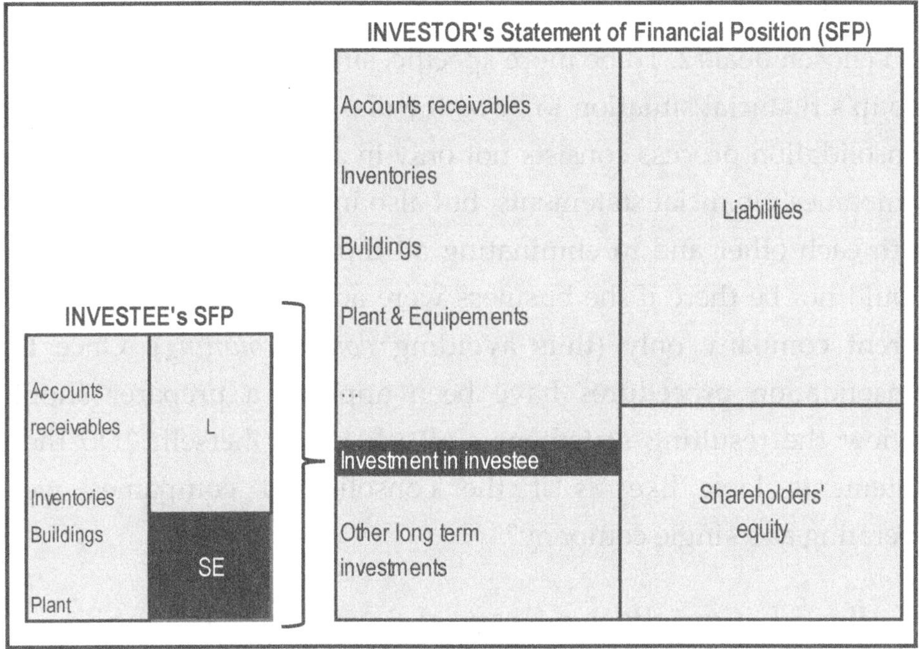

Source: Prepared by the Authors

5.2 The steps of the consolidation process

Having clarified the connection between the investment recognised in the investor's financial statements and the investee, let us go back to the notion of consolidation accounting we explained at the beginning of this chapter. We said that consolidation accounting is a method of combining the parent's financial statements with those of its subsidiaries into an overall set of statements as if the parent and its subsidiaries were a single entity. Moreover, the subsidiaries' assets, liabilities, revenues, expenses and other accounting items are added to the parent's accounts *as if the parent had acquired directly the assets and liabilities* of the subsidiary instead of investing in its shares. Therefore, independently of your previous choice of deal#2 or deal#1, consolidation accounting will always treat any investment as if you had chosen deal#2. To be more specific, since we want the resulting group's financial situation to be as the one of a single company, the consolidation process consists not only in adding up the individual companies' financial statements, but also in making them consistent with each other and in eliminating all those items and effects that would not be there if the business were actually carried out by the parent company only (thus avoiding *double counting*). Once the consolidation procedures have been applied, a preparer should review the resulting statement and ask his or herself: "Do these statements look like as if the consolidated companies were operating as a single company?"

Box 5.1 - Consolidated financial statements in the IASB's framework

The IASB's Framework looks at the concepts that underlie the preparation of financial statements together with their use. It is in fact concerned not only with separate financial statements, but also with consolidated financial statements. [Framework par. 6]. The Framework observes that such financial statements are generally produced annually and that although some users may have the power to obtain certain information in addition to the financial statements, many have to rely on the financial statements as their major source of financial information.

Surprisingly, other than this passing comment, there is no further consideration of consolidated financial statements in the Framework.

IAS 1 deals with the presentation of financial statements, and it applies equally to all entities irrespective of the preparation of consolidated financial statements as required by IFRS 10 or separate financial statements as required by IAS 27. [IAS 1 par. 2, 4].

We can now move on and analyse the steps needed to prepare consolidated financial statements.

The consolidation process includes the following steps:

1. Collect the individual companies' financial statements;
2. Make them *uniform* as concerns:
   - 2.1. the accounting period they refer to (differences between reporting dates cannot be longer than 3 months);
   - 2.2. the accounting policies;
   - 2.3. the reporting currency (if necessary, translation must take place);
   - 2.4. the layout.
3. Combine assets, liabilities, equity, income, expenses and cash flows of the parent with those of its subsidiaries; each item shall be added according to its accounting category (i.e. accounts receivable with accounts receivable, PPE with PPE,

etc). The outcome of this process is what is called the 'aggregate situation' (see below);

4. a. Offset (eliminate) the carrying amount of the parent's investment in each subsidiary against the parent's proportionate share of equity of each subsidiary (IFRS 3 explains how to account for any related goodwill) and recognise any surplus in subsidiaries' assets and liabilities;
4. b. Recognise and measure the share of equity attributable to other shareholders in non wholly-owned subsidiaries (i.e. non-controlling interests);
5. Eliminate any intra-group assets, liabilities, equity, income, expenses and cash flows relating to transactions between consolidated entities;
6. Calculate and allocate the group's and non-controlling interests' results;
7. Prepare the final consolidated financial statements.

Figure 5.3- Steps in the Consolidation Process

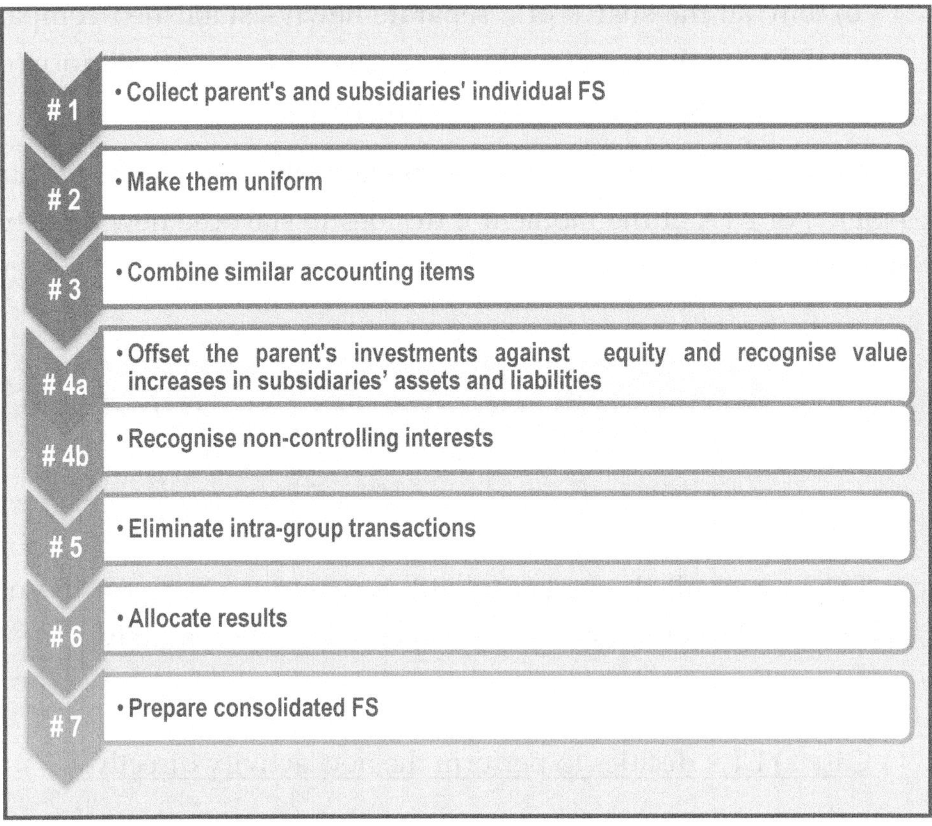

Source: Prepared by the Authors

In order to understand better the meaning of consolidation and to put the procedure just described into practice, let us continue our former example. In this case, our company ETA wants to start a new activity. Similarly to what we have seen before, in order to perform the new activity, ETA can either decide to:

a) buy the necessary assets and perform the activity directly; or

b) buy all the shares of a separate newly-established company, BETA, which owns the necessary assets, and perform the activity indirectly by controlling BETA.

Now let us suppose that the Statement of Financial Position ("SFP") of ETA at the moment it decides to start the new activity is the following:

ETA SFP case a)			
Cash	400	Liabilities	600
Other Assets	600	Owners' equity	400

The cost of all the assets (plant) necessary to perform the new activity is 100. Let us analyse case a) and case b) separately.

<u>Case a) ETA decides to perform the new activity directly.</u>

After the purchase of the assets (e.g. plant),

	Debit	Credit
Plant (+A)	100	
Cash (–A)		100

this is the resulting Statement of Financial Position:

ETA SFP case a)			
Cash	300	Liabilities	600

Other Assets	600	Owners' equity	400
Plant	100		

In this case there is only one legal entity (ETA) and no consolidation issue arises.

<u>Case b) ETA decides to buy all the shares of BETA.</u>

After the purchase of all of BETA's ordinary shares,

	Debit	Credit
Investment (+A)	100	
Cash (-A)		100

this is the resulting Statement of Financial Position of ETA and below that of BETA

ETA SFP case b)			
Cash	300	Liabilities	600
Other Assets	600	Owners' equity	400
Investments	100		

SFP BETA			
Plants	100	Owners' equity	100

In this case we have two legal entities and some consolidation issues may arise. We have already learned that, if we want to prepare consolidated financial statements under case b), we need all the assets, liabilities, revenues and expenses of each subsidiary to be added to the parent's accounts as if the parent had acquired the assets and liabilities of the subsidiary directly instead of investing in its shares. Hence, the consolidated financial statements (in this example, the consolidated SFP) in case b) should look exactly as the SFP of ETA in case a).

But let us proceed step by step. First, we should ask ourselves: "Do we really need to consolidate?" Based on what we saw in the previous chapter, we must prepare consolidated financial statements if ETA controls BETA. Since here ETA has acquired 100% of the ordinary shares of ETA which represent substantive voting rights, we are dealing with a group (ETA and BETA) in which the parent company (ETA) needs to prepare consolidated financial statements including all its subsidiaries (in this example, only BETA). Once we have established that we are before a group of companies and we need to prepare consolidated financial statements, we can apply the steps just seen in the consolidation process (for simplicity, we assume the first two steps to have already been accomplished).

Box 5.2 – Consolidation Process I

Step	Operation	Status
1	Collect financial statements	Done
2	Check if they are uniform and, if otherwise, harmonise them	Done
3	Combine like accounting items of ETA with those of BETA	To Do

We combine the accounting items of ETA with those of BETA by adding each item in its own accounting category. In this initial example, this operation is quite straightforward, since we have to add to ETA's SFP only one asset (i.e. Plant) and BETA's owners' equity. As a result, we obtain an aggregate SFP.

Aggregated ETA-BETA SFP			
Cash	300	Liabilities	600
Other Assets	600	Owners' equity	500
Investments	100		
Plant	100		

Box 5.3 - Consolidation Process II

Step	Operation	Status
1	Collect financial statements	Done
2	Check if they are uniform and, if otherwise, harmonise them	Done
3	Combine like accounting items of ETA with those of BETA	Done
4a	Offset (eliminate) the carrying amount of ETA's investment in BETA	To Do

Since the investment in BETA (i.e. the accounting item "Investments") already incorporates the value of BETA's assets and liabilities, we need to make sure that we are not counting those values twice. Our purpose is to represent the situation as if ETA had acquired the assets and liabilities of BETA directly. In order to do so, we need to offset the item 'Investments' against Beta's equity value (to find out why we need to write-off Beta's equity value refer to Box 5.3).

Aggregated ETA-BETA SFP			
Cash	300	Liabilities	600
Other Assets	600	Owners' equity	~~500~~ → 400
Investments	~~100~~		
Plant	100		

By eliminating investments for 100 and owners' equity for 100, we are in fact rebuilding the SFP as if ETA had acquired the plant directly (as in case a)).

In this easy example, we are preparing the consolidated statements at the date of the acquisition. Note that when consolidated accounts are prepared at a date subsequent to acquisition, the investments in the subsidiaries and the subsidiaries' owners' equity are not the only items to be eliminated in the consolidation process. All intercompany items (also called *mirror items*) such as receivables and payables with other subsidiaries, costs and revenues, profits and losses deriving from transactions carried out between two companies included in the same consolidated financial statements must be eliminated, since they would not appear in the financial statements if the subsidiaries' activities were performed by the parent company directly.

Box 5.4 – Shareholders' equity of the subsidiaries and consolidated SFP

When we combine the accounting items of the parent with those of the subsidiaries in the statement of financial position, we need to add all the assets and liabilities of the subsidiaries and initially their equity values. However, we still have the accounting item 'investment' referring to the subsidiary's value recognised in our assets. Given that there is no longer a subsidiary and, instead, we have recognised its assets and liabilities separately, we need to eliminate this item. Since we use a *double-entry* system, we need a suitable contra entry to balance the decrease in assets due to the derecognition of the investment. Can you think of any? What about the subsidiary's shareholders' equity?

Remember, the consolidation method assumes that there is no separate subsidiary, and consequently there cannot be any owner's equity belonging to it!

The next steps in this example are easily accomplished since we are dealing with two completely unrelated companies (see box 13 if the companies are related) and the acquisition involves 100 per cent of the subsidiary's shares. Therefore, there are no non-controlling interests and no intra-group transactions to eliminate.

Box 5.5 - Consolidation Process III

Step	Operation	Status
1	Collect financial statements	Done
2	Check if they are uniform and, if otherwise, harmonise them	Done

3	Combine like accounting items of ETA with those of BETA	Done
4a	Offset (eliminate) the carrying amount of ETA's investment in BETA	Done
4b	Recognise and measure non-controlling interests	None
5	Eliminate any intra-group transactions	None
6	Allocate group results	None
7	Close the consolidation process and prepare the statements	To Do

Here is the final consolidated SFP the group:

ETA Consolidated SFP			
Cash	300	Liabilities	600
Other Assets	600	Owners' equity	400
Plant	100		

which looks identical to the SFP of ETA under case a), i.e. as if the parent had acquired the assets and liabilities of the subsidiary directly instead of investing in its shares.

Box 5.6 - What if companies are not unrelated parties?

Companies are not totally independent when they have had some business together (e.g. sold products to each other, or granted intragroup financing) in the accounting period in which consolidation occurs. Those transactions or relationships between consolidated entities are not reflected in the consolidated financial statements because they are viewed as occurring within a single entity and, therefore, do not qualify for inclusion in the consolidated statements. We will learn more on such adjustments in the following chapter.

In this simple example, we have used both journal entries and the classical representation of the statement of financial positions readers are already familiar with from many other accounting textbooks. However, when companies prepare their consolidated financial statements in practice, they do not usually prepare a 'journal book' for their consolidation entries, since they are not required to. Most of them use worksheets similar to the one reported below to go through all the steps described above.

Item	ETA	BETA	Aggregate	(1)	Consolidated
Assets					
Cash	300		300		300
Investments	100		100	-100	
Plant		100	100		100
Other Assets	600		600		600

Total Assets	1,000	100	1,100	-100	1,000
Liabilities & SE					
Liabilities	600		600		600
SE	400	100	500	-100	400
Total Liab. & SE	1,000	100	1,100	-100	1,000

(1) Elimination of investments and related SE

The first two columns of the worksheet report the individual financial statements of all the companies included in the consolidation area (steps #1 and #2): the parent first and then all the subsidiaries. After that, we have a column presenting the 'aggregate' situation, which simply results from the sum of all the values reported in each item (i.e. line) of the individual financial statements, proceeding line by line from the top to the bottom (step #3). Next to the aggregate situation, we have the adjustments we need to make, according to the steps illustrated before (steps #4 to #6); these adjustments are sometimes referred to as 'consolidation entries'. For each adjustment we use a different column in order to understand the specific effect of each entry on the overall consolidated situation. Note that, thanks to the double-entry system, total assets always equal total liabilities + owners' equity.[3] This must be true in each column of the worksheet. Finally, the consolidated SFP comes out as the sum, for each item, of the aggregate situation and all the consolidation entries (step #7).

[3] From now on we will use shareholders' equity ("SE") and owner's equity ("OE" or "O.E.") as synonyms.

6

MORE ON CONSOLIDATION ACCOUNTING

Contents of this Chapter

- Consolidation accounting for subsidiaries
- The consolidation process in detail
- Intragroup transactions
- Intragroup profit
- Non-controlling interests

Under IFRS, there is a number of ways a company may use to account for an investment in another entity in its consolidated financial statements. It depends on the size of the investment and how much control or influence the investor has over the investee. The possible different situations are summarised below:

i. If the investor does not exercise significant influence or control over the other entity (normally holdings of below 20 per cent), its investment is a 'simple' investment in another entity, which does not require the preparation of consolidated financial reports.[1]

ii. If the investor has significant influence over the investee (presumed for holdings of over 20 per cent and below 50 per cent), its investment is generally considered to be in an 'associate entity' or in a joint venture, accounted for using the equity method.

iii. If the investor has the power to control the other entity (normally holdings of more than 50 per cent, but we have seen that this requirement may be neither necessary nor sufficient, depending on the specific situation), its investment is consolidated in full as a subsidiary and any non-controlling interests are recognised.

IFRS 10 deals specifically with the last of the three situations, i.e. when the investor has control over the investee. In this case we talk about 'consolidation accounting for subsidiaries'. We will deal with accounting for associates and joint ventures in the following chapter.

---

[1] Under IFRS such an investment is usually recorded at fair value as either an available-for-sale financial asset or as a financial asset at fair value through profit or loss (if permitted by IAS 39).

6.1 Consolidation accounting for subsidiaries

When an entity has control over another, IFRS 10 establishes that "the parent entity prepares consolidated financial statements using uniform accounting policies for like transactions and other events in similar circumstances" [IFRS 10 par. 19]. IFRS 10 provides only limited operative indications on how to proceed with the preparation of consolidated statements, as outlined in the previous chapter. In order better to understand the mechanisms behind consolidation accounting, we need to refer to another standard, namely IFRS 3, which deals with business combinations.

Box 6.1 - IFRS3 and business combinations

A business combination is a transaction or other event in which a reporting entity (the acquirer) obtains control of one or more businesses (the acquiree). Since control, as defined by IFRS 10, is the fundamental element that lets us define business combinations, we see that there is a close connection between IFRS 10 and IFRS 3. In particular, any transaction or event in which a reporting entity obtains *control* over one or more businesses is a business combination to which IFRS 3 applies.

Note that the control gained must be over a *business*, not only over an asset or a group of assets.

In a business combination, an entity (the acquirer) obtains control over another entity (the acquiree). In particular, through a business combination, the acquirer gains control over the acquiree's assets and assumes the obligations resulting from its liabilities; consequently, the acquirer recognises in its financial statements the assets acquired and the liabilities assumed.

When we deal with consolidation, we can think of the acquirer as the parent entity and of the acquiree as the subsidiary. As we saw in the previous chapter, in the consolidated financial statements the parent recognises the assets and liabilities of the subsidiary. The question is *how* the parent should do it: how does the parent *measure* those assets and liabilities? Also, shall the parent recognise *only* the assets and liabilities reported in the subsidiaries' financial statements (based on the applicable accounting standards) or shall it recognise *all* the assets and liabilities that belong to the subsidiaries (e.g. goodwill or other intangibles), even if not reported in the individual financial statements of the subsidiary?

Definitions 6.1 - Useful definitions [IFRS 3, Appendix A]

Acquiree: the business or businesses that the acquirer obtains control of in a business combination.

Acquirer: the entity that obtains control of the acquiree.

Business Combination: a transaction or other event in which an acquirer obtains control of one or more businesses.

Non-controlling Interest: the equity in a subsidiary that is not attributable, directly or indirectly, to a parent.

Intangible Asset: an identifiable non-monetary asset without physical substance.

Goodwill: an asset representing the future economic benefits arising from other assets acquired in a business combination that are not identified separately. It is measured as the difference between the acquisition price and the fair value of acquiree's net assets.

Fair Value: the price that would be received to sell an asset or paid to transfer a liability in an orderly transaction between market participants at the measurement date.

According to IFRS 3, all the *identifiable* assets and liabilities of the subsidiaries must be recognised and measured at their *fair values* at the time of the acquisition (i.e. the moment in which the parent gained control over the subsidiaries). This is the so-called **acquisition method**, which applies to all the new assets and liabilities with very few exceptions (see the Box below).

Box 6.2 - Exceptions to the acquisition method [IFRS 3, IN9]

The IFRS provides limited exceptions to the recognition and measurement principles which form the acquisition method. The exceptions include (but are not limited to):

(a) Leases and insurance contracts, which have to be classified on the basis of the contractual terms and other factors at the inception of the contract (or when the terms changed) rather than on the basis of the factors that exist at the acquisition date.

(b) Some contingent liabilities which are not a present obligation or cannot be measured reliably.

(c) Some assets and liabilities are required to be recognised or measured in accordance with other IFRSs, rather than at fair value. The assets and liabilities affected are those falling within the scope of IAS 12 Income Taxes, IAS 19 Employee Benefits, IFRS 2 Share-based Payment and IFRS 5 Non-current Assets Held for Sale and Discontinued Operations.

According to this method, all identifiable assets and liabilities - including assets and liabilities which were not previously recognised in the financial statements of the subsidiaries (typically intangible assets, such as goodwill, trademarks, etc.) - will now be included in the consolidated financial statements. Moreover, all the assets and liabilities must be measured at 100% of their fair value even if the investment of the parent company in the subsidiaries is less than 100%. In these cases, i.e. when dealing with non-fully-owned subsidiaries, a non-controlling interest must be recognised separately in the consolidated statements. The acquirer may choose to measure non-controlling interests in the acquiree either at fair value or as the net assets value of the non-controlling interest (e.g. if the parent's investment in the subsidiary is 90%, non-controlling interests are 10%, and they are recognised either at their fair value or as 10% × [acquired assets at fair value - acquired liabilities at fair value]).

Depending on the method chosen to measure non-controlling interests, goodwill will be recorded either in full or only for the part belonging to the parent entity: if the non-controlling interests are measured at their fair value, this implies that the value of goodwill is recognised in full, i.e. including the part belonging to the parent and the part belonging to non-controlling shareholders (this is the so called 'full goodwill method'). In such a case, non-controlling interests are viewed as having an equity interest in the consolidated reporting entity. If, instead, we choose to measure the non-controlling interests only as the percentage of net assets that does not belong to the parent, the share of goodwill attributable to non-controlling shareholders is ignored, therefore its recognition will not be 'full'.

6.2 The acquisition method in detail

The method applied to account for all business combinations (and, therefore, for consolidation accounting) is the **acquisition method** [IFRS 3 par 4]. This method looks at a business combination from the perspective of the acquirer. As a consequence, it requires - as a first step - to identify the acquirer and to determine the date from which the combination should be accounted for, i.e. the **acquisition date**. As a second step, the acquisition method requires the recognition and measurement of the components of the business combination, i.e. the assets acquired and liabilities assumed, any non-controlling interests, the consideration transferred, and the goodwill or gain on the purchase [IFRS 3 par. 5]. In particular, this method requires the assets acquired and the liabilities assumed to be those attributable to the acquiree at the acquisition date, usually measured at fair value. Recognising assets and liabilities acquired at fair value gives better information about market expectations of the future cash flows related to the assets and liabilities and to their future performance. Therefore, through the acquisition method, users of the financial statements are able to make a better assessment of the investment made by the acquirer and of the subsequent performance of the investment.

Fair values are key parts of the acquisition method. Indeed:

- The fair value of almost all identifiable net assets acquired will be used as the carrying amount of the assets and liabilities acquired in the acquirer's financial statements.
- Non-controlling interest may be measured at fair value.
- All components of the consideration transferred are measured at fair value.

In detail, the implementation of the acquisition method can be divided into the following steps:

a) Identifying the acquirer. Within consolidation accounting, this step translates into identifying the parent company and defining the 'consolidation area' or 'consolidation perimeter', i.e. the subsidiaries that will be included in the consolidated financial statements;

b) Determining the acquisition date (the date of the acquisition of control);

c) Recognising and measuring the identifiable assets acquired, the liabilities assumed (i.e. owned by subsidiaries) and the non-controlling interests;

d) Recognising and measuring the consideration transferred (e.g. the price paid) for the acquiree, including any previously held interests;

e) Recognising and measuring goodwill or gain from a bargain purchase.

Note that these steps are not substitutes for those seen with respect to the consolidation process; they are, indeed, complementary. In particular, steps a) and b) are needed to achieve step #1 (collecting parent's and subsidiaries' individual financial statements), steps c) to e) help accomplish steps #3 to #5 (the preparation of the aggregate statements and of the consolidation adjustments).

Under the acquisition method, all adjustments made to the aggregate financial statements in order to obtain the consolidated financial statements must be made for 100% of their values. This is true even when the stakes in the subsidiaries are lower than 100%, as non-controlling interests (consolidation step #4b) are recorded and computed with reference to 100% of the values of all recognised assets and liabilities, with the only exception of goodwill (which - as mentioned before - may be recognised in full or not).

Box 6.3–Different consolidation approaches

Over time, several conceptual frameworks have been developed and used in consolidation accounting. In particular, three main theories have emerged: the 'Entity Theory', which is mainly concerned with recognising and measuring the value created by the group companies as a single entity; the 'Proprietary Theory', which is primarily interested in measuring value creation for the owners of the group; and the 'Parent Company Theory', which is mainly concerned with providing the most appropriate financial information on the group from the parent company's perspective. A fourth theory has recently been developed as a branch of the Parent Company Theory, i.e. the 'Modified Parent

Company Theory'.

The theory adopted by the IFRS was the last one (Modified Parent Company Theory) until the revised IFRS 3 was published in January 2008. Since then, the IASB has allowed companies to use either the Modified Parent Company Theory or the Entity Theory.

The main features of the consolidation theory adopted by IFRS are the following (we will discuss them more in detail later on in this chapter):

a) <u>The full accounting method</u>:

The assets, liabilities, costs and revenues of all companies included in the consolidation must be accounted for at their full amount (100%), regardless of the share held by the parent company in the subsidiaries. Separate recognition is given in the consolidated balance sheet to the non-controlling interests' claim on the subsidiary's net assets, and in the consolidated income statement to the earnings attributed to the non-controlling shareholders. The share attributable to non-controlling shareholders should be reported separately in equity and in net income;

b) <u>Recognition of 100% of the fair value of the assets and liabilities of the subsidiaries at the date of acquisition</u>:

Fair value is defined in IFRS 3 as the amount for which an asset could be exchanged or a liability settled in an arm's length transaction between knowledgeable and willing parties. This valuation method often entails the emergence of positive or negative surpluses compared with the book values of the assets and liabilities as reported in the individual financial statements of the subsidiaries. In the consolidated balance sheet, the fair values of the assets and liabilities of the subsidiaries are stated at

100%, regardless of the parent's stake. The share attributable to non-controlling shareholders shall then be recognised separately. IAS 12 (Income taxes) states that when the fair value recognised in a business combination (including consolidation) is not recognised for tax purposes (i.e. the fiscal regulations do not consider the adjustment to fair values for their purposes), the deferred tax effect shall be recorded. For example if an increase in plant is recorded while applying the acquisition method but is not recognised by the tax regulations, a deferred tax liability shall be recorded. This liability represents an adjustment to the fair value recognised in the asset due to the loss of a "fiscal benefit" that the acquirer would have through depreciation if, instead of buying the shares of the subsidiary, it had bought the asset directly (when assets are bought directly, the fiscal regulations recognise the whole fair value paid for them). The deferred tax effect can give rise to either deferred tax liabilities and deferred tax assets but no tax effect must be recognised on goodwill (in order not to increase its value).

c) <u>Recognition of goodwill</u>:

According to the traditional approach followed by IFRS 3, goodwill is the difference between: (i) the consideration paid for the stake in a subsidiary, and (ii) the acquirer's interest in the fair value of the assets/liabilities of the subsidiary at the acquisition date. If the difference is *positive* (i.e. consideration paid > acquirer's interest in the fair value of the assets/liabilities of the subsidiary) it is recorded as an asset in the consolidated accounts and will be referred to as "goodwill"; if the difference is *negative* (i.e. consideration paid < acquirer's interest in the fair value of the assets/liabilities of the subsidiary) several actions need to be taken. First, the fair value estimation of assets and liabilities of the subsidiary should be reviewed, making sure that there is no overstated fair value of the acquired assets and/or all liabilities have been taken into account, including potential ones. Second, if the negative difference persists at the end of that process of "fair value review", this must be recorded in the income statement as a gain. Remember that, according to the most recent version of IFRS 3, goodwill attributable to non-controlling interests may also be recognised under the 'full goodwill method'. In such a case, goodwill is calculated as (consideration paid + fair value of non-controlling interests at the acquisition date) - 100% of the fair value of the assets/liabilities of the subsidiary.

d) Recognition of non-controlling interests:

According to the traditional approach followed by IFRS, these are determined as a proportion of the fair value of the assets and liabilities of the subsidiary at the acquisition date. The most recent version of IFRS 3 allows non-controlling interests to be measured at fair value, with the consequent full recognition of goodwill (see above).

6.3 The consolidation process in detail

As illustrated before, the consolidation process is subdivided into the following steps:

Figure 5.3 b - Steps in the Consolidation Process

Pre-consolidation Adjustments

- # 1 • Collect parent's and subsidiaries' individual FS
- # 2 • Make them uniform
- # 3 • Combine like accounting items

Consolidation Adjustments

- # 4a • Offset the parent's investments in the consolidated subsidiaries
- # 4b • Recognise non-controlling interests
- # 5 • Eliminate intra-group transactions

- # 6 • Allocate results
- # 7 • Prepare consolidated FS

Source: Prepared by the Authors

Step #1 is rather intuitive so long as the control issue is addressed correctly. For the sake of simplicity, we will assume this step has already been done.

As far as step #2 is concerned, there are several reasons why a parent may have to make consolidation adjustments to its subsidiaries' individual financial statements before preparing the group's consolidated financial statements, as shown here below.

i **Pre-consolidation Adjustments**

The consolidated financial statements incorporate the information contained in the individual financial statements of the entities included in the consolidation, subject to certain adjustments. For this purpose, it is necessary to standardise all financial statements of the companies included in the consolidation area. This is usually done by "adapting" the subsidiaries' financial statements to that of the parent so that their items are uniform to those of the other consolidated entities and can be merged correctly. The problem of 'uniformity' usually involves:

a) the form and content of financial statements;

b) the closing date of the financial statements;

c) the reporting currency;

d) the accounting principles and policies adopted.

a) Form and content of Financial Statements

For obvious reasons, the format of the financial statements of the parent and the subsidiaries must be consistent in order to allow 'line by line' aggregation. Different entities may use different formats in their individual financial statements. This is especially true when the group includes companies that apply different accounting standards. However, even when all consolidated companies apply IFRS, there may be differences in the formats as IAS1 prescribes only the minimum content of the financial statements.

Therefore, before starting the consolidation, the individual financial statements are all reformulated according to the group's format, following the parent company's instructions.

b) Closing date of financial statement

The financial statements of the parent and its subsidiaries used in the preparation of consolidated financial statements shall refer to the same date. In this respect:

- When the closing date of the financial statements of one or more subsidiaries is different from that of the parent company, the subsidiary (or subsidiaries) prepares, for consolidation purposes, interim financial statements at the closing date of the parent company.
- When drawing up interim financial statements is not feasible, the closing date of the financial statements of the subsidiary (or subsidiaries) and the parent company is allowed to be different on condition that:
  - i. the difference between the closing dates does *not exceed three* months;
  - ii. the duration of the financial year and the difference between the closing dates remain *constant over time;*
  - *iii.* adjustments are made for *significant transactions* and *events* which occur between the closing date of the subsidiary and the closing date of the parent company.

c) Currency adopted

If the scope of consolidation includes companies that keep their accounts in a functional currency that is different from the reporting currency of the consolidated financial statements, it is necessary to translate financial statements denominated in currencies other than the reporting currency of the consolidated financial statements. The method of translation used is the so-called *current exchange rate* method.

The current exchange rate method provides that:

- Income statement items (including the profit for the year) are translated at:
  - The effective exchange rate at the date of each transaction, or
  - The average exchange rate of the financial year;
- Balance sheet items, except for the profit for the year, are translated at:
  - The exchange rate at the reporting ("closing") date of the consolidated financial statements (so-called "exchange rate").

If the rate used for translating income statement values does not coincide with the one used for the balance sheet, it causes a 'translation difference' to be classified in a special owners' equity reserve named 'translation reserve'.

d) Accounting principles and policies adopted

Consolidated financial statements are prepared based on the assumption that instead of separate entities we have one only entity. Under this assumption, the different entities are similar to divisions of the same company. If this is the case, there is no room for allowing different accounting policies for similar transactions. For example, similar raw materials cannot be measured using different standards or criteria only because they have been stocked in two different divisions of the same company. By the same token, consolidated financial statements must be based on individual financial statements prepared according to a consistent set of principles and accounting policies.

Example 6.1 – Different accounting principles and policies

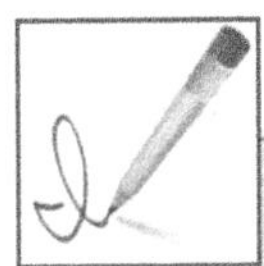

To illustrate the point better we provide the following example. Suppose two companies operate in the same industry, let us say fashion. The first company expenses the costs incurred for the development of the new collection lines directly in the income statement as incurred; the other one, considering that comparable lines are technically and commercially feasible, decides to capitalise them. If no pre-consolidation adjustment were made, the aggregate (and consequently the consolidated) situation would have part of development costs expensed, and part recognised among intangibles. Another example of an incorrect representation occurs when one company within the group accounts for its construction contracts on the basis of the percentage of completion method, and another company in the same group uses the completed contract method to measure the same type of transaction.

When one or more subsidiaries use different accounting policies than those adopted by the group for similar transactions, then appropriate pre-consolidation adjustments are made as part of the consolidation process. Operationally this can be achieved:

- By applying in the subsidiaries' individual accounts the accounting policies adopted by the group, to the extent that these are not in contrast with local law;
- By requiring the subsidiaries to provide individual statements for the consolidation process appropriately adjusted to be consistent with the accounting policies used for the consolidated financial statements.

Once all the necessary pre-consolidation adjustments (step #2) have been made, we can effectively combine like accounting items (step #3) and prepare the aggregate financial statements.

ii Consolidation Adjustments

When the aggregate statements are ready, we can start our consolidation adjustments. These form step #4a, step #4b, and step #5. We are going to see these steps in more detail in this section.

Step #4a - Elimination of the parent's investment and equity share and recognition of value increases in subsidiaries' assets and liabilities

As we saw in the simple example of company ETA and BETA, the first adjustment we need to make in consolidated financial statements consists in offsetting the carrying amount of the parent's investment in each subsidiary against the parent's proportionate share in the shareholders' equity of each subsidiary. To understand the meaning of this adjustment, consider another simple example.

Let us take a newly established company, DUFFY, , which has the following balance sheet at 01.01.X.

DUFFY SFP (01.01.X)			
Cash	1,500	Equity	1,500

DUFFY's shareholders decide to enter the business of snack manufacturing. They can choose between purchasing the necessary equipment to perform this activity directly, and investing in a company that already carries out this activity. They choose to buy a 100% stake in DUCK, which already has the plant needed for production.

DUCK SFP (02.01.X)			
Plant	600	Equity	600

Therefore, on 02.01.X DUFFY acquires all the ordinary shares of DUCK at a price of 600 equal to the carrying amount of the plant.

02.01.X	Debit	Credit
Shares of DUCK (+A)	600	
Cash (-A)		600

After the purchase, the financial position of DUFFY is the following.

DUFFY SFP (02.01.X) hp: investment in DUCK			
Investment in DUCK	600	Equity	1,500
Cash	900		

Now assume that you want to prepare consolidated financial statements for the group composed of DUFFY and DUCK as of 02.01.X, after the purchase. The situation is almost identical to the one seen in relation to companies ETA and BETA.

First, we need to add up all the accounting items of the two companies.

DUFFY – DUCK SFP (02.01.X) aggregate SFP			
Investment in DUCK	600	Equity	2,100
Cash	900		
Plant	600		

Suppose that the individual financial statements of DUFFY and DUCK are all uniform so that there is no need for any pre-consolidation adjustment.[2] As we know from what we have already seen in the previous chapter, to achieve consolidation all the accounting items of each subsidiary must be added to the parent's ones as if the parent had acquired the assets and liabilities of the subsidiary directly, instead of investing in its shares. Under the assumption of direct purchase of the plant by DUFFY, the balance sheet of the company would look as follows.

---

[2] Suppose for simplicity that both companies close their books at the same date.

DUFFY SFP (02.01.X) hp: direct purchase of the plant by DUFFY			
Cash	900	Equity	1,500
Plant	600		

To achieve this "ideal situation", we need effectively to take step #4a, by offsetting the investment and decreasing owner's equity. In this simple example, this is actually enough in order to get straight to the desired financial statements; however, in most cases the cost of the investment does not match the book value of the subsidiary's equity.

Figure 6.1–Comparison between the hypothetical and aggregate financial statements

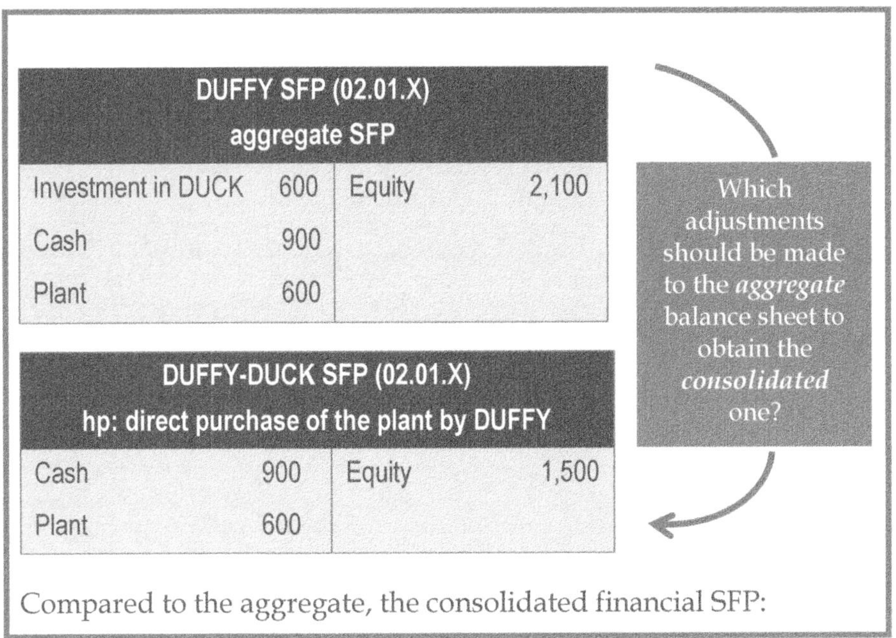

- does not contain the item 'Investment in DUCK';
- has a lower equity amount.

The case just described is an extremely simple one, in which DUFFY acquired the shares of DUCK at a price that is equal to the book value of DUCK's equity (i.e. 600). However, if readers have any basic knowledge of valuation theory, or have some first-hand exposure to financial markets and M&A, they should know that such a situation is very rare. Normally, when acquiring a company, we pay prices that are much higher than simply the book value of the acquiree. This is due to the fact that we are not paying only for the *recognised* assets, but also for all the value created which could not be recognised under the accounting principles (e.g. due to conservatism in financial reporting); classic examples are goodwill and other unrecognised intangibles. Figure 6.2 summarises this issue in a graphical form.

Figure 6.2 - Accounting and Market Values

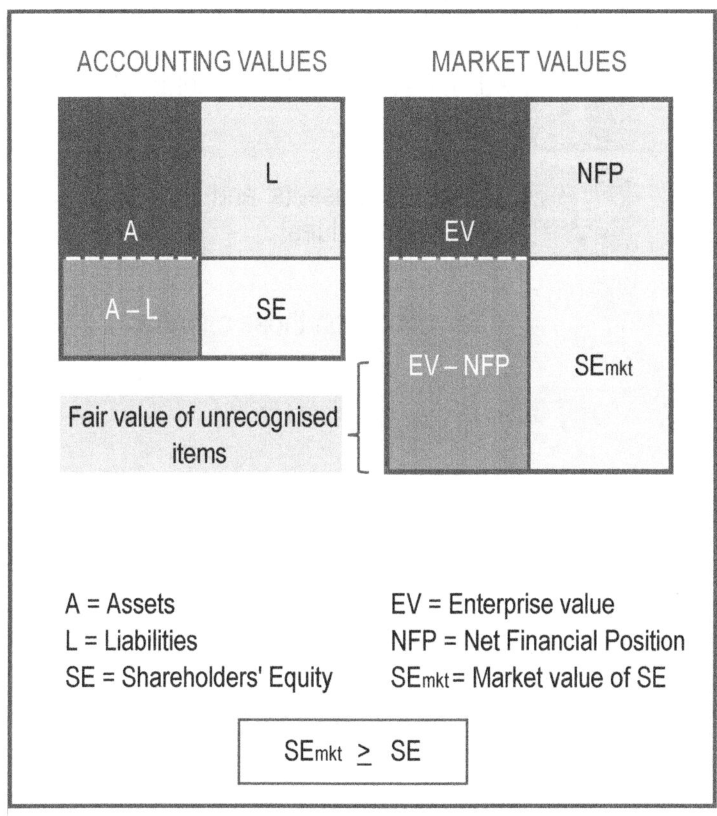

Note: The last relationship holds in the majority of instances but it is not mathematically true. Source: Prepared by the Authors

To understand the point better, let us break down the price paid for the acquisition into its determinants. The **purchase price** paid for the investment is ideally attributable to the following components:

Figure 6.3 - Purchase Price components

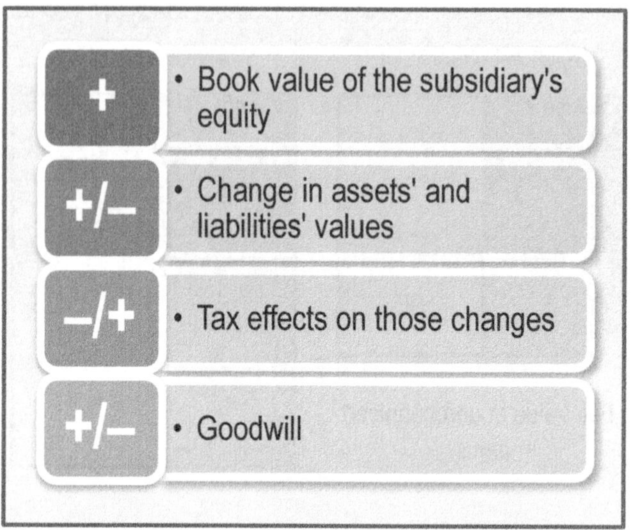

Source: Prepared by the Authors

The components in Figure 6.3 can be explained as:

1. The book value of the subsidiary's equity, equal to the difference between the book values of the (recognised) assets and liabilities of the acquiree;

2. The unrecognized increase (surplus) or, rarely, decrease (negative surplus) in assets' and liabilities' values or fully new unrecognized assets and liabilities which meet particular conditions (i.e. which are 'separable' according to IFRS 3) of the acquiree (or, in case of the consolidation, of the subsidiaries);

3. The tax effects on such surpluses in assets' and liabilities' values, in order to take into consideration the implicit tax loss/benefit;

4. Goodwill, i.e. the expectations of future earnings or losses of the acquiree (subsidiaries, in the case of consolidation). Goodwill is calculated as the difference between (i) the consideration paid for the purchase of a stake in a subsidiary, and (ii) the proportionate interest in the fair value of the acquiree's net assets. In case the expectations are positive, we pay an extra amount for the value that will be generated by the acquiree and we talk of "goodwill"; if we expect losses, instead, we discount them in the price we are willing to pay. We might also pay less because we close a very convenient deal (however, this is unlikely to happen in reality).

Although the consideration paid is made of all these components (and more), in our examples up to now we have only seen the basic case where the purchase price is entirely comprised of the first component. When, as it usually happens, we find differences between the consideration paid and the book value of the subsidiary's equity, we need to understand by which other factors this difference is generated, and choose the correct accounting treatment for it. In particular, we should do the following (the numbers recall the components listed above):

2. For unrecognized surpluses in assets' and liabilities' values or new unrecognized assets and liabilities of the subsidiary:

   a. We add the surpluses (positive or negative) to the subsidiary's assets and liabilities values, so that all the subsidiary's assets and liabilities are recognized at their fair values at the time control is acquired;

b. We recognize all new assets' (and rarely liabilities') values which were not recognized in the subsidiary's individual financial statements in accordance with its accounting principles (e.g. internally generated intangible assets). In order to do this, specific conditions required by IFRS 3 must be met.

3. For the tax effects on such surpluses: the differences between the book and fair values of the recognized items may create 'temporary differences' that will give rise to (or will lower) taxes in the future. We want to recognize such future obligation (or benefit) though the separate recognition of deferred tax liabilities (or assets).

4. For the expectations of future earnings of the subsidiary: the difference between (i) the cost of acquisition, i.e. the consideration paid, and (ii) the parent's interest in the fair value of the subsidiary's net assets/liabilities at the acquisition date must be treated in the following way:

   a. If <u>positive</u> (consideration paid > fair value of equity attributable to the parent), it must be included as an asset, the so called 'goodwill', in the consolidated financial statements;

   b. If <u>negative</u> (consideration paid < fair value of equity attributable to the parent), estimates of the fair values of assets/liabilities of the subsidiary should be reviewed; the negative difference - if still existing - must be allocated to the income statement as a gain.

c. In case we recognize goodwill, we do not account for any related deferred tax liabilities.

Note also that:

- The elimination of the investment and the recognition of the fair values of the subsidiary's assets and liabilities should be made with reference to the values *reported at the acquisition date* (in consolidation accounting, the date on which control is acquired) by the parent company. We shall not take into consideration changes in book value and fair value of assets and liabilities that may have occurred between the date of acquisition and the date on which the consolidation occurs;
- The acquisition date is also the time when the revenues and expenses of the subsidiaries start being included in the consolidated financial statements;
- The surpluses on assets and liabilities of the subsidiary follow the treatment of the assets or liabilities they refer to. In particular:
    - If they are related to *depreciable assets*, the surpluses are amortized over the useful life of the asset to which they relate;
    - If they are related to *non-depreciable assets*, the surpluses may, together with the assets to which they relate to, be subjected to impairment testing in accordance with IAS 36.[3]

[3] This is a 'value audit' of whether the carrying amount of an asset is less than its 'recoverable amount', i.e. the value which can be reasonably obtained from the asset. Due to the prudence principle according to which financial statements are prepared, if the asset's carrying amount is greater than its recoverable amount, the company shall recognize an impairment loss and decrease (i.e. 'impair') the value of the asset accordingly.

In particular, every year goodwill shall be tested for impairment.

Examples 6.2 – Consolidation of a subsidiary at the date of acquisition (with goodwill)

On 31 December X company MICKEY buys 100% of shares in company MOUSE. The cost of the investment is 2,700. The balance sheet of the two companies at the date of the acquisition is reported in the worksheet.

Balance Sheet	Mickey	Mouse
ASSETS		
Non-current assets		
Property, plant and equipment	1,000	1,500
Goodwill		
Other intangible assets	3,000	2,000
Deferred tax assets		
Investments	2,700	
TOTAL ASSETS	6,700	3,500
LIABILITIES and OWNERS' EQUITY		
Owners' equity		
Common Stock	3,000	1,500
Retained earnings	600	500
Non-controlling interests		
Deferred tax liabilities		
Current and non-current liabilities (incl. Provisions)	3,100	1,500

LIABILITIES and OWNERS' EQUITY	6,700	3,500

On the same date, the fair value of the assets and liabilities of MOUSE equals their book value, except for plant, whose fair value is 1,000 higher that the carrying amount, and provisions, whose fair value is 200 higher than the book value. The difference between the cost of the investment and owners' equity is recorded as goodwill.

Consider that the tax rate applied by the two companies is 50%.

Prepare the consolidated financial statements at the date of the acquisition.

First, we prepare the aggregate financial statements by adding up, line by line, the amounts in the individual statements of financial positions (column 'Aggregate'). We assume that the individual financial statements are already uniform so that we can proceed straight away to the consolidation adjustments, in particular, step #4a, which we perform in column '(1)'. Finally, by adding up the columns 'Aggregate' and '(1)' we obtain the desired consolidated financial statements.

Balance Sheet	Mickey	Mouse	Aggregate	(1)	Consol.
ASSETS					
Non-current assets					
Property, plant and equipment	1,000	1,500	2,500	1,000	3,500
Goodwill				300	300
Other intangible assets	3,000	2,000	5,000		5,000
Deferred tax assets				100	100
Investments	2,700		2,700	-2,700	0

TOTAL ASSETS	6,700	3,500	10,200	-1,300	8,900
LIAB. and OWN. EQUITY					
Owners' equity					
Common Stock	3,000	1,500	4,500	-1,500	3,000
Retained earnings	600	500	1,100	-500	600
Minority interests					
Deferred tax liabilities				500	500
Current and non-current liabilities (incl. Provisions)	3,100	1,500	4,600	200	4,800
LIAB. and OWN. EQUITY	6,700	3,500	10,200	-1,300	8,900

(1) Recognition of surplus on PPE and provisions [1,000 and 200, respectively]

Elimination of investment [2,700] and subsidiary's equity [1,500+500 = 2,000]

Recognition of deferred tax liabilities [1,000×0.5 = 500] and deferred tax assets [200×0.5 = 100]

Recognition of goodwill = 300 calculated as follows:

purchase price [2,700] – book value of equity of subsidiary [2,000] – increase in PPE's value [1,000] + deferred tax liabilities [500] + decrease in provisions' value [200] - deferred tax asset [100].

Remember that the accounting item containing the value of the parent's investment in the consolidated subsidiaries which we want to offset is nothing other than the purchase price we have just seen, measured at the time control was acquired. Hence, in order to account for its components, we need to perform the following consolidation adjustments:

1. Write-off of the investment's carrying amount (i.e. the investment originally recognized in the parent's statement of financial position);
2. Write-off of the aggregate equity for an amount equal to the equity of the subsidiaries at the acquisition date;
3. Recognition of surpluses on the assets and liabilities of the subsidiary at the acquisition date;
4. Recognition of deferred tax on those surpluses at the acquisition date;
5. Recognition of goodwill among consolidated assets, if positive, or in the consolidated income statement, as a gain, if negative.

Step #4b – Non-controlling interests

Now, let us have a look at the computation of non-controlling interests. How should we treat non-controlling interests in consolidated subsidiaries? When a subsidiary is less than wholly owned, the general approach to recognising and measuring all (separable) assets and liabilities of the acquiree is the same as the one discussed above. However, the consolidation procedures must be slightly modified as concerns the recognition of goodwill and of the non-controlling interests.[4] For example, if a parent owns 85 per cent of a subsidiary, it has to consolidate 100 per cent of the

---

[4] In this book, 'non-controlling' and 'minority' interests are used as synonyms. As seen in the chapter on control, the definition of non-controlling interest is given in appendix A of IFRS 10 as "equity in a subsidiary not attributable, directly or indirectly, to a parent".

subsidiary's results and net assets and report non-controlling interests of 15 per cent.

The non-controlling interests are reported as part of the equity of the consolidated group, recorded separately from the other equity components and clearly identified and labelled (for example, 'non-controlling interests in subsidiaries' or 'equity attributable to third parties'). However, an entity with non-controlling interests in more than one subsidiary may aggregate its various non-controlling interests in the consolidated financial statements. Since the non-controlling interests are classified separately in the consolidated statement of financial position, the net income resulting from the income statement must also distinguish the profit or loss that is attributable to the parent from the share attributable to the non-controlling interests, so that each component will be added separately where it belongs (in step #6 of the consolidation procedure). With regard to the *measurement* of the non-controlling interests, as already specified, the acquirer may choose to measure a non-controlling interest in the acquiree either at fair value (so called 'full goodwill accounting') or at the non-controlling interest's proportionate share of the acquiree's identifiable net assets [IFRS 3 par. 19].

Let us go back to the purchase price components. In the case of non-fully-owned subsidiaries, not only shall we break down each component and account separately for each of them (i.e. increase in subsidiaries' assets and liabilities, deferred taxes and goodwill), but we must also take into account that the consideration paid by the parent only refers to a portion (specifically the stake acquired, e.g. 80%) of the subsidiary's. The breakdown of the purchase price of the investment is the same as the one illustrated above in Figure 6.3, with the only difference that we now need to recognize the non-controlling interests according to one of the two methods outlined. The example in the Box shows how the two different methods have different accounting impacts on the consolidated accounts.

Example 6.3 - Recognition of non-controlling interests at the acquisition date

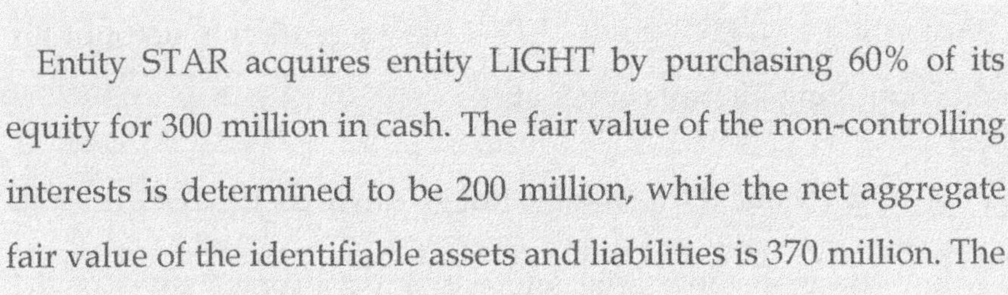

Entity STAR acquires entity LIGHT by purchasing 60% of its equity for 300 million in cash. The fair value of the non-controlling interests is determined to be 200 million, while the net aggregate fair value of the identifiable assets and liabilities is 370 million. The company's tax rate is on a 40% basis.

The key figures included in the Balance Sheet of entity LIGHT at the date of acquisition are summarized in the table below:

Balance Sheet LIGHT			
Assets	290	Liabilities	100
		Equity	190

At the date of acquisition, the fair values for all assets and liabilities of LIGHT are equal to their book values, except for a parcel of land, a building and an internally generated trademark. The fair values of those assets are given in the following table:

100%	Book Value	Fair Value
Building	50	140
Land	30	75
Trademark (Internally generated)	90	255
Total	170	470

According to IFRS 3, Entity STAR has the option to account for non-controlling interests either at:

i. fair value (i.e. using the full goodwill method); or

ii. the non-controlling interests' proportionate share of the acquiree's identifiable net assets at fair value.

Let us see how to proceed by looking at each of the two options.

(i) FULL GOODWILL RECOGNITION

If the company chooses to apply the full goodwill method, the non-controlling interests' value is equal to their fair value. The resulting value is therefore 200 million.

In such a case, we calculate the total value of the company (as if 100% had been acquired at the acquisition date) which will be useful to calculate the full goodwill:

Consideration paid by the parent company (60%)	300
Fair value of non-controlling interests (40%)	200

Total Value (100%) **500**

The total value of entity LIGHT can be broken down into the following components:

+ Book value of equity	190
+ Net surpluses on identifiable assets (net of tax effects)	180
+ Goodwill	130
= Total Value (100%)	**500**

The calculation of the net surpluses on identifiable assets is summarized in the table below:

100%	Book Value	Fair Value	Diff	Tax effect	Net Amounts
Building	50	140	90	36	54
Land	30	75	45	18	27
Trademark (Internally generated)	90	255	165	66	99
Total	170	470	300	120	**180**

Goodwill has been computed as:

+	Consideration paid (60% of subsidiary value)	300
+	Fair value of the non-controlling interests (40%)	200
-	Fair value of 100% of the identifiable net assets	-370
=	**Goodwill recognized**	**130**

For the purpose of consolidation, the parent company would account for the elimination of the investment in LIGHT and for the different determinants of its value by making the following journal entries:

	Debit	Credit
Land (+A)	45	
Building (+A)	90	
Trademarks (+A)	165	
Goodwill (+A)	130	
Equity (-SE)	190	
Investments (-A)		300
Deferred Tax Liabilities (+L)		120
Non-controlling Interests (+SE)		200

Where:

- Land, Building and Trademarks are increased by the surpluses arising from comparing the fair values of the assets to their carrying amounts, net of tax (Deferred Tax Liabilities)
- Goodwill is determined as the difference between the value of the whole company (500) and the fair value of the company's net assets (190 + 180)
- Non-controlling interests are accounted for at their fair value, which indirectly is composed of:
  - the proportionate share of the book value of equity;
  - the proportionate share of the surpluses on the value of net assets, net of tax, and
  - the goodwill attributable to the non-controlling interests.

Remember: Since the non-controlling interests are recorded at fair value, goodwill is effectively recognized for both the controlling and non-controlling interests (i.e. 'fully' recognized).

(ii) NON-CONTROLLING INTERESTS MEASURED AT THE PROPORTIONATE SHARE OF THE ACQUIREE'S IDENTIFIABLE NET ASSETS

If entity STAR chooses to record the non-controlling interests at their proportionate share of the amount of the acquiree's identifiable net assets, the goodwill recognised and measured in the consolidated financial statements is only the amount attributable to the portion belonging to the parent company (i.e. STAR).

In such a case, the process would work similarly to the one described above, but with different values for Goodwill and Non-controlling interests.

First, we need to calculate the surpluses on assets and liabilities by comparing their fair values with their carrying amounts, as we did before:

100%	Book Value	Fair Value	Diff	Tax effect	Net Amounts
Building	50	140	90	36	54
Land	30	75	45	18	27

Trademark (Internally generated)	90	255	165	66	99
Total	170	470	300	120	**180**

Next, we identify the portion of net surpluses belonging to the controlling entity:

180 x 60% = 108

Finally, we determine the goodwill implicit in the consideration paid by the parent company (STAR) as follows:

+ Consideration paid (60%)	300
+ Book value of equity (60%)	-114
+ Net surpluses on identifiable assets (60%)	-108
= Goodwill (60%)	**78**

In this case, the parent company will consolidate its investment in LIGHT by making the following journal entries:

	Debit	Credit
Land (+A)	45	
Building (+A)	90	
Trademarks (+A)	165	
Goodwill (+A)	78	
Equity (-SE)	190	
Investments (-A)		300
Deferred Tax Liabilities (+L)		120
Non-controlling Interests (+SE)		148

Where:

- Land, Building, Trademarks and Deferred Tax Liabilities are increased by the same amount as calculated in the full goodwill method;
- Goodwill is recognized only for the portion acquired by the parent company;
- Non-controlling interests are calculated by attributing to them:
  - the proportionate share of the book value of equity;
  - the proportionate share of the net surpluses on the assets and liabilities of LIGHT: [190*40%] + [180*40%] = 148.

In this case, no goodwill is recognized for the non-controlling interests.

We now see two examples using the classic worksheets; in the first one, the companies use the full goodwill method, whilst in the second example the companies opt for the partial recognition of goodwill, i.e. only for the portion acquired by the parent company.

Example 6.4 – Full goodwill recognition with non-controlling interests

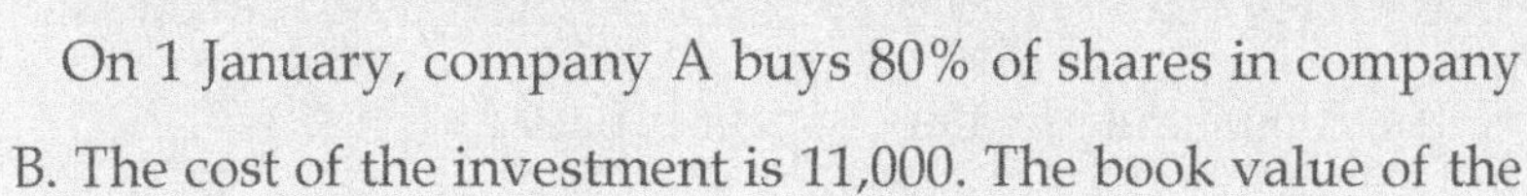

On 1 January, company A buys 80% of shares in company B. The cost of the investment is 11,000. The book value of the

equity of B at the same date is 10,000.

The fair values of assets and liabilities of B equal their book values, except for the following:

	Book value	Fair value	Gross surplus
Property	6,000	8,000	2,000
Patents	1,000	3,000	2,000

Consider that the tax rate applied by the two companies is 50%.

We start by eliminating the investment in B in accordance with IFRS 3, recognising the positive difference as goodwill. The company applies the full goodwill method. In this case, assume that the fair value of the non-controlling interests at the acquisition date is 2,750.

	Debit	Credit
B equity (-SE)	10,000	
Property (+A)	2,000	
Patents (+A)	2,000	
Goodwill (+A)	1,750	
Investment in B (-A)		11,000
Deferred tax liabilities (+L)		2,000
Minority interests (+SE)		2,750

The consolidated balance sheet is built as follows:

SFP	A	B	Aggregate	(1)	Consol.
ASSETS					
Non-current assets					
Property, plant and equipment	5,000	6,000	11,000	2,000	13,000
Patents and trademarks	2,000	4,000	6,000	2,000	8,000
Goodwill				1,750	1,750
Investments	11,000		11,000	-11,000	0
TOTAL ASSETS	18,000	10,000	28,000	-5,250	22,750
LIAB. and OWN. EQUITY					
Owners' equity					
Common stock	18,000	10,000	28,000	-10,000	18,000
Non-controlling interests				2,750	2,750
Deferred tax liabilities				2,000	2,000
TOTAL LIAB and EQUITY	18,000	10,000	28,000	5,250	22,750

(1) Recognition of surpluses [4,000] on property and patents

Elimination of investment [11,000] and subsidiary's equity [10,000]

Recognition of deferred tax liabilities [4,000*0.5=2,000]

Recognition of (full) goodwill [1,750]: 13,750 [consideration paid + fair value non-controlling interests] - 10,000 [BV equity] - net surplus value [2,000].

Example 6.5 – Proportionate recognition of goodwill with non-controlling interests

On Dec. 31, company A buys 90% of shares in company B.

The cost of the investment is 2,100. The individual balance sheets of the two companies on the date of the acquisition are reported in the worksheet. On the same date, the fair values of assets and liabilities of B equal their book values, except for patents, whose fair value is 400.

	Book value	Fair value	Gross surplus
Patents	200	400	200

The difference between the cost of the investment and the owners' equity is recorded as goodwill. Consider that the tax rate applied by the two companies is 50%. Prepare the consolidated financial statements on the date of the acquisition in accordance with IFRS 3, assuming that the company recognizes only the goodwill acquired by the parent company.

We start by eliminating the investment in B in accordance with IFRS 3. Remember that, in this case, we shall not consider the goodwill of the non-controlling interests.

	Debit	Credit
B equity (-SE)	1500	
B Retained Earnings (-SE)	500	
Patents (+A)	200	
Goodwill (+A)	210	
Investment in B (-A)		2,100
Deferred tax liabilities (+L)		100

Non-controlling interests (+SE)	210

The consolidated balance sheet is built as follows:

SFP	A	B	Aggregate	(1)	Consol.
ASSETS					
Non-current assets					
Goodwill				210	210
Investments	2,100		2,100	-2,100	0
Patents		200	200	200	400
Other assets	4,000	3,300	7,300		7,300
TOTAL ASSETS	6,100	3,500	9,600	-1,690	7,910
LIAB and EQUITY					
Owners' equity					
Common stock	3,000	1,500	4,500	-1,500	3,000
Retained earnings	600	500	1,100	-500	600
Non-controlling interests				210	210
Current and non-current liabilities (including deferred tax liabilities)	2,500	1,500	4,000	100	4,100
TOTAL LIAB and EQUITY	6,100	3,500	9,600	-1,690	7,910

Recognition of surplus [200] on patents

Elimination of investment [2,100] and subsidiary equity [1,500+500=2,000]

Recognition of deferred tax liabilities [200×0,5=100]

Recognition of goodwill = 210 = 2,100 [consideration paid] - 90%×2,000 [equity B] - 100 [net surplus on patents]

Step #5– Elimination of intra-group transactions

As we have said several times now, the purpose of consolidation accounting is to have one set of financial statements as if there was only one reporting subject (i.e. the group). This is why IFRS 10 requires the full elimination of intra-group assets and liabilities, equity, income, expenses and cash flows relating to transactions *between* entities of the group [IFRS 10, appendix B86(c)].

The elimination of intra-group transactions consists of:

a) the elimination of intra-group receivables and payables, costs, and revenues;

b) the elimination of intercompany profits and losses, i.e.:

  b1) the elimination of intercompany profits and losses included in the value of inventories;

  b2) the elimination of intercompany profits and losses included in the value of fixed assets;

c) the elimination of intra-group dividends.

The consolidated financial statements present the financial situation and result of operations of the group as a single entity. The different entities included in the consolidation area may be seen as divisions of the same company from a substantial point of view. Therefore, from the perspective of the consolidated financial statements, the transactions that occur between group companies are equivalent to transactions between divisions/functions within a single company. Such transactions cannot be presented in the consolidated financial statements, as these must present only those transactions that group companies have made with third parties, i.e. outside the group. If you think about it, it makes perfect sense not to consider such transactions: if you start selling goods to yourself you are not getting richer! The same goes with groups: if one company sells goods or provides services to another, the group in not creating any economic value. Therefore, we want to make sure that the effects of such intra-group transactions are not reported in the consolidated reports.

Some examples:

- The supply of goods from one company to another within the group is equivalent, from a consolidation point of view, to the 'transfer' of goods from one warehouse to another, within the same company. This should not be identified by the general ledger system as a sale of goods and, by the same token, intra-group supplies should leave the consolidated financial statements untouched;
- Financing provided by a holding company to subsidiaries is equal, in terms of the consolidated financial statements, to a 'cash transfer' from a division to another within the same company. This operation does not qualify as financing and consequently it should not be recognised in the group financial statements.

In the following section we will see how consolidation accounting eliminates (a) intra-group receivables and payables, (b) intra-group profits and losses, and (c) intra-group dividends.

a) The elimination of intra-group payables and receivables , costs and revenues

When group companies carry out trade or financing transactions with other companies of the group, payables and receivables accounts are opened and costs and revenues are recognised. When the individual financial statements are collected and added up, these items end up in the aggregate statements. Their impact on the group's results should be nil: if for instance one company sells an asset or a product to another, the aggregate situation will contain both the revenues recognised by the selling company and the cost incurred by the buying company. The same goes for credit and debit components. However, since in consolidation accounting we prepare the consolidated statements by adding up all the items line by line, we end up with an undue 'inflating' of the accounts affected by the intercompany transaction: e.g. in an intercompany sale we have higher revenues (from the selling company), higher expenses (of the buying company) for the same amount. Even though the net effect on income is zero, the aggregate item "revenues" will be too high, and so will the aggregate item "expenses". Therefore, we want to remove the effects of such transactions, to present accurately not only the net results, but also each of the lines forming the income statement and the balance sheet. In particular, we should eliminate:

- intra-group receivables and payables not yet settled at the end of the year;
- intra-group revenues and expenses recognised during the financial year.

Box 6.4 – Intra-group transactions and accounts' equivalence

The procedure to remove intra-group transactions is based on the assumption that there is equivalence between the amounts recorded by each company. This equivalence exists if all group companies have reported the transactions correctly. If, due to error or imperfect information, there is no equivalence between the amounts, we need to 'reconcile' the values of intra-group transactions, ensuring that they are properly recognised by all companies. After the reconciliation, we can proceed with their elimination.

The adjustments posted to eliminate intercompany payables and receivables, revenues and expenses follow the steps below:

1) Identify which values of credit/debit and costs/revenues arising from intra-group transactions are recorded in the financial statements of the companies included in consolidated financial statement;
2) Make sure there is mutual equivalence between the accounts; if this equivalence is not present, reconcile intra-group values;
3) Delete the mutual accounts (receivables and payables, costs and revenues).

It should be noted that:

- Adjustments for the purpose of elimination of intra-group receivables and payables, costs and revenues are made at 100%;
- The write-off of intra-group receivables and payables, costs and revenues does not require the reporting of intra-group deferred tax effects; these consolidation adjustments, in fact, do not cause changes in the operating result.

Example 6.6 – Elimination of intra-group payables and receivables

Company A has an 80% stake in Company B (acquired on 1 January X). During the year, A provided services to B for a total amount of 500. Company A has recognised the related revenue under 'operating revenues' while company B recognised the related costs under 'operating costs'. On 31.12.X the transaction is settled only partially, and intercompany payables and receivables are recognized for 300.

We proceed to the elimination of intra-company costs and revenues, receivables and payables to prepare consolidated financial statements at 31.12.X.

	Debit	Credit
Revenues from services (-R, -SE)	500	
Service costs (-E, SE)		500

	Debit	Credit
Payables to parent (-L)	300	
Receivables from subsidiary (-A)		300

b) <u>The elimination of intra-group profits and losses</u>

Consistently with what we have seen above, any intercompany profit or loss shall be eliminated in the consolidated financial statements, as these must present only transactions between the group and third parties. This is achieved by:

1) adjusting the carrying values of assets that have been the subject of the intra-group transaction and that are still recognised in the balance sheet of the acquiring company; the value of these goods must be 'brought back' to the original value as if they had never been sold;
2) adjusting the income items related to those goods that are 'generated' by the intra-group transaction. The result of operations of companies involved in the transaction, in fact, may be changed as a result of the intra-group transaction, and this change must be eliminated.

Note that:

- Intercompany losses expressing an actual decrease in the value of any asset shall not be eliminated.
- From the elimination of intra-group profit and losses temporary differences emerge and we must calculate the associated deferred tax assets or liabilities.

As a matter of fact, when we talk about the elimination of intercompany profits and losses we are dealing mainly with two cases: the elimination of intercompany profits and losses included in the value of inventories and the elimination of intercompany profits and losses included in the value of long-lived assets. Let us see each of the two cases.

b1) The elimination of intra-group profits and losses included in the value of inventories

In the case of profits (or losses) included in the value of inventories, those values must be adjusted in order not to account for the goods that still are in the inventory of the buyer at year-end.

In particular, when dealing with intercompany sales of goods, we can face the three following situations:

1. All inventories are 100 per cent **still on hand** at the buying company at the end of the year. In this case it is necessary to:
   a. decrease aggregate revenues *by the full amount of the goods at the intercompany selling price;*
   b. decrease aggregate COGS (which we debit in the perpetual inventory system when we sell goods) *by the full amount at the original purchase cost from third parties;*
   c. reduce the value of ending inventory by the *full amount of* intercompany profit;
   d. account for the related fiscal effects.
2. All inventories **have been sold by** the buying company at the end of the year. In this case, there is no unrealised profit from the group point of view and, consequently, we make only the following adjustments:
   a. decrease aggregate revenues *by the full amount at the intercompany sell price;*
   b. decrease aggregate COGS *by the full amount at the intercompany acquisition cost.*
3. **Part** of inventories **has been sold** by the buying company at the end of the year. In order properly to adjust the effects of this internal transaction, we must split the transaction into two parts: the one referring to inventories still on hand and the one referring to inventories sold at the end of the year. The adjustments follow the steps described in situation 1 and

2 above, respectively, for the part of goods still unsold (situation 1) and sold (situation 2) to third parties.

Example 6.7 – Intra-group profits and losses included in the value of inventories

Alfa is a manufacturing company producing custom t-shirts. It has a subsidiary, Beta, also producing custom t-shirts and located in Russia. During year X, Alpha sells white t-shirts to Beta so that they can be customised for the Russian market for a total amount of 120 mil. Those t-shirts were bought by Alpha from external parties at a cost of 100 mil in the same accounting period.

CASE A : AT YEAR-END 100% OF T-SHIRTS ARE STILL IN BETA'S INVENTORY

Suppose that both companies use a perpetual inventory system and all transactions are settled in cash (i.e. no receivables or payables). Since all goods are still in the group's inventory (Beta's inventory), we want the consolidated financial statements to represent the following situation:

Revenues	=	0
COGS	=	0
Inventory	=	100

What we have instead in the aggregate situation is the following:

Revenues	=	120	since Beta sold the t-shirts to A for

		120
COGS	= 100	since Beta's inventory decreased by 100
Inventory	= 120	since Beta's inventory decreased by 100 and Alpha's inventory increased by 120

Therefore, we need therefore to make the following adjustments:

(–) Revenues	= –120	since the group did not sell any t-shirt to third-parties
(–) COGS	= –100	since the group's inventory has not decreased
(–) Inventory	= –20	since we need to rebuild the original value of the inventory, moving from 120 back to 100

Notice that:

- since we assume all payments were made in cash we do not need to adjust the values of receivables and payables;
- since the adjustments to revenues and COGS do not add up to zero, earnings before taxes are modified, therefore, we need to compute the fiscal effect of the adjustment. Assuming a tax rate of 50 per cent, we need to decrease tax expense by 50 and recognize a deferred tax asset of 50.

CASE B: AT YEAR-END NO T-SHIRTS IS IN BETA'S INVENTORY

Again, suppose that both companies use a perpetual

inventory system and all transactions are settled in cash (i.e. no receivables or payables). Suppose that Beta sells all the t-shirts it has purchased at a price of XXX. In this case, we want the consolidated financial statements to represent the following situation:

Revenues	= XXX	
COGS	= 100	i.e. 100% of the value of the beginning inventory that has decreased
Inventory	= 0	since the group has sold all the inventory to third-parties, no inventory is left

What we have instead in the aggregate situation is the following:

Revenues	= 120 + XXX	
COGS	= 220	i.e. 100 from the decrease in Alpha's inventory and 120 from the decrease in Beta's inventory
Inventory	= 0	

We need therefore to do the following adjustments to pass from the aggregate to the consolidated situation:

(-) Revenues	= -120	the selling price applied by Alpha
(-) COGS	= -120	the decrease in inventory recognised by Beta
(-) Inventory	= 0	

Note that:

- since we assume all payments were made in cash, we do not need to adjust the values of receivables and payables;

- the adjustments to revenues and COGS add up to zero, so we do not need to account for any fiscal effect of the adjustment;
- the price at which Beta sold the t-shirts in Russia is not relevant in terms of the adjustments we need to perform;
- we do not adjust the value of the group's inventory as it is already consistent with the consolidation purposes.

CASE C: AT YEAR-END ONLY PART OF THE T-SHIRTS ARE STILL IN BETA'S INVENTORY

This case is a "mix" of the two cases discussed above. Again, suppose that both companies use a perpetual inventory system and all transactions are settle in cash (i.e. no receivables or payables). Suppose that Beta has sold only 60% of the t-shirts it has purchased to third-parties at a price of XXX, i.e. 40% is still in the group's inventory (Beta's inventory). In this case, we want the consolidated financial statements to represent the following situation:

Revenues	= XXX	
COGS	= 60	i.e. 60% of the beginning inventory
Inventory	= 40	i.e. the original value of the inventory still left in the group at the end of the year.

What we have instead in the aggregate situation is the following:

Revenues	=	120 + XXX

COGS	=	172	i.e. 100 from the decrease in Alpha's inventory and 72 [= 120 × 60%] from the decrease in Beta's inventory
Inventory	=	48	i.e. = 120 × 40%

Since this situation is a mix of 'case a' and 'case b', in order better to understand the adjustments we can split the transaction into two parts: the part related to the 'sold t-shirts' case (i.e. case b) and the part related to the 't-shirts still in the group's inventory' case (case a).

For the part of t-shirts sold to third-parties (60%), we have learnt from case b that we do not need to adjust the ending inventory but only to correct the revenues and COGS accounts:

(-) Revenues	=	-72	60% of the selling price recognized by Alpha
(-) COGS	=	-72	60% of the decrease in Beta's inventory
(-) Inventory	=	0	

For the part of t-shirts still in Beta's inventory (40%) we need to make the same adjustments seen in case a (naturally only for the 40% of the total amount):

(-) Revenues	=	-48	40% of the selling price recognised by Alpha
(-) COGS	=	-40	40% of Alpha's inventory decrease
(-) Inventory	=	-8	To return to the original value of the inventory (40%) still on hand

> Note that:
>
> - Since we assume all payments were made in cash, we do not need to adjust the values of receivables and payables;
> - Since the adjustments to revenues, expenses, and COGS do not add up to zero, earnings before taxes are affected and therefore we need to compute the fiscal effect of the adjustment.

b2) The elimination of intercompany profits and losses included in the value of long-lived assets

If companies within the same group sell long-lived assets to each other, generating profits (or losses), we must:

- Report the assets transferred (still held by the buyer at year-end) at the carrying amount at which they would have been recognised absent any intercompany transaction;
- Reverse any gains/losses realised as a result of disposal;
- Adjust depreciation expenses and accumulated depreciation to restore their values as if no transaction had occurred.

Therefore, elimination entries are needed in the consolidation worksheet to restate the assets, associated accumulated depreciation, and depreciation expense to the amounts that would appear in the financial statements if there had been no intra-group transfer.

In order to undertake such adjustments it is necessary to:

1. Identify the accounting effects that the intra-group transaction has generated, with particular reference to gains/losses, assets sold and their depreciation;
2. Identify the values that the items affected by the transaction (gains/losses, assets sold and depreciation) would have if the transaction had not taken place;
3. As a result of the differences found between values (1) and (2), identify corrections to be made to the aggregate financial statements in order to obtain the consolidated financial statements.

Example 6.8 – Downstream sale of a depreciable asset

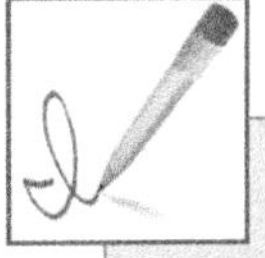

When a parent sells assets (or goods) to one of its subsidiaries we say that there is a '*downstream sale*'. In the opposite situation, i.e. when the sale is made by a subsidiary to its parent, we say that there is an '*upstream sale*'.

Let us make an example of a downstream sale of a depreciable asset.

MICKEY holds 70% of MOUSE stock. Assume that MICKEY sells a building to MOUSE on 1 January X for 400. The building originally had a cost to MICKEY of 1,500 and, at the time of the sale, had been depreciated for 900. MICKEY depreciated the asset using a constant rate (i.e. straight line depreciation method) of 10%, while now MOUSE is depreciating the building with a constant rate of 20%. The tax rate for the two companies is 50%.

When we deal with intra-group sales of long-lived assets, we always need to make two adjustments. First we need to eliminate any gain or loss arising from the intra-group transaction and restore the sold asset's value to the one before the sale. Remember that, since we are changing an income statement account, we need to consider the fiscal impact of the sale: if the buying company realised a gain from the transaction it paid taxes on the gain and now we need to recognise a deferred tax asset; on the other hand, we have a deferred tax liability if the acquirer realised a loss from the transaction.

Original cost of the equipment to MICKEY = 1,500

Accumulated depreciation = 900

Net carrying amount of the building = 1,500 – 900 = 600

Gain (Loss) on the sale = Selling price – Book value = 400 – 600 = –200

	Debit	Credit
PPE (+A)	200	
Deferred Tax Asset (+A)	100	
Operating Expenses (-E, +SE)		200
Income tax (-E, +SE)		100

Second, we need to deal with the different depreciation rates. In fact, if the building had not been sold, it would have been depreciated by 10 per cent, not 20. Therefore, depreciation expense needs to be adjusted by the following amount:

Depreciation rate used by MOUSE = 400 × 20% = 80

Depreciation rate that MICKEY would have used (assume zero residual value) = 1,500 × 10% = 150

Difference between the depreciation rates (MOUSE – MICKEY) = 80 – 150 = –70

Hence we should increase (i.e. debit) the depreciation expense account by 70 in the following way (again, since we are modifying costs we should account for the related fiscal impact):

	Debit	Credit
Operating Expenses (+E, +SE)	70	
Deferred Tax Asset (+A)	35	
PPE (+A)		70
Income tax (-E, +SE)		35

c) The elimination of intra-group dividends

Companies usually (or at least once in a while) pay dividends to their shareholders. When this happens, money flows out of companies and is paid to an external subject (shareholders) so that it is no longer part of the companies' assets. However, if a subsidiary pays dividends to its parent, the cash flow related to dividends stays within the group and the overall entity is neither richer nor poorer (its assets did not decrease). The situation changes a little when there are non-controlling interests since, in this case, the non-controlling investors receives some dividends and part of the cash effectively flows out of the group. The accounting effects connected with the distribution of intra-group dividends are the following:

- Recognition of financial income by the company of the group that receives the dividends;
- Reduction in reserves of the company that distributes the dividends;

- Recognition of the portion of the dividends attributable to non-controlling shareholders.

The logical process to be followed for the adjustment in question is as follows:

1. Identify the effects of the transaction listed above;
2. Eliminate these effects through:
   - the elimination of financial income, recognized by the company that receives the dividends;
   - the reintegration of the reserves of the company that distributes the dividends;
   - the decrease in shareholders' equity attributable to non-controlling interests by the amount of dividends received by them.

It should be noted that:

- In the elimination of the investment, the amount of equity allocated to non-controlling interests was determined with reference to the equity of the subsidiary at the acquisition date, without considering any reduction in reserves during the year following the distribution of dividends. The non-controlling interests should therefore be reduced in the consolidation by the amount already received by them as a dividend. In fact, they have already received 'cash' as dividends distributed and, therefore, this reduces their share of equity.
- Temporary differences that would lead to the formation of deferred taxes may arise from the elimination of intra-group dividends. However, such differences are usually very low

due to favourable fiscal treatments (e.g. the participation exemption rule).

- The distribution of dividends by a parent company to its shareholders does not constitute an intra-group transaction. In this case, those who receive the dividends (the parent's shareholders) are external to the group (except in those cases where there are cross-shareholdings between the parent and its subsidiaries), since the group is made only of the parent company and its subsidiaries.

Example 6.9 – Elimination of intra-group dividends

A holds a 100% stake in B. During the year, B uses reserves previously accumulated to distribute a dividend of 2,000. A accounts for the amount received as financial income. We proceed to eliminate the effect of the distribution of intra-group dividends.

	Debit	Credit
Financial income (-R, -SE)	2,000	
Reserves (+SE)		2,000

***

A holds a 70% stake in B. During the year, B distributes 5,000 in dividends. A accounts for the amount received as financial income. We proceed to eliminate the effect of distribution of intra-group dividends.

Dividends received by A: 5,000 × 70% = 3,500

Dividends received by non-controlling shareholders = 5,000 x 30% = 1,500

	Debit	Credit
Financial income (-R, -SE)	3,500	
Reserves (+SE)		3,500
Non-controlling interests (-SE)	1,500	
Reserves (+SE)		1,500

Step #6 – Allocation of results

After going through all the steps down to #5, we are now able to compute the final consolidated balance sheet and income statement. In order to do this, we only need a last step i.e. to compute and account separately for the net income attributable to the non-controlling interests, similarly to what we did in step #4a-b for the balance sheet.

The question then is: how do we compute the non-controlling shareholders' share of net income? For sure we need to start from the net income of the subsidiary, since the non-controlling interests are shareholders of the latter;[5] then we need to consider each of the adjusting entries we went through in the consolidation process, from step #4a to step #5, and see whether they had an impact on the portion of net income we are trying to pin down. Specifically, we are interested in spotting all gains/losses realized by the subsidiary that are attributable to the non-controlling interests. Then we need not only to look separately at each entry but also to look at the *direction* of any intra-group transaction occurred during the period.

[5] If Alpha owns 80% of Beta, the non-controlling interests are the subjects representing the remaining 20% of Beta. Hence Alpha's results are independent of any non-controlling interests in its subsidiaries.

Examples might be a parent company selling part of its manufactured goods to one of its subsidiaries ('downstream sale') or a plant sold by the subsidiary to its parent ('upstream PPE sale'). Depending on whether the transaction is an upstream or a downstream one, we compute the non-controlling interests differently. In fact, only one of those two types of transactions gives rise to a (potential) gain/loss for the subsidiary. Can you guess which one? (see the following Box for the answer)

Example 6.10 – Downstream and upstream transactions

Let us make a simple example. Suppose company A owns a 75% stake in B. During period X, A sold an intangible asset (e.g. a brand) to B for 100,000. The historical cost of the brand was 150,000 with a 20-year useful life and 0 terminal value. Suppose the parent company has been using the brand for the last 8 years and sells it at the end of the 8th one. The brand's net carrying amount is: 150,000 – 8/20 x 150,000 = 90,000 and so the parent realises a gain of 10,000 (for simplicity we assume no tax rate). The two companies will then make the following journal entries in their individual systems:

Company A Journal		
	Debit	Credit
Cash (+A)	100,000	
Brand (–A)		90,000
Operating revenue (+R, +SE)		10,000

Company B Journal

	Debit	Credit
Brand (+A)	100,000	
Cash (-A)		100,000

Given that there is no tax effect (remember we assumed the tax rate = 0) the gain of 10,000 translates into a higher net income of company A which we (as per step #5) need to reduce to zero (i.e. as if the brand had never been sold). Our adjustment does not impact B's net income, hence when we allocate the results to the non-controlling interests (i.e. the other shareholders of B) we should not consider the adjustment of -10,000.

On the other hand, if the transaction were an *upstream transaction* (B selling the brand to A) the gain would be reported in B's individual financial statements, and so the adjustment would have an impact on B's net income.

Our objective is to separate the net income attributable to the group from the part of it that is attributable to the non-controlling interests. Our starting point is the net income of the subsidiary where the non-controlling interests are. Then, depending on the type of transaction (i.e. downstream or upstream) we include only the adjustments made in the consolidation process that had an impact on the subsidiary's net income.

Special mention has to be made of the treatment of the surpluses on assets and liabilities arising from the consolidation process (the first consolidation adjustments, step #4a-b). As we all know by now, any asset or liability surplus affects directly only the balance sheet, having no impact on the non-controlling interests' net income by definition.

However, any such surpluses might have to be depreciated or amortised according to the group's criteria. The depreciation/amortisation expenses do pass through the income statement; the question is whether they influence non-controlling interests (i.e. the subsidiary's net income). Since they originate from a revaluation of the *subsidiary's* assets and liabilities, it is safe to assume that they do.

The initial net income of the subsidiary and the selected adjustments have then to be multiplied by the non-controlling interests' percentage and recognised on a separate line usually called "Net Income of Non-controlling Interests" or "Non-controlling NI". Figure 6.4 summarizes the allocation procedure.

Figure 6.4 – Non-controlling interests' Net Income allocation scheme

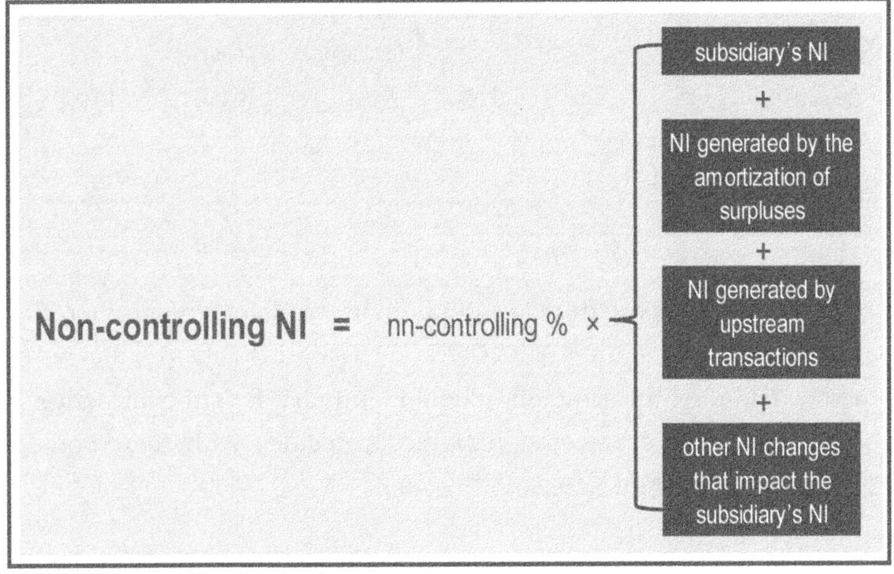

Source: Prepared by the Authors

Step #7 – Prepare Consolidated Financial Statements

The company, after going through the steps highlighted above (1 to 6), is now ready to prepare the consolidated financial statements.

Now that we have gone through all the main steps of the consolidation process we can have a look at a comprehensive example.

Example 6.11 – Comprehensive Example

On 1 January X company CIP acquires an 80% stake in company CIOP for 12,000. The balance sheet of the subsidiary at the date of acquisition was as follows:

Balance Sheet CIOP 1.1.X			
PPE	10,000	Payables	4,500
Intangibles	5,000	Other liabilities (including provisions)	7,500
Other assets (including receiv. and cash)	7,000	Equity	10,000
TOTAL	22,000	TOTAL	22,000

When we compare the individual financial statements prepared at year-end, the equity of CIOP is increased solely by the net income (500). At the acquisition date (1 January 1 X), the fair value of all of CIOP's assets and liabilities coincides with their book value, except for buildings and brands.

	Book value	Fair value	Gross surplus
Property	10,000	14,000	4,000
Brands	0	3,000	3,000

Please note that the capital gains are to be considered before the tax effect of 50%. The useful life of the buildings is estimated as 20 years, while that of the brands is 10 years. The company applies the full goodwill method; for this purpose, assume that the fair value of the non-controlling interests at the acquisition date is 2,700.

During year X, the companies experience the following events relevant to the preparation of consolidated financial statements:

1. CIOP capitalises research and development costs for 180 and writes them down at year-end for a third of their value (direct amortization method). Based on the group's accounting policies, these costs should be charged to the income statement as incurred for the full amount.
2. CIP, in line with the internal pricing policy strategy, sells 200 tons of copper to CIOP for 1,500, a price equivalent to the total cost incurred by purchasing it from third parties outside the group, therefore no intra-group profit arises. However, at the year-end CIOP has not yet received either the goods or the related invoice.
3. Company CIOP sells 30 units of steel rods to CIP at a price per unit of 150. CIOP paid a unit cost of 100 for the purchase of the goods. At 31/12/X only 30% of the goods purchased by CIP has been sold to third parties.
4. CIP sells 40 units of ball bearings to CIOP at a price per unit of 160. CIP in turn has purchased the goods from third parties at a unit price of 140. At the year end, all the merchandise is still in the inventory of CIOP. For the

calculation of intra-group profits keep in mind that CIOP, in the preparation of its individual financial statements, in accordance with its accounting principles, measures the goods not at cost per unit (160), but at 145 as estimated realizable value.

5. CIOP sells one piece of machinery to CIP at a price of 2,500. In determining the net carrying amount in CIOP balance sheet, note that:

	Historical cost	Accumulated depreciation
Machinery	5,000	3,000

Keep in mind that CIOP depreciated the machinery on a straight line at 4%, while CIP uses a straight-line amortisation rate of 20%. Any deferred tax assets and liabilities are accounted for on the basis of a tax rate of 50%.

We now prepare the consolidated income statement and the consolidated statement of financial position following the steps we have seen so far. Please note that step #6 (i.e. the allocation of non-controlling interests' results) is included in consolidation adjustment No. 11.

Here are the pre-consolidation and consolidation adjustments, numbered according to their order, and in the next page we give the usual spreadsheet which we use to pass from the aggregate to the consolidated situation (each number in the 'adjustment description' represents the corresponding column in the spreadsheet). For a better understanding, you should read the description of each adjustment and right after that look at the effects on the spreadsheet. Where the adjustment refers to an event that occurred during the year (1 to 5 listed above) it is reported in square brackets.

Description of Adjustments

[event # 1] (1) This adjustment shall be performed to homogenise the valuation criteria. Company CIOP has to expense the entire cost of research and development (R&D) for 180 in the income statement. The costs, however, increase only by 120, as CIOP already accounted for the R&D amortisation of 60 at year-end. An increase in costs leads to a reduction of income (which of course is reflected in the statement of financial position), and taxes. In the balance sheet we then have an increase in deferred tax assets of 60 and an adjustment of the assets value for a net value of 120 (i.e. 180–60).

[event # 2] (2) This adjustment is made to ensure the reconciliation of intercompany transactions. CIOP accounts for the invoice related to the purchase of goods from CIP. This, in the income statement, is reflected in an increase in operating expenses and inventories (the goods purchased by CIOP had not yet been received at their warehouse at year-end). Note that the increase in operating costs and the value of inventories offset each other, so the impact on operating income is zero. In the balance sheet, an increase in trade payables and an increase in the value of inventory are reported for 1,500.

[event # 2] (3) This adjustment is done to eliminate the intra-group payable and receivable of 1,500 which arise after the reconciliation.

[event # 2] (4) With this adjustment, the related costs and revenues are cancelled out for a value of 1,500.

(5) This adjustment consists in the elimination of the investment reported in CIP's balance sheet (12,000) against the net book value of CIOP (10,000). Surpluses on the property and trademarks are also recognised with the related deferred tax effect.

Deferred tax liabilities amount to 3,500.

To calculate any difference in the consolidation it is necessary to compare the cost of the investment (i.e. the consideration paid) with the proportionate share of equity of CIOP expressed at fair value:

+ Consideration paid	+12,000
+ fair value of non-controlling interests	+2,700
– book value equity of CIOP	-10,000
– net surplus in property's value	- 2,000
– net surplus in brand's value	-1,500
= Goodwill (100%)	**1,200**

In accordance with IFRS 3, the remaining difference is attributed to goodwill.

(6) Now that we have recognised the surpluses on property and brands, we also have to treat them consistently with the items they refer to: the surplus in property will be treated in accordance with the accounting policies for property and the surplus in brand will follow the accounting treatment of intangibles. This correction ensures assets are depreciated as before. The depreciation charge on the surplus value of the property is equal to 200 [= 4,000 × 5%, i.e. the gross surplus divided by the property's useful life (20 years); we assume zero residual value]. The depreciation charge on the surplus of the brand is 300. It is obtained by dividing the gross surplus by the useful life (10 years) and considering a residual value of zero [3,000 × 10%].

The charging of depreciation determines a reduction in the operating result of 500 and a decrease in income and taxes, which are reflected, of course, in the statement of financial position (a reduction in property and brands due to depreciation and an adjustment for the related deferred tax liability for 250 are reported in the SFP). Goodwill is not subjected to impairment testing because its recoverable amount is greater than its book value.

[event # 3] (7) This adjustment makes it possible to eliminate intra-group profits. At year-end, 70% of the merchandise that was purchased by CIP from CIOP is still in CIP's inventory, generating some intra-group profit. We want to make sure that this profit is eliminated. In order properly to reflect the effects of this transaction, we must split it into two parts. First, we should consider the adjustment referred to the percentage of inventories which are still on hand at the buying company CIP (70%). By consequence, we should:

a. decrease aggregate revenues by 70% of 4,500 [30 units * 150 Euro] = 3,150;

b. decrease aggregate COGS by 70% of 3,000 [30 units * 100 Euro] = 2,100.

Since the adjustment to revenues and expenses has an impact on earnings before taxes (-1,050), we should account also for the related fiscal effect.

[event # 3] (8) The second adjustment, instead, considers the part of the transaction that is referred to the percentage of the inventories sold to third parties (30%). In this case, we should:

a. decrease aggregate revenues by 30% of 4,500= 1,350;

b. decrease aggregate COGS by the same amount.

The net impact on earnings before taxes is zero.

[event # 4] (9) Again, we need to write off the intra-group profit. Since goods purchased by CIOP from CIP are all in stock at year end, we want to eliminate 100 per cent of the revenues realised by CIP (6,400) and the CGS recorded by the same company at the time of the sale (5,600). However, we also need to eliminate the impairment recorded by the buying company as, had the sale not taken place, there would have not been any need for a write-down of the inventory. This implies that we have to eliminate also the 600 recorded by CIOP in its CGS.

All in all, as a consequence, we eliminate the residual intra-group profit net of the write-down, which can also be calculated as follows:

Intercompany profit (100%)	[40 × (160 – 140)] =	800
Impairment which CIOP already recorded	[40 × (160-145)] =	600
= Residual intra-group profit		**200**

The elimination of intra-group profit generates: a) a reduction in the value of inventories (CIOP) for 200 – to be reported in the IS as an operating cost and in the SFP as a reduction of inventory; b) a reduction in the income for the year – to be reported in the IS and impacting SFP through the SE; c) its impact on taxes – to be reported both in the IS as a lower income tax expense and in SFP as a deferred tax asset.

[event # 5] (10) We now need to take into account the intra-group sale of machinery. This is the first of the two adjustments which eliminates the intercompany gain. CIOP, in fact, recorded a gain of 500 [2,500 – (5,000 – 3,000)] on the sale of a piece of machinery to CIP. It is necessary to eliminate the gain in the IS, and to reduce the value of machinery in the SFP by the same amount. The elimination of capital gains gives rise to a reduction of operating income and taxes and thus the recognition of deferred tax liabilities for 250 in the SFP.

[event # 5] (11) The second adjustment is made to correct the different depreciation rate on the machinery transferred from CIOP to CIP. CIOP's depreciation expense was 200 (4% of 5,000), while CIP's depreciation expense is 500 (20% of 2,500). It is therefore necessary to reduce the depreciation by 300. This results in a reduction of operating costs and thus an increase in operating income (also to be identified in the SFP) of 300 (machinery) and a decrease in the related deferred tax asset of 150; although an adjustment to deferred tax assets is preferable, it may be also acceptable to report an increase in deferred tax liabilities.

[event # 5] (12) In accordance with step #6, we now allocate the share of net income to non-controlling interests. To do that, we need to consider only the events and the consolidation adjustments that have an impact on the subsidiary's net income, since the non-controlling shareholders only hold part of it (and not part of the parent's equity). The events and the consolidation adjustments are: (a) the harmonisation of accounting policies (adjustment 1), (b) the depreciation/amortization of the surpluses of property and brands (adjustments 6), and the intercompany profits recorded by CIOP (adjustments 7, 9, and 10). Hence, the total adjusted result of CIOP is the following:

+ Reported Net income (from CIOP's financial statements)	+800
- adjustment 1	-60
- adjustment 6	-250
- adjustment 7	-525
- adjustment 9	-250
+ adjustment 10	+150
= Adjusted Net Income of CIOP (total)	**-135**

This is the total result of CIOP, which for 80 per cent belongs to its parent [–135 × .80 = –108] CIP, and for the remaining 20% belongs to CIOP's non-controlling shareholders [–135 × .20 = –27]. As in this case we have a loss, we add 27 to the total net income and report separately -27 on the line "Non-controlling interests' net income". The same goes for the non-controlling interests' share of equity.

INCOME STATEMENT	CIP	CIOP	Aggregate	(1)	(2)	(3)	(4)	(5)	(6)	(7)	(8)	(9)	(10)	(11)	(12)	Consol
Operating revenues	20,000	24,000	44,000				-1,500			-3,150	-1,350	-6,400	-500			31,100
Operating expenses	16,000	21,000	37,000	+180-60	+1,500 -1,500		-1,500		500	-2,100	-1,350	-6,200		-300		26,170
Operating income	4,000	3,000	7,000	-120	0		0		-500	-1,050	0	-200	-500	300		4930
Financial income	6,000	3,000	9,000													9,000
Financial expenses	8,000	5,000	13,000													13,000
Earnings before taxes	2,000	1,000	3,000	-120	0		0		-500	-1,050	0	-200	-500	300		930
Income tax expenses	1,000	500	1,500	-60					-250	-525		-100	-250	-150		165
Net income	1,000	500	1,500	-60	0		0		-250	-525	0	-100	-250	150	27	492
Non-contr interest' inc															-27	-27

BALANCE SHEET	CIP	CIOP	Aggregate	(1)	(2)	(3)	(4)	(5)	(6)	(7)	(8)	(9)	(10)	(11)	(12)	Consol.
ASSETS																
Non Current assets																
PPE	40,000	20,000	60,000					4,000	-200				-500	300		63,600
Goodwill								1,200								1,200
Other intangible	11,000	9,000	20,000	-180+60				3,000	-300							22,700
Investments	12,000		12,000					-12,000								
Deferred tax assets	2,000	850	2,850	60						525		100	250	-150		3,635
Current assets																
Cash	10,000	21,000	31,000													31,000
Inventories	9,500	2,500	12,000		1,500					-1050		-200				12,250
Trade receivables	8,500	6,650	15,150			-1,500										13,650
TOTAL ASSETS	93,000	60,000	153,000	-60	1,500	-1,500	0	-3,800	-500	-525	0	-100	-250	150	0	147,975

BALANCE SHEET	CIP	CIOP	Aggregate	(1)	(2)	(3)	(4)	(5)	(6)	(7)	(8)	(9)	(10)	(11)	(12)	Consol.
TOTAL LIAB and EQUITY																
Group Owners' Equity																
Common stock	25,000	7,000	32,000					-7,000								25,000
Reserves	5,000	3,000	8,000					-3,000								5,000
Net income	1,000	500	1,500	-60	0		0		-250	-525	0	-100	-250	150	27	492
Non-controlling inter																
C. Stock and reserves								2,700								2,700
Net income															-27	-27
Non Current liabilities																
Deferred tax liabilities	3,500	1,650	5,150					3,500	-250							8,400
Current liabilities																
Trade payables	16,200	11,500	27,700		1,500	-1,500										27,700
Other liabilities	42,300	36,350	78,650													78,650
TOTAL LIAB and	93,000	60,000	153,000	-60	1,500	-1,500	0	-3,800	-500	-525	0	-100	-250	150	0	147,975

7

CONSOLIDATING ASSOCIATES AND JOINT-VENTURES

Contents of this Chapter

- Associates and Joint Ventures: definition
- Accounting for associates and joint ventures
- The Equity Method
- Additional Issue on Accounting for Associates and Joint Ventures

7.1 Introduction

In the previous chapters we dealt with the consolidation of subsidiaries, i.e. entities on which the reporting entity (parent company) has *control*. However, an entity may have other types of strategic investments apart from subsidiaries. This is the case, for example, of associates or joint-ventures.

The consolidation of associates and joint-ventures is regulated by the following accounting standards:

- IAS 28 – *Investments in Associates and Joint Ventures*
- IFRS 11 – *Joint Arrangements*
- IFRS 12 – *Disclosure of Interests in Other Entities*

In this chapter we will refer to the most recent versions of these standards, which are effective for annual periods beginning on or after 1 January 2013 or 2014. As already mentioned in Chapter 2, these standards are the result of a major revision project undertaken by the IASB that involved all standards directly and indirectly related to consolidation.

The structure of the chapter is as follows: we first provide a definition of associates and joint-ventures. We then provide an overview of the main standards regarding the consolidation of associates and joint-ventures. Finally, we introduce and describe the "equity method", which is the method now required for the consolidation of these two types of investments.

7.2 Associates and joint-ventures

IAS 28 provides formal definitions of associates and joint ventures, as reported in the Box below [IAS 28 par. 3].

Definitions 7.1 - Associates and Joint-Ventures

An ***associate*** is an entity over which the investor has significant influence.

Significant influence is the power to participate in the financial and operating policy decisions of the investee, but is not control or joint control of those policies.

A ***joint venture*** is a joint arrangement whereby the parties that have joint control of the arrangement have rights to the net assets of the arrangement.

Joint control is the contractually agreed sharing of control of an arrangement, which exists only when decisions about the relevant activities require the unanimous consent of the parties sharing control.

Based on the definitions reported above, it is clear that associates and joint ventures refer to different types of investments.

Associates are investments in entities over which the investor (in our case the reporting entity) is able to exercise a so-called "significant influence", i.e. the power to participate in (but not to control!) the main financial and operating decisions. This is, for example, the case where another investor has control over the investee, but our reporting entity has the power to participate in the main decisions and, potentially, to influence them.

In order to help practitioners to identify the existence of a significant influence and to reduce discretionality, IAS 28 [par. 5-6] provides some practical indicators and examples (see Box 7.1).

Box 7.1 – Significant influence

If an entity holds, directly or indirectly (e.g. through subsidiaries), 20 per cent or more of the voting power of the investee, it is presumed that the entity has significant influence, unless it can be clearly demonstrated that this is not the case. Conversely, if the entity holds, directly or indirectly (e.g. through subsidiaries), less than 20 per cent of the voting power of the investee, it is presumed that the entity does not have significant influence, unless such influence can be clearly demonstrated. [IAS 28, par. 5]

The existence of significant influence by an entity is usually evidenced in one or more of the following ways:

(a) representation on the board of directors or equivalent governing body of the investee;

(b) participation in policy-making processes, including participation in decisions about dividends or other distributions;

(c) material transactions between the entity and its investee;

(d) interchange of managerial personnel; or

(e) provision of essential technical information [IAS 28, par. 6]

Therefore, holding 20 percent or more of the voting power is considered to be enough to presume the existence of a significant influence on the investee. Conversely, holding less than 20 percent of the voting power indicates no significant influence. When calculating the voting power, the investor should take into consideration the shares held directly and those held indirectly through *subsidiaries*, while holdings by other associates or joint ventures shall be excluded from the computation. Moreover, similarly to what IFRS state for *control*, potential voting rights (e.g. warrants, options, convertible debt or equity instruments) that are currently exercisable or convertible are to be taken into consideration when assessing significant influence

Figure 7.1 - Voting power examples

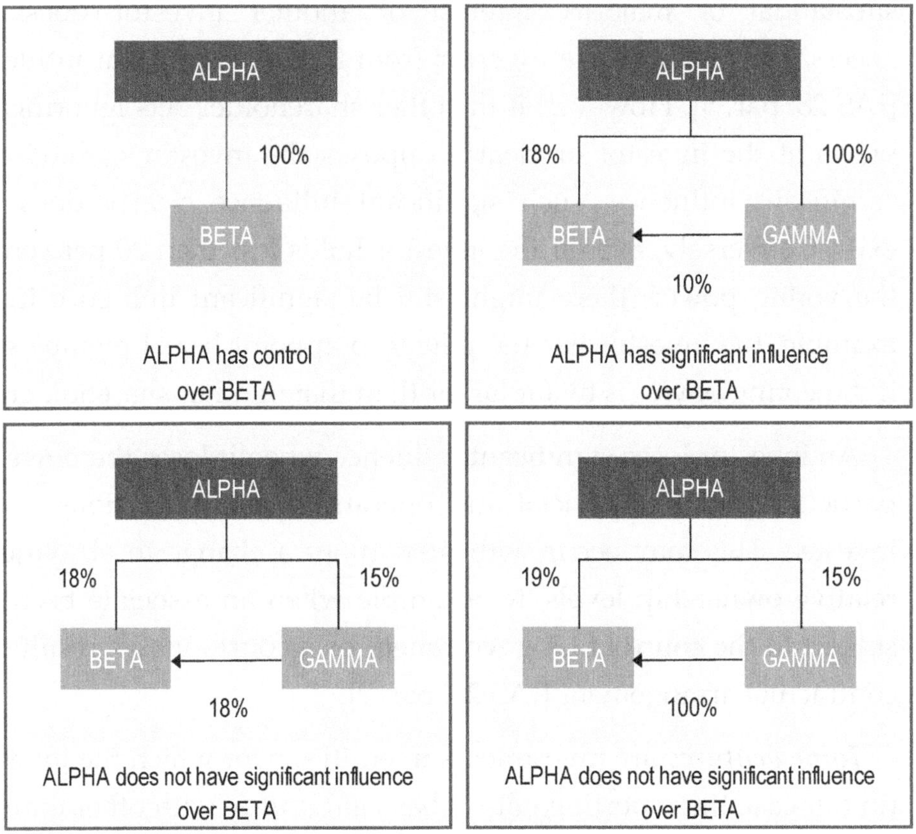

ALPHA
100%
BETA
ALPHA has control over BETA

ALPHA
18%
100%
BETA
GAMMA
10%
ALPHA has significant influence over BETA

ALPHA
18%
15%
BETA
GAMMA
18%
ALPHA does not have significant influence over BETA

ALPHA
19%
15%
BETA
GAMMA
100%
ALPHA does not have significant influence over BETA

Source: Prepared by the Authors

It should be noted that, even in the presence (absence) of at least 20 percent of the voting power, it is still possible to demonstrate that the significant influence does not exist (exists). For this purpose, the indicators suggested by IAS 28 [par. 6] are very useful. For example, the presumption of significant influence may be overcome when an investor, in spite of owning more than 20 per cent of the voting power, has no representation on the board of directors, or when the investor has no power to obtain timely financial information from the investee. Moreover, the existence of a substantial or majority interest of another investor does not necessarily preclude the investor from having significant influence [IAS 28, par. 5]. However, if the other shareholder acts ignoring the views of the investor or clearly opposes the investor's exercise of significant influence, such significant influence clearly does not exist. Conversely, even if the investor holds less than 20 per cent of the voting power, there might still be significant influence if, for example, the investor has the power to appoint board members, or if the voting power is by far larger than that of other shareholders.

An investor loses significant influence when it loses the power to participate in the financial and operating policy decisions of the investee. This may occur with or without a change in absolute or relative ownership levels, for example when an associate becomes subject to the control of a government or a court, or as a result of a contractual arrangement [IAS 28, par. 9].

Joint ventures are investments in entities over which the investor (in our case the reporting entity) has *joint control* with other entities. The definition of joint ventures is within the scope of IFRS 11 - *Joint arrangements*. Indeed, joint ventures are one of the two types of joint arrangements identified by IFRS 11, the other type being the so-called *joint operations* (see Definitions 7.2).

Definitions 7.2 – Joint arrangements

A ***joint arrangement*** is an arrangement of which two or more parties have joint control. [IFRS 11, par. 4]

A ***joint operation*** is a joint arrangement whereby the parties that have joint control of the arrangement have rights to the assets, and obligations for the liabilities, relating to the arrangement. Those parties are called joint operators. [IFRS 11, par. 15]

A ***joint venture*** is a joint arrangement whereby the parties that have joint control of the arrangement have rights to the net assets of the arrangement. Those parties are called ***joint venturers***. [IFRS 11, par. 16]

In order to have a joint arrangement, the following conditions must be fulfilled [IFRS 11, par. 5]:

1. the parties are bound by a contractual arrangement;
2. the contractual arrangement gives two or more of those parties joint control of the arrangement.

In other words, for a joint arrangement to exist, there must be a *contractual arrangement* establishing *joint control*. As mentioned above, *joint control* is the contractually agreed sharing of control among two or more parties.[1] When joint control exists, relevant decisions require the unanimous consent of the parties sharing

[1] For, a definition of *control*, please see Chapter 4. The definition of control given by IFRS 10 applies also to joint ventures. [IFRS 11, B5]

control, and no single party controls the arrangement on its own. Note that there may be a joint arrangement even if not all of its parties (but at least two of them) have joint control.

A joint arrangement is classified as either a joint operation or a joint venture. The classification depends on the rights and obligations of the parties to the arrangement. While in joint operations the parties have joint control over the individual assets and liabilities within the scope of the arrangement, in joint ventures the parties have joint control over the net assets of an investment (which is always a separate entity).

As joint operations do not give rise to consolidation issues (each operator accounts for its share of the operation's assets, liabilities, revenues and expenses directly), they are out of the scope of this book. In contrast, joint ventures - which are a special type of investment - are relevant for consolidation purposes. Therefore, from now on, we will focus on this type of joint arrangement.

Figure 7.2 – Joint agreements and equity consolidating accounting

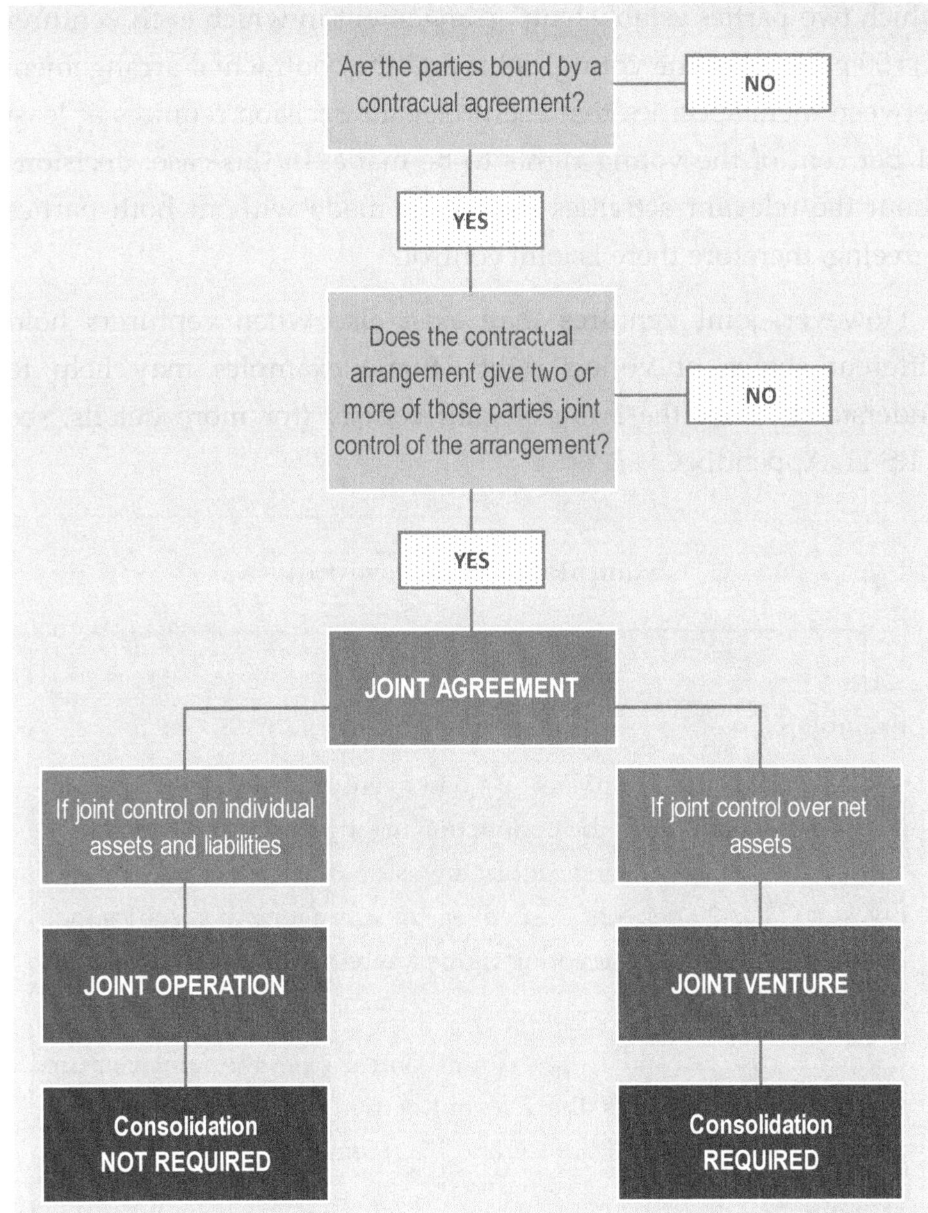

Note: (i) In the table, any time we get a "NO" outcome, this means a joint arrangement does not exist; (ii) "Consolidation not required" means no equity method is required. Other consolidation procedures might apply. Source: Prepared by the Authors.

The typical case where we have a joint venture is the one in which two parties establish an arrangement in which each venturer has 50 per cent of the voting rights and the contractual arrangement between them specifies that each relevant decision requires at least 51 per cent of the voting rights to be made. In this case, decisions about the relevant activities cannot be made without both parties agreeing, therefore there is joint control.

However, joint ventures may exist also when venturers hold different shares of voting rights. Some examples may help to understand better the issue of joint control (for more details, see IFRS 11, Appendix C).

Example 7.1 – Joint control

Example 1

Three investors establish a joint venture to perform R&D activities. According to the contractual arrangement, investor A has 50 per cent of the voting rights, investor B has 30 per cent and investor C has 20 per cent. Moreover, the arrangement specifies that at least 80 per cent of the voting rights are required to make relevant decisions.

In this case, A and B have joint control over the joint-venture because decisions about the relevant activities of the arrangement cannot be made without both A and B agreeing.

Example 2

A company is established in which two parties, A and B, have 30 per cent each of the voting rights, with the remaining 40 per cent being widely dispersed.

The arrangement specifies that all relevant decisions require the approval of both A and B. In such a case, A and B have joint control over the entity.

Example 3

Using the case described in Example 2, let us assume that the arrangement simply specifies that relevant activities require approval by a majority of the voting rights. In such a case, there is no joint control, as there are too many different combinations with the other investors for either A or B to control relevant decisions, and decisions may be made even with the two parties disagreeing.

7.3 Accounting for associates and joint-ventures

The accounting treatment of both associates and joint ventures is set out in IAS 28. Investments in associates and joint ventures shall be accounted for using the so-called *equity method*. [IAS 28, par. IN8]

The equity method is a sort of intermediate form of consolidation accounting. The reason for introducing a special accounting treatment for investments in entities over which the investor has significant influence or joint control can be understood better if we have a brief look at the historical development of the equity method. In the early times of consolidation accounting, entities over which there was no full control were carried at cost. The related revenues were recognised only when dividends were received. In the 1960s - as the number of investments with significant influence was increasing - practitioners started questioning the adequacy of the historical cost as the measurement criterion for this type of investment. In particular, the recognition of dividends was considered an inadequate solution to report the investee's results in the investor's financial statements, because distributions received might bear little relation to the real performance of the former. In the light of this, in 1964 the Royal Shell Group started a new accounting treatment for its investments, something in between cost and full consolidation, which later on became known as the *equity method*. The equity method allows the investor to recognise its share of the profit or loss of the investee in its financial statements, regardless of whether dividends are paid on that result.

Based on the most recent version of IAS 28, an entity shall account for its investment in an associate or a joint venture using the equity method except when that investment qualifies for exemptions (see Box 7.2).

Box 7.2 – Exemptions from applying the equity method

An entity does not need to apply the equity method to its investment in an associate or a joint venture if the entity is a parent that is exempted from preparing consolidated financial statements by the scope exception in IFRS 10, or if all the following apply:

The entity is a wholly-owned subsidiary, or is a partially-owned subsidiary of another entity and its other owners, including those not otherwise entitled to vote, have been informed about, and do not object to, the entity not applying the equity method;

The entity's debt or equity instruments are not traded in a public market (a domestic or foreign stock exchange or an over-the-counter market, including local and regional markets);

The entity did not file, nor is it in the process of filing, its financial statements with a securities commission or other regulatory organisation, for the purpose of issuing any class of instruments in a public market; and

The ultimate or any intermediate parent of the entity produces consolidated financial statements available for public use that comply with IFRS. [IAS 28, par. 17]

It is easy to note that the exemptions provided by IAS 28 are very similar to those provided for consolidated financial statements and already discussed in Chapter 4.[2]

After introducing the relevance and scope of the issue, we now turn to a better understanding of the equity method's details and its implications on the investor's financial statements.

7.4 Application of the equity method

A brief description of the equity method can be found in IAS 28 [par. 10].

Definitions 7.3 – Equity method

Under the *equity method*, on initial recognition the investment in an associate or a joint venture is recognised at cost, and the carrying amount is increased or decreased to recognise the

[2] In addition to the exemptions mentioned above, in certain circumstances, when an investment in an associate or a joint venture is held by, or indirectly through, an entity that is a venture capital organisation, or a mutual fund, unit trust or a similar entity including an investment-linked insurance fund, the entity may be exempted from applying the equity method and measure investments in those associates and joint ventures at fair value through profit or loss in accordance with IFRS 9 [IAS 28, par. 18].

investor's share of the profit or loss of the investee after the date of acquisition. The investor's share of the investee's profit or loss is recognised in the investor's profit or loss.[3]

Distributions received from an investee reduce the carrying amount of the investment.

Adjustments to the carrying amount may also be necessary for changes in the investor's proportionate interest in the investee arising from changes in the investee's other comprehensive income. Such changes include those arising from the revaluation of property, plant and equipment and from foreign exchange translation differences. The investor's share of those changes is recognised in the investor's other comprehensive income.

Let us try to understand better how the equity method works in practice.

Under the equity method of accounting, the investment (either in an associate or in a joint venture) is initially recognised at acquisition cost, like all other assets. After the acquisition, at each reporting date, the value of the investment is increased (decreased) in proportion to the profit (loss) realised by the investee. In this way, the results of the investee are recognised immediately in the financial statements of the investor (in proportion to the share held) rather than waiting for the time of distribution. From a different point of view, the equity method aims to mirror the changes in the owners' equity of the investee in the financial statements of the

[3] The exact definition of IAS 28, par. 3 reports: "The equity method is a method of accounting whereby the investment is initially recognised at cost and adjusted thereafter for the post-acquisition change in the investor's share of the investee's net assets. The investor's profit or loss includes its share of the investee's profit or loss and the investor's other comprehensive income includes its share of the investee's other comprehensive income."

investor. As profits (losses) increase (decrease) the equity of the investee, the related changes shall be recorded proportionally in the value of the investment reported in the financial statements of the investor.

A basic example may help to clarify the accounting implications of this procedure.

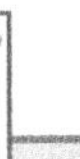

Example 7.2 – Basic example on equity method

On 1 January X company ALPHA acquires 30% of the share capital of a new established company (BETA). ALPHA is able to exercise significant influence on BETA, which therefore is classified as an associate. The acquisition cost is 50 million, paid cash.

On 31 December X BETA reports a profit of 10 million in its income statement.

The equity method requires the investment in BETA to be initially recognised at cost. Therefore, ALPHA will make the following journal entry on 1 January X:

	Debit	Credit
Investment in BETA (+A)	50	
Cash (-A)		50

On 31 December X ALPHA adjusts the value of the investment in BETA, increasing it by 3 million (= 30% × 10 million), even though profit has not been distributed to shareholders.

	Debit	Credit
Investment in BETA (+A)	3	
Investment income - Equity method (+R, +OE)		3

At the end of the accounting period, the value of the investment will be equal to 53 million, i.e. 30% of the value of BETA's equity at the acquisition date.

What would have happened if ALPHA had not adjusted for BETA's profits? Since no dividends were distributed, now the investment (50 million) would represent less than 30% of BETA's equity, which increased thanks to the positive result.

However, adjusting the value of the investment is not always so simple. Profits (losses) are not the only events that affect the owners' equity of the investee. IAS 28 explicitly indicates that any distribution from the investee to the investor reduces the carrying amount of the investment recorded in the financial statements of the investors. A typical example of distribution are dividends. When dividends are paid, the owners' equity of the investee decreases. Consistently, under the equity method the value of the investment in the investor's financial statements will be reduced, as shown in the example below.

Example 7.3 – Basic example on equity method (cont'd)

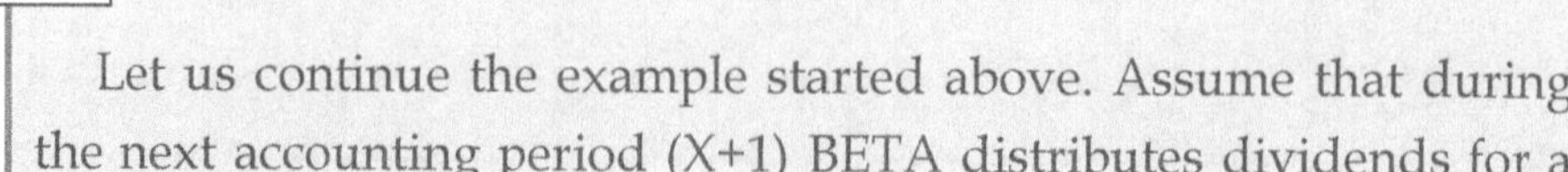

Let us continue the example started above. Assume that during the next accounting period (X+1) BETA distributes dividends for a total amount of 5 million. Also, assume that at the end of X+1 BETA reports a new profit of 7 million.

When dividends are paid, ALPHA will make the following journal entry:

	Debit	Credit
Cash (+A)	1.5	
Investment in BETA (-A)		1.5

On 31 December X+1 ALPHA will adjust again the value of the investment in BETA for the new profit realised by the latter. The increase will be 2.1 million (= 30% × 7 million).

	Debit	Credit
Investment in BETA (+A)	2.1	
Investment income - Equity method (+R, +OR)		2.1

At the end of the accounting period, the value of the investment will be equal to 53.6 million (= 53 - 1.5 + 2.1).

Another adjustment to the carrying amount of the investment under the equity method may arise from changes in the investee's owners equity following the revaluation of property, plant and equipment (PPE) in accordance with IAS 16.

Box 7.3 – Revaluation of property, plant and equipment

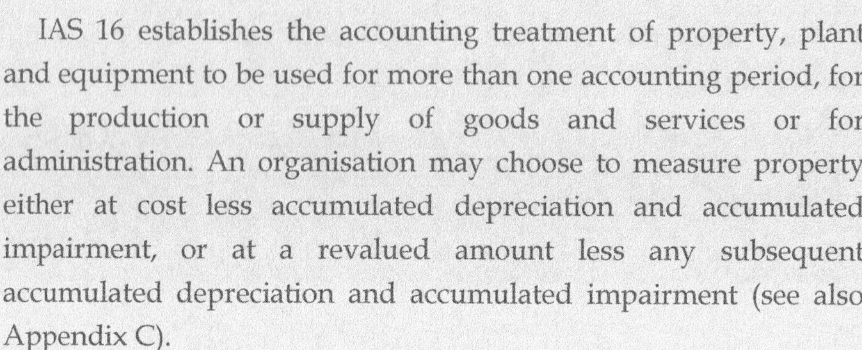

IAS 16 establishes the accounting treatment of property, plant and equipment to be used for more than one accounting period, for the production or supply of goods and services or for administration. An organisation may choose to measure property either at cost less accumulated depreciation and accumulated impairment, or at a revalued amount less any subsequent accumulated depreciation and accumulated impairment (see also Appendix C).

When the investee opts for the revaluation model for its PPE, upward revaluations are recorded as a "revaluation surplus" in its owners' equity. Following the logic underlying the equity method, such an increase in the investee's owners' equity shall be mirrored in the value of the investment recorded in the financial statements of the investor. However, differently from what we have seen for profits, such an increase shall be recorded in the equity of the investor rather than as income in the income statement, as shown in the example below.

Example 7.4 – Basic example on equity method (cont'd)

Let us continue the example started above. Assume that BETA applies the revaluation model to some of its PPE and that, at the end of period X+1, a revaluation surplus of 3 million is recorded.

In relation to the revaluation recognised by BETA, ALPHA will adjust the carrying amount of its investment in the associate as follows (= 30% × 3 million):

	Debit	Credit
Investment in BETA (+A)	0.9	
Revaluation surplus - equity method (+OE)		0.9

To summarise, when the investee realises a profit (loss) the value of the investment recorded by the investor will increase (decrease) proportionally to mirror the increase (decrease) in the investee's equity. An income statement item will be recorded as a contra entry. Consistently, dividends distributed reduce the value of the investment because they decrease the value of the equity of the investee. The contra entry is cash or dividends receivable. Other changes in the equity of the investee such as those due to the application of the revaluation method or to the translation of foreign currency financial statements shall be mirrored proportionally in the carrying amount of the investment. Such changes will affect the owners' equity of the investor and will be reported within its other comprehensive income ("OCI").[4]

7.5 Equity method: beyond the basics

In the previous section we introduced the basic logic underlying the application of the equity method. It is now time to go beyond the basics, trying to understand how the equity method works in more complex situations.

For this purpose, a useful start is provided directly by IAS 28 [par. 26], which states "Many of the procedures that are appropriate for the application of the equity method are similar to the consolidation procedures described in IFRS 10. Furthermore, the concepts underlying the procedures used in accounting for the acquisition of a subsidiary are also adopted in accounting for the acquisition of an investment in an associate or a joint venture." In other words, the equity method being a sort of intermediate form of consolidation the same logic and procedures adopted for the latter should be employed when addressing valuation issues under the equity method.

The first complexity that we will address is related to the case where the acquisition cost - i.e. the cost incurred to acquire the share of the associate or the joint venture - exceeds the proportionate share of the book value of the investee. Unless the investor acquires its ownership at the time the investee is established, paying an amount equal to book value is extremely

---

[4] Other Coprehensive Income is defined by IAS 1, par. 7 as a statement comprising "items of income and expense (including reclassification adjustments) that are not recognised in profit or loss as required or permitted by other IFRSs". A list of items is provided by the same standard to which we address interested readers for further reference [IAS 1 par. 7].

rare, therefore this case is very common in practice. In the previous chapters we learned what are typical reasons for the acquisition cost differing from the book value. For example, the book values of individual assets and liabilities may differ from the respective fair values, or the investee may have unrecognised intangible assets, or the investor may be willing to pay for goodwill.

Similarly to full consolidation, also under the equity method a proper understanding of the source of the excess of the acquisition cost over book value is very important. Indeed, the recognition of income from the investee requires the proper matching of the income generated from the investment to its costs. These costs include, for example, depreciation/amortisation or impairment of the unrecognised surpluses on depreciable assets paid upon acquisition, or the impairment of goodwill (if any). Therefore, when the investee realises a profit (loss), the adjustment to the value of the investment recorded by the investor will not be a mere proportion of the profit (loss) reported, but an adjusted amount which takes into consideration all the costs implicit in the difference between the acquisition cost and the value of the investee.

Let us use an example to understand this issue better.

Example 7.5 – Equity method with allocation of acquisition Cost

On 1 January X company ALICE acquires 40% of company ROSE, which is classified as an associate. The acquisition cost is 220 million, paid cash. On the date of acquisition, the net book value of ROSE is

400 million. The difference between the cost and the net book value of the investment is due to the existence of unrecorded patents, whose fair value is estimated to be 50 million, and to some property which is undervalued by 70 million. The remaining difference is allocated to goodwill. The patents have a remaining useful life of 20 years, while the undervalued property has a remaining useful life of 7 years. The tax effect is calculated at a rate of 50%.At 31 December X ROSE reports a profit of 25 million.

***

On 1 January X the investor (ALICE) records the investment at cost, posting the following accounting entry:

	Debit	Credit
Investment in ROSE (+A)	220	
Cash (-A)		220

In order properly to apply the equity method, we need to allocate the acquisition cost to its different components. This allocation will be useful later on to calculate the *adjusted income* from the investment, to be used to increase/decrease the value of the investment.

ALLOCATION OF THE ACQUISITION COST

Net book value of ROSE	40% × 400	160
Unrecorded patents	40% × 50 × (1 - 0.5)	10
Undervalued property	40% × 70 × (1 - 0.5)	14
Goodwill		36
TOTAL COST		220

The computation above shows that the acquisition cost includes not only the book value of ROSE's equity, but also unrecognised assets (patents), and undervalued assets (property). The remaining difference, if any, is assigned to goodwill, similarly to what we have seen for full consolidation. Note that on the unrecorded values we need to consider also the implicit tax effect due to the fact that those values are not recognised for tax purposes.

Once the cost has been allocated, we can use the different components to calculate the adjusted income at the end of the accounting period.

CALCULATION OF THE ADJUSTED INCOME

Net income	40% × 25	10
Amortisation of patents	10 / 20	(0.5)
Depreciation of property	14 / 7	(2)
ADJUSTED INCOME		**7.5**

The corresponding entry will be:

	Debit	Credit
Investment in BETA (+A)	7.5	
Investment income – Equity method (+R,+OE)		7.5

The share of net income, therefore, is adjusted for amortisation/depreciation of unrecognised assets and undervalued assets. Goodwill is not amortised, but remember that all assets, including goodwill, are subject to impairment testing. When we consider the amortisation/depreciation expense, the income from the investment is indeed matched with all the related costs implicit in the acquisition, and we are able to give a more consistent picture of the real return from the associate.

At the end of period X, the value of the investment is equal to 227.5 million.

A second complexity arises with the occurrence of transactions between the investor and the investee. In this regard, IAS 28 [par. 28] provides specific directions, as indicated in the box below.

Box 7.4 – Unrealised gains and losses

Gains and losses resulting from **'upstream'** and **'downstream' transactions** between an entity (including its consolidated subsidiaries) and its associate or joint venture are recognised in the entity's financial statements only to the extent of unrelated investors' interests in the associate or joint venture.

'Upstream' transactions are, for example, sales of assets from an associate or a joint venture to the investor. 'Downstream' transactions are, for example, sales or contributions of assets from the investor to its associate or its joint venture. The investor's share in the associate's or joint venture's gains or losses resulting from these transactions is eliminated.

In other words, the transactions that are relevant to application of the equity method are those related to the sale of assets (e.g. inventory, fixed assets, etc.) with unrealised gains or losses. The proportionate share of the unrealised gains and losses arising from upstream or downstream transactions must be eliminated.

Again, the procedure followed for the equity method mimics those applied for the full consolidation. However, because the investment is not consolidated line by line, intra-group transactions that generate only intra-group revenues and expenses, or accounts receivable and accounts payable, with no net effect on 'consolidated' profits or losses do not need to be eliminated. What is eliminated is only the proportionate share of the unrealised gains or losses that typically arise in relation to the sale of assets.

The most common way to eliminate such unrealised gains or losses consists in making an additional adjustment to the income from the investment, similarly to what we have seen for depreciation. An example may help to clarify this procedure.

Example 7.6 – Unrealised gains on inventory

Let us continue the previous example (Example 7.5).

Assume that at the end of period X+1, ROSE reports a profit of 30 million. Consider also that, during period X+1, ALICE sold merchandise to ROSE realising revenue of 20 million. The cost of the goods sold was 12 million. At the end of the period, 80% of that merchandise is still unsold in ROSE's inventory.

***

Using the data of the previous example, at the end of period X the value of the investment in ROSE is equal to 227.5 million (=220 + 7.5, see the previous Box).

We are now in period X+1. ROSE reports again a profit that we need to adjust in order properly to apply the equity method.

CALCULATION OF ADJUSTED INCOME X+1

Net income	40% × 30	12
Amortisation of patents	10 / 20	(0.5)
Depreciation of property	14 / 7	(2)
Elimination of unrealised intra-group profit		(1.28)
ADJUSTED INCOME		8.22

The *unrealised intra-group profit* was calculated as follows:

Total gross profit	20 – 12	8
Total net of tax profit	8 × (1 – 0.5)	4
Total unrealised profit	80% × 4	3.2
SHARE OF UNREALISED PROFIT	40% × 3.2	1.28

At the end of period X+1, ALICE will make the following journal entry:

	Debit	Credit
Investment in BETA (+A)	8.22	
Investment income – Equity method (+OE)		8.22

The share of net income, therefore, is adjusted not only for the depreciation on unrecognised assets and undervalued assets, but also for unrealised gains and losses arising from downstream transactions.

The value of the investment at the end of X+1 is equal to 235.72 million.

Note that the adjustment would have been identical had ROSE sold the merchandise to ALICE, i.e. in the case of an upstream transaction.

Example 7.7 – Unrealised gains on fixed assets

Let us keep using the example above. Assume now that at the end of period X+2, ROSE reports a profit of 40 million. During period X+2, ROSE sold equipment to ALICE realising revenue of 10 million. The equipment sold had a net book value of 6 million (historical cost = 15 million, accumulated depreciation = 9 million). ROSE used to depreciate the equipment at 10%. ALICE applies a depreciation rate of 20%.

***

CALCULATION OF ADJUSTED INCOME X+2

Net income	40% × 40	16
Amortisation of patents	10 / 20	(0.5)
Depreciation of property	14 / 7	(2)
Elimination of unrealised intra-group profit		(0.7)
ADJUSTED INCOME		12.8

The *unrealised intra-group profit* was calculated as follows:

Total gross profit from the sale	10 – 6	4
Higher depreciation calculated by ALICE	(10 × 20%) – (15 × 10%)	0.5
Total net profit	4 – 0.5	3.5
Total profit after tax	3.5 × (1 – 0.5)	1.75
SHARE OF UNREALISED PROFIT	40% × 1.75	0.7

At the end of period X+2, ALICE will make the following journal entry:

	Debit	Credit
Investment in BETA (+A)	12.8	
Investment income – Equity method (+R, +OE)		12.8

The share of net income, this time, has been adjusted for the unrealised gain (net of the change in depreciation) related to the sale of equipment. The profit is always considered net of tax and in proportion to the share held in ALICE.

The value of the investment at the end of period X+2 is equal to 248.52 million.

The ones described above are the most popular approaches to eliminating unrealised gains and losses when applying the equity method in practice. However, some companies prefer to use a different approach that adjusts directly the items that were affected by the transaction in the financial statements of the investor rather than including them in the income from the investment. An example of this alternative approach is provided in Appendix C.

7.6 Some additional issues

Financial statements to be used for the application of the equity method

IAS 28 [par. 33-34] requires the most recent available financial statements of the associate or joint venture to be used in applying the equity method. Similarly to what has been discussed for the consolidation of subsidiaries, when the end of the reporting period of the investor is different from that of the investee, the latter prepares financial statements as of the same date as the financial statements of the investor. When it is impracticable to do so, adjustments shall be made for the effects of significant transactions or events that occur between that date and the date of the entity's financial statements. In any case, the difference between the end of the reporting periods cannot be more than three months and shall be the same from period to period.

The financial statements used for the application of the equity method shall be prepared using uniform accounting policies, similarly to what we have seen for the consolidation of subsidiaries [IAS 28, par. 35]. When needed, adjustments shall be made to the investee's financial statements to achieve uniformity.

Excess of net fair value over acquisition cost

In the illustrations reported above, we have always assumed the acquisition cost of the investment to be equal to or higher than the entity's share of the net fair value of the investee's identifiable assets and liabilities. This is not necessarily the case. It may happen that the acquisition cost is lower than the proportionate share of the net fair value of the investee's identifiable assets and liabilities. In this case, IAS 28 [par. 32] requires the excess to be included as income in the determination of the entity's share of the associate or joint venture's profit or loss for the period in which the investment is acquired. In other words, the investment is first recorded at cost, then increased by including the difference between the cost and the net fair value in the income of the first period.

Reporting investee losses

Although the illustrations reported so far are based on the recording of profits, accounting for losses incurred by the investee shall be addressed in a similar manner. The investor recognises its share of loss and reduces the carrying amount of the investment.

However, through the recognition of losses reported by the investee, the value of the investment can eventually be reduced to zero. In such a case the investor discontinues recognising its share of further losses. Once the investment has been reduced to zero, additional losses are provided for, and a liability is recognised, only to the extent that the investor has a commitment to the investee. If the associate or joint venture subsequently reports profits, the entity resumes recognising its share of those profits in accordance with the equity method only after its share of the profits equals the share of losses not recognised [IAS 28, par. 38-39].

8

EXERCISES ON CONSOLIDATION ACCOUNTING

Contents of this chapter:

We think it may be a good idea to end the book with a chapter containing exercises. Consolidation accounting, as many other issues in accounting and in other corporate studies, is a topic that requires some practice to gain proper knowledge of the main mechanisms behind its preparation. The exercises give readers a chance to get used to the different aspects covered in this book and are presented in an increasing order of difficulty. Each exercise has its set of individual financial statements and a few empty columns to allow readers to practice before looking at the solutions, which are shown at the end of each exercise and are meant to be 'reasoned' to guide readers through all the main steps of the exercise.

***

We may decide to prepare consolidated financial statements exactly on the date of the acquisition or later (typically at the end of each accounting period after the acquisition takes place). Let us start by considering the case of consolidation ***on the date of the acquisition***. This is the simplest case since no intra-group transactions have taken place yet, so the only consolidation entry to be made is the elimination of the investment against the subsidiary's equity. Also, there is no consolidated income statement on the date of the acquisition. The consolidated income statement actually shows the consolidated results achieved by the holding company and its subsidiaries as a group *after* the acquisition has taken place. On the date of the acquisition, no transaction has been performed by the group yet, so there is no need to prepare the income statement.
Let us now start with examples.

EXERCISE 1 – CONSOLIDATION OF A SUBSIDIARY ON THE ACQUISITION DATE (WITH NO GOODWILL)

On 31 December X company ALPHA buys 100% of shares in company BETA. The cost of the investment is 2,300. The balance sheets of the two companies on the date of the acquisition are reported in the worksheet.

BALANCE SHEET	ALPHA	BETA	Aggregate	(1)	Consolidated
Non-current assets					
Property plant and equipment	1,000	1,500			
Intangible assets	3,000	2,000			
Investment	2,300				
Total assets	6,300	3,500			
Owners' equity					
Common stock	3,000	1,500			
Retained earnings	600	500			
NC Interests					
Liabilities					
Deferred tax liabilities					
Other Current and non - current liabilities	2,700	1,500			
Total liabilities and equity	6,300	3,500			

On the same date, the fair value of the assets and liabilities of BETA equals their book value, except for plant, whose fair value is 600 higher than the carrying amount as illustrated in the following table:

	Book Value	Fair Value
Plant	1,500	2,100
Total	**1,500**	**2,100**

Consider that the tax rate applied by the two companies is 50%. Prepare the consolidated balance sheet on the date of the acquisition.

EXERCISE 1 - SOLUTION

According to the steps illustrated in Chapter 6, the first thing to do is to compute the "Aggregate" column as the plain sum, line by line, of each item in the individual financial statements. Since the exercise mentions nothing about it, we assume that the individual financial statements are already uniform so that we can proceed straight away to the consolidation adjustments, i.e. step #4a of Chapter 6, which we perform in column (1). Finally, we add up, again line by line, the columns Aggregate and (1) to obtain the requested consolidated balance sheet.

To understand the process of step #4a properly, we need to break down the price paid for the acquisition in all its determinants. The consideration paid for the investment is ideally attributable to the following components:

a) The book value of the subsidiary's equity;
b) Any change in assets and/or liabilities values (i.e. any surplus between the fair values of the assets and/or liabilities acquired and their book values);
c) The tax effects on those surpluses;
d) Goodwill (if any).

In this exercise, the acquisition cost can be broken down as follows:

a)	BETA's Equity	2,000
b)	Surplus on Plant	600
c)	Tax effect on surplus	(300)
d)	Goodwill	-
	Consideration paid	**2,300**

Where:

a) is the equity of BETA (Common Stock + Retained earnings): 1,500 + 500 = 2000;

b) is the difference between the fair value of BETA's plant and its book value: 2,100 – 1,500 = 600;

c) is the deferred tax effect on BETA's plant, computed as the marginal tax rate (50%) times the surplus of point b) (600): 50% × 600 = 300

d) is the Goodwill that justifies the remaining difference (if any) between the consideration that is paid to acquire BETA and what can be recognised separately in BETA's assets, less the deferred tax effect: 2,300 – 100% × {2000 + [600 × (1 – 50%)]} = 2,300 – {2,300} = 0.

The spreadsheet below shows the elimination of the investment in company BETA on the date of acquisition:

BALANCE SHEET	ALPHA	BETA	Aggregate	(1)	Consol.
Non-current assets					
Property plant and equipment	1,000	1,500	2,500	600	3,100
Intangible assets	3,000	2,000	5,000		5,000
Investment	2,300		2,300	(2,300)	0
Total assets	**6,300**	**3,500**	**9,800**	**(1,700)**	**8,100**
Owners' equity					
Common stock	3,000	1,500	4,500	(1,500)	3,000
Retained earnings	600	500	1,100	(500)	600
NC Interests					0
Liabilities					
Deferred tax liabilities				300	300
Other Current and non-current liabilities	2,700	1,500	4,200		4,200
Total liabilities and equity	**6,300**	**3,500**	**9,800**	**(1,700)**	**8,100**

The journal entries of the elimination of the investment are shown in the table below:

	Debit	Credit
Common Stock (-SE)	1,500	
Retained earnings (- SE)	500	
PPE (+A)	600	
Investment (-A)		2,300
Deferred tax liabilities (+L)		300

EXERCISE 2 - CONSOLIDATION OF A SUBSIDIARY ON THE ACQUISITION DATE (WITH GOODWILL)

On 31 December X company ALPHA buys 100% of shares in company BETA. The cost of the investment is 2,700. The balance sheets of the two companies on the date of the acquisition are reported in the worksheet.

BALANCE SHEET	ALPHA	BETA	Aggregate	(1)	Consol.
Non-current assets					
Property plant and equipment	1,000	1,500			
Goodwill					
Intangible assets	3,000	2,000			
Deferred tax assets					
Investment	2,700				
Total assets	**6,700**	**3,500**			
Owners' equity					
Common stock	3,000	1,500			
Retained earnings	600	500			
NC Interests					
Liabilities					
Deferred tax liabilities					
Other current and non-current liabilities (included provisions)	3,100	1,500			
Total liabilities and equity	**6,700**	**3,500**			

On the same date, the fair value of the assets and liabilities of BETA equals their book value, except for its plant, whose fair value is 1,000 higher than the carrying amount, and its provisions, whose fair value is 200 higher than their book value. The difference between the cost of the investment and the owners' equity is recorded as goodwill.

	Book Value	Fair Value
Property plant and equipment	1,500	2,500
Other current and non-current liabilities (included provisions)	1,500	1,700
TOTAL	3,000	4,200

Considering that the tax rate applied by the two companies is 50%, prepare the consolidated financial statements on the date of the acquisition.

EXERCISE 2 - SOLUTION

As in the previous exercise, we first compute the "Aggregate" column by adding up, line by line, each item of the individual statements. Again, we assume that the financial statements are uniform so that we can start form step #4a of Chapter 6 (*"Elimination of parent's investment, equity and recognition of value increase in subsidiaries' assets and liabilities"*) and break down the consideration paid for the acquisition in all its determinants. The consideration paid for the investment is attributable to the following components:

a) The book value of the subsidiary's equity;
b) Any change in assets and/or liabilities values (i.e. any surplus between the fair values of the assets and/or liabilities acquired and their book values);
c) The tax effects on those surpluses;
d) Goodwill (if any).

In the exercise at hand, the purchase price can be broken down as follows:

a)	BETA's Equity	2,000
b_1)	Surplus on Plant	1,000
b_2)	Surplus on Provisions	(200)
c)	Tax effect on surpluses	(400)
d)	Goodwill	300
	Consideration paid	**2,700**

Where:

a) is the equity of BETA (Common Stock + Retained earnings): 1,500 + 500 = 2000;

b_1) is the difference between the fair value of BETA's plant and its book value: 2,500 – 1,500 = 1,000;

b_2) is the difference between the fair value of BETA's provisions and their book values: 1,700 – 1,500 = 200;

c) is the deferred tax effect on BETA's plant, computed as the marginal tax rate (50%) times the surplus of point b): 50% × [1,000 + (-200)] = 400

d) is the Goodwill that justifies the remaining difference between the consideration paid to acquire BETA and what can be recognised separately in BETA's assets and liabilities, less the deferred tax effect: 2,700 – 100% × {2000 + [(1,000 – 200) × (1 – 50%)]} = 2,700 – {2,000 + 400} = 300.

The spreadsheet below shows the elimination of the investment in BETA and the related adjustments (step #4a) on the date of acquisition:

BALANCE SHEET	ALPHA	BETA	Aggregate	(1)	Consol.
Non-current assets					
Property plant and equipment	1,000	1,500	2,500	1,000	3,500
Goodwill				300	300
Intangible assets	3,000	2,000	5,000		5,000
Deferred tax assets				100	100
Investment	2,700		2,700	-2,700	0
Total assets	**6,700**	**3,500**	**10,200**	**-1,300**	**8,900**
Owners' equity					
Common stock	3,000	1,500	4,500	-1,500	3,000
Retained earnings	600	500	1100	-500	600
NC Interests					0
Deferred tax liabilities				500	500
Other current and non-current liabilities (included provisions)	3,100	1,500	4,600	200	4,800
Total liabilities and equity	**6,700**	**3,500**	**10,200**	**-1,300**	**8,900**

The journal entries of this step are shown in the table below:

	Debit	Credit
Common Stock (–SE)	1,500	
Retained earnings (– SE)	500	
PPE (+A)	1,000	
Deferred tax assets (+A)	100	
Goodwill (+A)	300	
Investment (–A)		2,700
Provisions (-L)		200
Deferred tax liabilities (+L)		500

EXERCISE 3 - CONSOLIDATION OF A SUBSIDIARY ON THE ACQUISITION DATE WITH NEGATIVE DIFFERENCE (i.e. "BARGAIN ACQUISITION")

On 31December X company ALPHA buys 100% of shares in company BETA. The cost of the investment is 2,700. The balance sheets of the two companies on the date of the acquisition are reported in the worksheet.

BALANCE SHEET	ALPHA	BETA	Aggregate	(1)	Consol.
Non-current assets					
Property plant and equipment	1,000	1,500			
Goodwill					
Intangible assets	3,000	2,000			
Deferred tax assets					
Investment	2,700				
Total assets	**6,700**	**3,500**			
Owners' equity					
Common stock	3,000	1,500			
Retained earnings	600	500			
Net earnings					
NC Interests					
Liabilities					
Other Current and non-current Liabilities (included deferred tax liabilities)	3,100	1,500			
Total liabilities and equity	**6,700**	**3,500**			

On the same date, the fair value of the assets and liabilities of BETA equals their book value, except for its buildings, whose fair value is 2,000 higher than the carrying amount.

	Book Value	Fair Value
Property plant and equipment (PPE)	1,500	3,500
TOTAL	**1,500**	**3,500**

Assuming a tax rate of 50%, prepare the consolidated balance sheet on the date of the acquisition.

EXERCISE 3 - SOLUTION

The situation is similar to the ones depicted in Exercise 1 and 2, so the same assumptions apply and we start from step #4a of Chapter 6. The most significant difference in this case is that, as we are going to see, the consideration paid is lower than the sum of the assets acquired and equity (i.e. we end up with a negative difference).

In this exercise, the acquisition cost can be broken down as follows:

a)	BETA's Equity	2,000
b)	Surplus on PPE	2,000
c)	Tax effect on surplus	(1,000)
d)	Bargain gain	(300)
	Consideration paid	**2,700**

Where:

a) is the equity of BETA (Common Stock + Retained earnings): 1,500 + 500 = 2000;

b) is the difference between the fair value of BETA's PPE and its book value: 3,500 – 1,500 = 2,000;

c) is the deferred tax effect on BETA's PPE: 50% × (2,000) = 1,000

d) is the remaining difference between the consideration paid to acquire BETA and what can be recognised separately in BETA's assets and liabilities, less the deferred tax effect: 2,700 – 100% × {2000 + [2,000 × (1 – 50%)]} = 2,700 – {3,000} = (300). As we can see, this is a case of negative difference. As noted in Chapter 6, sometimes the acquiring company has more bargaining power or better negotiation skills than the selling entity; it can also be the case that the selling company is acting under compulsion to complete the deal, so that the acquiring company is able to make the deal at a cheaper price. After double checking the purchase price allocation procedure as required by IFRS 3 [IFRS 3, par. 36], the negative difference is recognised as a gain in the acquirer's income statement.

The spreadsheet below shows step #4a on the date of acquisition:

BALANCE SHEET	ALPHA	BETA	Aggregate	(1)	Consol.
Non-current assets					
Property plant and equipment	1,000	1,500	2,500	2,000	4,500
Goodwill					0
Intangible assets	3,000	2,000	5,000		5,000
Deferred tax assets					0
Investment	2,700		2,700	-2,700	0
Total assets	**6,700**	**3,500**	**10,200**	**-700**	**9,500**
Owners' equity					
Common stock	3,000	1,500	4,500	-1,500	3,000
Retained earnings	600	500	1,100	-500	600
Net earnings				300	300
NC Interests					
Liabilities					
Other Current and non-current Liab. (included deferred tax liab.)	3,100	1,500	4,600	1,000	5,600
Total liabilities and equity	**6,700**	**3,500**	**10,200**	**-700**	**9,500**

The journal entries of the discussed step are shown in the box below:

	Debit	Credit
Common Stock (-SE)	1,500	
Retained earnings (- SE)	500	
Property (+A)	2,000	
Investment (-A)		2,700
Deferred tax liabilities (+L)		1,000
Negative difference (+R)		300

EXERCISE 4 – CONSOLIDATION OF A SUBSIDIARY ON THE ACQUISITION DATE (WITH NON-CONTROLLING INTERESTS)

On 31 December X company ALPHA buys 90% of shares in company BETA. The cost of the investment is 2,100. The balance sheets of the two companies on the date of the acquisition are reported in the worksheet.

BALANCE SHEET	ALPHA	BETA	Aggregate	(1)	Consol.
Non-current assets					
Goodwill					
Investments	2,100				
Patents		200			
Current assets					
Other assets	4,000	3,300			
Total assets	**6,100**	**3,500**			
Owners' equity					
Common stock	3,000	1,500			
Retained earnings	600	500			
NC Interests					
Liabilities					
Other Current and non-current liab. (included deferred tax liab.)	2,500	1,500			
Total liabilities and equity	**6,100**	**3,500**			

On the same date, the fair value of assets and liabilities of BETA equals their book value, except for patents, whose fair value is 200 higher than the carrying amount.

	Book Value	Fair Value
Patents	200	400
TOTAL	**200**	**400**

The remaining difference between the cost of the investment and the owners' equity is recorded as goodwill.

Consider that the tax rate applied by the two companies is 50% and prepare the consolidated financial statements on the date of the acquisition according to IFRS 3, assuming that:

A. the company recognises only the goodwill acquired by the parent company;
B. the company applies the "full goodwill method". In such a case, assume that the fair value of the non-controlling interests at the acquisition date is 300.

EXERCISE 4 - SOLUTION A

First, we need to prepare the "Aggregate" balance sheet of the company in the usual way. Since the individual financial statements are already uniform, we can proceed straight away to the consolidation adjustments and then to the consolidated statements.
To understand the process properly, we need to break down the consideration paid for the acquisition in all its determinants. The consideration paid for the investment is attributable to the following components:

a) The book value of the subsidiary's equity;
b) Any change in assets and/or liabilities values (i.e. any surplus between the fair values of the assets and/or liabilities acquired and their book values);
c) The tax effects on those surpluses;
d) Goodwill (if any).

In our case, the acquisition cost can be broken down as follows:

a)	BETA's Equity (90% of 2,000)	1,800
b)	Surplus on Patents (90% of 200)	180
c)	Tax effect on surplus	(90)
d)	Goodwill	210
	Consideration paid	**2,100**

Where:

a) is the equity of BETA (Common Stock + Retained earnings): 90% × (1,500 + 500) = 1,800;

b) is the difference between the fair and book values of BETA's patents: 90% × (400 – 200) = 180;

c) is the deferred tax effect on the surplus of BETA's patents: 50% × (180) = 90;

d) is the Goodwill that justifies the remaining difference between the consideration paid to acquire BETA and what can be recognised separately in BETA's assets and liabilities, less the deferred tax effect: 2,100 – 90% × {2,000 + [200 × (1 – 50%)]} = 2,100 – 90% × {2,100} = 210.

Moreover, since the share held is lower than 100%, we also need to recognise non-controlling interests: 10% × [2,000 (equity BETA) + 200 (gross surplus on patents) – 100 (tax effect on surplus)] = 210.
The spreadsheet below shows the consolidation entry (step #4a of Chapter 6) on the date of acquisition:

BALANCE SHEET	ALPHA	BETA	Aggregate	(1)	Consol.
Non-current assets					
Goodwill				210	210
Investments	2,100		2,100	- 2,100	0
Patents		200	200	200	400
Current assets:					0
Other assets	4,000	3,300	7,300		7,300
Total assets	**6,100**	**3,500**	**9,600**	**- 1,690**	**7,910**
Owners' equity					
Common stock	3,000	1,500	4,500	- 1,500	3,000
Retained earnings	600	500	1,100	-500	600
NC Interests				210	210
Liabilities					
Other Current and non-current liabilities (included deferred tax liab.)	2,500	1,500	4,000	100	4,100
Total liabilities and equity	**6,100**	**3,500**	**9,600**	**- 1,690**	**7,910**

The Journal Entries of the discussed step are shown in the box below:

	Debit	Credit
Common Stock (–SE)	1,500	
Retained earnings (– SE)	500	
Patents (+A)	200	
Goodwill (+A)	210	
Investment (–A)		2,100
Deferred tax liabilities (+L)		100
NC interests (+SE)		210

EXERCISE 4 - SOLUTION B

The steps followed are the same as the ones in Solution A. The difference lies in how we compute goodwill: not only we include the amount attributable to the controlling entity (i.e. 90%) but we also recognise the part which belongs to the non-controlling shareholders.

The consideration paid *and the fair value of the non-controlling interests* are then allocated as follows:

a)	BETA's Equity (100%)	2,000
b)	Surplus on Patents (100%)	200
c)	Tax effect on surplus	(100)
d)	Goodwill	300
	Consideration paid + NC interests	**2,400**

Where:

a) is the equity of BETA (Common Stock + Retained earnings): 100% × (1,500 + 500) = 2,000;

b) is the difference between the fair and book values of BETA's patents: 100% × (400 – 200) = 200;

c) is the deferred tax effect on the surplus of BETA's patents: 50% × (200) = 100;

d) is the Goodwill that justifies the remaining difference between the entity's value (i.e. the sum of the consideration paid to acquire the stake in BETA and the fair value of the non-controlling interests) and what can be recognised separately in BETA's assets and liabilities, net of the deferred tax effect: (2,100 + 300) – {2,000 + [200 × (1 – 50%)]} = 2,400 – 2,100 = 300.

Moreover, we are given the fair value of the non-controlling interests, which amounts to 300.

The spreadsheet below shows the consolidation entry (step #4a of Chapter 6) on the date of acquisition:

BALANCE SHEET	ALPHA	BETA	Aggregate	(1)	Consol.
Non-current assets					
Goodwill				300	300
Investments	2,100		2,100	-2,100	0
Patents		200	200	200	400
Current assets:					0
Other assets	4,000	3,300	7,300		7,300
Total assets	**6,100**	**3,500**	**9,600**	**-1,600**	**8,000**
Owners' equity					
Common stock	3,000	1,500	4,500	-1,500	3,000
Retained earnings	600	500	1,100	-500	600
NC Interests				300	300
Liabilities					
Other Current and non-current liabilities (included deferred tax liab.)	2,500	1,500	4,000	100	4,100
Total liabilities and equity	**6,100**	**3,500**	**9,600**	**-1,600**	**8,000**

The journal entries of this step are shown in the table below:

	Debit	Credit
Common Stock (-SE)	1,500	
Retained earnings (- SE)	500	
Patents (+A)	200	
Goodwill (+A)	300	

Investment (-A)	2,100
Deferred tax liabilities (+L)	100
NC interests (+SE)	300

Let us now move on to considering the case of consolidation ***after the acquisition date***. In this case, it is highly likely that some intra-group transactions have taken place, so that beside the elimination of the investment against the subsidiary's equity we also need to make sure that all the required adjustments to the Aggregate results are made. At this stage, we also start looking at the consolidated income statement and we have to allocate the non-controlling interests' result.

Better to isolate and learn the effects of the main intra-group transactions, exercises 5 to 7 focus only on such adjustments, ignoring the very first part of the consolidation process (step #4a, i.e. the elimination of the parent's investment against the subsidiary's equity and the recognition of any surplus including goodwill). Just remember that we always need to perform also step #4a when we intend to build the final consolidated financial statements. Starting from exercise 8, we will work with all the steps of the consolidation process.

EXERCISE 5 – ELIMINATION OF INTERCOMPANY PROFITS INCLUDED IN INVENTORIES

Company ALPHA holds 100% of company BETA. The income statements and the balance sheet of the two companies are reported below.

INCOME STATEMENT	ALPHA	BETA	Aggregate	(1)	Consol.
Operating revenues	15,000	6,000			
Operating expenses	9,000	3,000			
Operating Income	**6,000**	**3,000**			
Financial income and expenses	-100	-80			
Income before taxes	**5,900**	**2,920**			
Taxes	2,400	920			
Net Income	**3,500**	**2,000**			

BALANCE SHEET	ALPHA	BETA	Aggregate	(1)	Consol.
Non-current assets					
Property, plant and equipment	10,000	10,000			
Consolidation difference					
Other intangible assets	1,000	1,000			
Investments	11,000				
Deferred tax assets					
Current assets					
Inventories	3,000	7,500			
Receivables	4,500	2,000			
Cash & Other assets	3,000	1,500			
Total assets	**32,500**	**22,000**			
Equity and liabilities					
Owners' equity					
Common stock	20,000	9,600			
Retained earnings	1,000	400			
Net income	3,500	2,000			
NC Interests					
Common stock and Retained earnings					
Net income					
Non-current liabilities					
Provisions	2,500	1,500			
Deferred tax liabilities	200				
Current liabilities					
Trade and financial liabilities	4,800	7,000			
Other liabilities	500	1,500			
Total liabilities and equity	**32,500**	**22,000**			

During year X, ALPHA sold to BETA 100 units of product "Win" at a unit price of 50. For the purchase of those goods ALPHA incurred a unit cost of 40. At 31 December X, the reporting date, none of the units purchased by BETA has been sold to third parties. Assume also that the goods were paid cash by BETA (i.e. there are no intercompany receivable/payable accounts at the time of consolidation) and that the tax rate for both companies is 50%.

Eliminate the unrealised intercompany profits included in the value of BETA's inventories.

EXERCISE 5 - SOLUTION

First, we need to prepare the "Aggregate" column of the financial statements, in which we add up, line by line, the amounts in the individual reports. As always, we assume that the individual financial statements are already uniform so that we can proceed straight away to the consolidation adjustments.
In this exercise, the adjustment required is related to the elimination of the intercompany profit included in the value of inventory. The contra entry to the profit elimination is the reduction in the inventory value, which has been overstated due to the intra-group mark up on the goods sold. Since all inventories are still in the group at the end of the year, we need to reduce the value of the inventory in full. As this adjustment reduces the operating income, for consistency we also need to lower the tax amount. The contra entry will be a deferred tax asset to be reported in the balance sheet.

The computations are the following:

a)	Decreasing revenues	100% × (50 × 100)	5,000
b)	Decreasing costs	100% × (40 × 100)	4,000
c)	Net effect on operating income	–5,000 – (–4,000)	–1,000
d_1)	Tax effect	–1,000 × 50%	-500
	Net Income		**-500**

e)	Decreasing ending inventory	100% × (50 – 40) × 100	1,000
d_2)	Tax effect	–1,000 × 50%	-500
	Total assets		**-500**
f)	Net income (OE)		-500
	Total liabilities and equity		**-500**

The spreadsheet below shows the consolidation adjustment:

INCOME STATEMENT	ALPHA	BETA	Aggregate	(1)
Operating revenues	15,000	6,000	21,000	-5,000
Operating expenses	9,000	3,000	12,000	-4,000
Operating Income	**6,000**	**3,000**	**9,000**	**-1,000**
Financial income and expenses	-100	-80	-180	
Income before taxes	**5,900**	**2,920**	**8,820**	**-1,000**
Taxes	2,400	920	3,320	-500
Net Income	**3,500**	**2,000**	**5,500**	**-500**

BALANCE SHEET	ALPHA	BETA	Aggregate	(1)
Non-current assets				
Property, plant and equipment	10,000	10,000	20,000	
Consolidation difference				
Other intangible assets	1,000	1,000	2,000	
Investments	11,000		11,000	
Deferred tax assets				500
Current assets				
Inventories	3,000	7,500	10,500	-1,000
Receivables	4,500	2,000	6,500	
Cash & Other assets	3,000	1,500	4,500	
Total assets	**32,500**	**22,000**	**54,500**	**-500**
Liabilities and Own. equity				
Common stock	20,000	9,600	29,600	
Retained earnings	1,000	400	1,400	
Net income	3,500	2,000	5,500	-500
NC Interests				
Common stock and Retained earnings				
Net income				
Non-current liabilities				
Provisions	2,500	1,500	4,000	
Deferred tax liabilities	200		200	
Current liabilities			0	
Trade and financial liabilities	4,800	7,000	11,800	
Other liabilities	500	1,500	2,000	
Total liabilities and equity	**32,500**	**22,000**	**54,500**	**-500**

The journal entries related to this adjustment are shown in the box below:

	Debit	Credit
Operating revenues (-R)	5,000	
Deferred tax assets (+A)	500	
Operating expenses (-E)		4,000
Inventory (-A)		1,000
Income taxes (-E)		500

EXERCISE 6 – ELIMINATION OF INTERCOMPANY PROFITS INCLUDED IN INVENTORIES

Company ALPHA holds 100% of company BETA. The income statements and the balance sheets of the two companies are reported below:

INCOME STATEMENT	ALPHA	BETA	Aggreg.	(1)	(2)	Consol.
Operating revenues	25,000	16,000				
Operating expenses	19,000	13,000				
Operating income	**6,000**	**3,000**				
Financial income and expenses	-100	-80				
Income before taxes	**5,900**	**2,920**				
Taxes	2,400	920				
Net Income	**3,500**	**2,000**				

BALANCE SHEET	ALPHA	BETA	Aggreg.	(1)	(2)	Consol.
Non-current assets						
Property, plant and equipment	10,000	10,000				
Consolidation difference						
Other intangible assets	1,000	1,000				
Investments	11,000					
Deferred tax assets						
Current assets						
Inventories	3,000	7,500				
Receivables	5,000	2,000				
Cash & Other assets	2,500	1,500				
Total assets	**32,500**	**22,000**				
Owners' equity						
Common stock	20,000	9,600				
Retained earnings	1,000	400				
Net income	3,500	2,000				
NC Interests						
Common stock and Retained earnings						
Net income						
Non-current liabilities						
Provisions	2,500	1,500				
Deferred tax liabilities	200					
Current liabilities						
Trade and financial liabilities	4,800	7,000				
Other liabilities	500	1,500				
Total liabilities and equity	**32,500**	**22,000**				

During year X, ALPHA sold to BETA 200 units of product "Run" at the unit price of 100. In order to purchase those goods, ALPHA incurred a unit cost of 80. At 31 December X, 40% of the units purchased by BETA has been sold to third parties. Assume that there are no intercompany receivable/payable accounts at the time of consolidation and that the tax rate for both companies is 50%.

Eliminate the unrealised intercompany profits included in the value of BETA's inventories.

EXERCISE 6 – SOLUTION

As in the previous exercise, the adjustment we need to perform is related to the elimination of the intercompany profit included in the value of inventory. The difference is now that only 40% of the units has been sold to third parties, so that 60% is still in the inventory of the buying company at the end of the year. Again, as in the previous case, we need to account for the deferred tax effect related to the adjustment, since we change the group's income before taxes. For the sake of clarity, we split the adjustments into two: #1. the one that relates to the 60% of the goods which are still in the group and that we will treat as in the previous case; #2. the one that relates to the 40% of the good that have been sold to third parties which do not impact the group profit.

The necessary computations are then the following:

First adjustment (60% of the goods)

a)	Decreasing revenues	60% × (200 × 100)	12,000
b)	Decreasing costs	60% × (200 × 80)	9,600
c)	Net effect	−12,000 – (−9,600)	−2,400
d_1)	Tax effect	−2,400 × 50%	−1,200
	Net Income		**−1,200**

e)	Decreasing ending inventory	60% × (100 – 80) × 200	−2,400
d_2)	Tax effect	−2,400 × 50%	1,200
	Total assets		**−1,200**
f)	Net income (OE)		−1,200
	Total liabilities and equity		**−1,200**

Second adjustment (40% of the goods, net impact = 0)

a)	Decreasing revenues	40% × (200 × 100)	8,000
b)	Decreasing costs	40% × (200 × 80) 40% × (20,000 – 16,000)	6,400 1,600
c)	Net effect	–8,000 – (–8,000)	0
d_1)	Tax effect	0 × 50%	0
	Net Income		**0**

The spreadsheet below shows the consolidation adjustments:

INCOME STATEMENT	ALPHA	BETA	Aggreg.	(1)	(2)
Operating revenues	25,000	16,000	41,000	-12,000	-8,000
Operating expenses	19,000	13,000	32,000	-9,600	-6,400 -1,600
Operating income	**6,000**	**3,000**	**9,000**	**-2,400**	**0**
Financial income and expenses	-100	-80	-180		
Income before taxes	**5,900**	**2,920**	**8,820**	**-2,400**	
Taxes	2,400	920	3,320	-1,200	
Net Income	**3,500**	**2,000**	**5,500**	**-1,200**	**0**

BALANCE SHEET	ALPHA	BETA	Aggreg.	(1)
Non-current assets				
Property, plant and equipment	10,000	10,000	20,000	
Consolidation difference				
Other intangible assets	1,000	1,000	2,000	
Investments	11,000		11,000	
Deferred tax assets				1,200
Current assets				
Inventories	3,000	7,500	10,500	-2,400
Receivables	5,000	2,000	7,000	
Cash & Other assets	2,500	1,500	4,000	
Total assets	**32,500**	**22,000**	**54,500**	**-1,200**
Owners' equity				
Common stock	20,000	9,600	29,600	
Retained earnings	1,000	400	1,400	
Net income	3,500	2,000	5,500	-1,200
NC Interests				
Common stock and Retained earnings				
Net income				
Non-current liabilities				
Provisions	2,500	1,500	4,000	
Deferred tax liabilities	200		200	
Current liabilities				
Trade and financial liabilities	4,800	7,000	11,800	
Other liabilities	500	1,500	2,000	
Total liabilities and equity	**32,500**	**22,000**	**54,500**	**-1,200**

The journal entries related to the adjustment described above are shown in the box below:

Account	Debit	Credit
Operating revenues (-R)	12,000	
Operating revenues (-R)	8,000	
Deferred tax assets (+A)	1,200	
Operating costs (-E)		17,600
Income taxes (-E)		1,200
Inventory (-A)		2,400

EXERCISE 7 - ELIMINATION OF INTERCOMPANY PROFITS FROM THE SALE OF FIXED ASSETS AND DEPRECIATION ADJUSTMENT

Company ALPHA holds 100% of company BETA. The income statements and the balance sheets of the two companies are reported below:

INCOME STATEMENT	ALPHA	BETA	Aggreg.	(1)	(2)	Consol.
Operating revenues	10,000	6,000				
Other op. revenues	1,600					
Operating Expenses	4,400	3,000				
Depreciation		400				
Operating Income	**7,200**	**2,600**				
Financial income & expenses	-100	-80				
Income before taxes	**7,100**	**2,520**				
Taxes	3,000	720				
Net Income	**4,100**	**1,800**				

BALANCE SHEET	ALPHA	BETA	Aggreg.	(1)	(2)	Consol.
Non-current assets						
PPE (net of accumulated depr.)	8,200	13,600				
Consolidation difference						
Other intangible assets	1,000	1,000				
Investments	11,000					
Deferred tax assets						
Current assets						
Inventories	3,000	2,500				
Receivables	4,000	2,000				
Cash & Other assets	5,900	1,700				
Total assets	**33,100**	**20,800**				
Equity and liabilities						
Owners' equity						
Common stock	20,000	9,600				
Retained earnings	1,000	400				
Net income	4,100	1,800				
NC Interests						
C.S.& Retained earnings						
Net income						
Non-current liabilities						
Provisions	2,500	1,500				
Deferred tax liabilities	200					
Current liabilities						
Trade and Fin. liabilities	4,800	6,000				
Other liabilities	500	1,500				
Total liabilities and equity	**33,100**	**20,800**				

At the beginning of year X ALPHA sold to BETA, at the price of 4,000, plant already partially amortised and accounted for the following values:

Historical cost	6,000
Accumulated depreciation	3,600
Net book value at 1.1.X	**2,400**

At year end the plant is still recognised in the financial statements of BETA. The parent ALPHA used to depreciate the asset at an annual rate of 10% (on straight-line basis); the subsidiary BETA depreciates the asset at an annual rate of 20% (on a straight-line basis).

Assume that the tax rate is 50%, and that the plant was paid for in cash.

Eliminate the unrealised intragroup gain, and adjust the depreciation of the asset sold by ALPHA to BETA.

EXERCISE 7 - SOLUTION

In this exercise, the adjustments required are related to the *"Elimination of intercompany profit included in the value of long-lived assets"*.

When we deal with a sale of inter-company long-lived assets, we always need to make two adjustments:

1. Through the first adjustment we eliminate the gain recognised by the selling company -ALPHA- in its income statement. In this case, the gain is of 1,600 (the plant's selling price of 4,000 less the net carrying amount of 2,400). The contra entry is a reduction of the asset's value on the balance sheet for the same amount. Remember that, since we are changing an income statement account, we need to consider the fiscal impact of the sale.

c)	Decreasing plant value	-(4,000 - 2,400)	-1,600
b_2)	Tax effect	1,600 × 50%	800
	Total assets		**-800**
d)	Net income (OE)		-800
	Total liabilities and equity		**-800**

2. Through the second adjustment we reset the depreciation expenses to the original level, prior to the intra-group transaction. If we went back to the pre-sale situation, ALPHA would report depreciation expense for 600 (10% of the plant's historical cost, equal to 6,000); on the other hand, BETA recognised an actual cost of 800 (price paid = historical cost = 4,000, times its depreciation rate of 20%). Therefore

depreciation expense needs to be decreased by 200 (800 - 600) and the contra entry will be an increase in the asset's value. Also this adjustment requires the recognition of the deferred tax liability (100 in this exercise: 200 × 50%). In this case, since we have already generated a deferred tax asset with the first adjustment and given the same nature of the underlying business transaction, it is more appropriate to decrease the value of that asset rather than recognising a separate deferred tax liability.

a)	Decreasing depreciation expenses	(10% × 600) – (20% × 400)	-200
b_1)	Tax effect	200 × 50%	100
	Net Income		**-100**

c)	Increasing plant value	(10% × 600) – (20% × 400)	-200
b_2)	Tax effect	200 × 50%	100
	Total assets		**-100**

The spreadsheet below shows the consolidation adjustments:

INCOME STATEMENT	ALPHA	BETA	Aggregate	(1)	(2)
Operating revenues	10,000	6,000	16,000		
Other op. revenues	1,600		1,600	-1,600	
Operating Expenses	4,400	3,000	7,400		
Depreciation		400	400		-200
Operating Income	**7,200**	**2,600**	**9,800**	**-1,600**	**200**
Financial income and expenses	-100	-80	-180		
Income before taxes	**7,100**	**2,520**	**9,620**	**-1,600**	**200**
Taxes	3,000	720	3,720	-800	100
Net Income	**4,100**	**1,800**	**5,900**	**-800**	**100**

BALANCE SHEET	ALPHA	BETA	Aggregate	(1)	(2)
Non-current assets					
PPE (net of accumulated depr.)	8,200	13,600	21,800	-1,600	200
Consolidation difference					
Other intangible assets	1,000	1,00	2,000		
Investments	11,000		11,000		
Deferred tax assets				800	-100
Current assets					
Inventories	3,000	2,50	5,500		
Receivables	4,000	2,00	6,000		
Cash & Other assets	5,900	1,70	7,600		
Total assets	**33,100**	**20,8**	**53,900**	**- 800**	**100**
Owners' equity					
Common stock	20,000	9,60	29,600		
Retained earnings	1,000	400	1,400		
Net income	4,100	1,80	5,900	-800	100
NC Interests					
C.S.& Retained earnings					
Net income					
Non-current liabilities					
Provisions	2,500	1,50	4,000		
Deferred tax liabilities	200		200		
Current liabilities					
Trade and Fin. liabilities	4,800	6,00	10,800		
Other liabilities	500	1,50	2,000		
Total liabilities and equity	**33,100**	**20,800**	**53,900**	**-800**	**100**

	Debit	Credit
Operating revenues (-R)	1,600	
Deferred tax assets (+A)	800	
PPE (-A)		1,600
Income tax (-E)		800

	Debit	Credit
PPE (+A)	200	
Income tax (+E)	100	
Depreciation (-E)		200
Deferred tax assets (-A)		100

EXERCISE 8 – COMPREHENSIVE EXERCISE

On 1 January X company ALPHA acquires 80% of the share capital of company BETA. The cost of the investment is 5,000. On the date of the acquisition, company BETA's owners' equity is 5,400. The income statements and the balance sheet of the two companies are reported at the end of the exercise.
On the same date, the fair value of the assets and liabilities of BETA equals their book value, except for plant, whose fair value is higher than the carrying amount for 1,000.

	Book Value	Fair Value
Plants	6,000	7,000
TOTAL	**6,000**	**7,000**

The expected remaining useful life of the plants is 10 years. The difference between the cost of the investment and the fair value of the subsidiary's owners' equity is allocated to goodwill. Consider that the company recognises goodwill only for the share acquired by the parent company and that, on the date of consolidation, there is no impairment loss on goodwill.
During the accounting period X, the two companies carry out the following intra-group transactions:

A. ALPHA sells BETA services for a total amount of 300; at the end of the accounting period the transaction has not been settled yet;
B. ALPHA lends money to BETA; the total amount lent is 1,000 and this will be paid back in its entirety in 10 years. In relation to this transaction, the two companies record interest

for 100, and this has already been paid at the end of the current accounting period;

C. BETA sells goods to ALPHA for a total amount of 600. All goods are still in ALPHA's inventory. The intra-group profit included in these goods is 250, i.e. the cost of goods sold for BETA is 350. The transaction has already been settled at the end of the accounting period.
D. ALPHA sells a building to BETA. The carrying amount of the building sold was 500 [historical cost = 900]. The selling price, collected cash, is 800. ALPHA applied a yearly depreciation rate of 10%, while BETA applies 20%.
E. The tax rate for the two companies is 50%.

Prepare the consolidated financial statements of the ALPHA BETA group as of 31 December X.

INCOME STATEMENT	ALPHA	BETA	Aggr.	(1)	(2)	(3)	(4)	(5)	(6)	(7)	(8)	Consol.
Operating revenues	150,000	130,000	280,000									
Operating expenses	141,000	121,000	262,000									
Operating income	9,000	9,000	18,000									
Financial income	2,000	6,500	8,500									
Financial expenses	4,000	10,000	14,000									
Income before taxes	7,000	5,500	12,500									
Income tax expense	1,200	3,000	4,200									
Net income	5,800	2,500	8,300									
NC share of Income												

BALANCE SHEET	ALPHA	BETA	Aggr.	(1)	(2)	(3)	(4)	(5)	(6)	(7)	(8)	Consol.
Non-current assets												
Property, plant and equipment	29,000	6,000	35,000									
Goodwill												
Investments	5,000	1,000	6,000									
Financial receivables	10,000	2,800	12,800									
Deferred tax assets												
Current assets												
Inventories	2,600	4,000	6,600									
Trade receivables	5,000	2,000	7,000									
Total assets	**51,600**	**15,800**	**67,400**									
Owners' equity												
Common stock	17,000	3,000	20,000									
Retained earnings	13,500	2,400	15,900									
Net income	5,800	2,500	8,300									
NC Interests												
NC Common stock and reserves												
NC Net income												
Non-current liabilities												
Financial payables	2,300	900	3,200									
Deferred tax liabilities												
Current liabilities	13,000	7,000	20,000									
Total liabilities and equity	**51,600**	**15,800**	**67,400**									

EXERCISE 8 – SOLUTION

Assuming that the individual financial statements are uniform, the first thing to do is to compute the "Aggregate" column as the plain sum, line by line, of each item in the individual financial statements. Then, we need to break down the consideration paid for the acquisition into all its determinants to proceed according to step #4a of Chapter 6. As usual, this is our starting point. We present now each of the adjustments, as they appear in the financial statements' columns.

Adjustment # (1)

In this exercise, the acquisition cost can be broken down as follows:

a)	BETA's Equity (80% × 5,400)	4,320
b)	Surplus on Plant (80% × 1,000)	800
c)	Tax effect on surplus	-400
d)	Goodwill	280
	Consideration paid	**5,000**

Where:

a) is the equity of BETA at acquisition [80% × (Common Stock + Retained earnings)]: 80% × (3,000 + 2,400) = 4,320;

b) is the difference between the fair value of BETA's plant and its book value: 80% x (7,000 – 6,000) = 800;

c) is the deferred tax effect on BETA's plant, computed as the marginal tax rate (50%) times the surplus of point b) (800): 50% × 800 = 400;

d) is the Goodwill that justifies the remaining difference between the consideration that is paid to acquire BETA and what can be recognised separately in BETA's assets, less the deferred tax effect: 5,000 - 80% × {5,400 + [1,000 × (1 - 50%)]} = 5,000 - {4,720} = 280.

Moreover, since the stake held is lower than 100%, we also need to recognise non-controlling interests: 20% × [5,400 (equity BETA) + 1,000 (gross surplus on PPE) - 500 (tax effect on surplus)] = 1,180.

Adjustment # (2)

Recognition of depreciation of surplus on plant [10% × 1000 = 100], since the expected remaining life is 10 years. This adjustment requires the recognition of the deferred tax effect, as the group's income is affected. Specifically, income before taxes decreases by 100, therefore taxes have to be reduced by 50 [100 × 50%].

Adjustment # (3)

Elimination of intra-group service revenues [300] and expenses [300] and related payables/receivables.

Adjustment # (4)

Elimination of intra-group financial payable/receivable [1,000].
Elimination of the related interest [Financial income/expenses 100].

Adjustment # (5)

Elimination of intra-group revenues and expenses related to the sale of goods. Decreasing revenues [600], decreasing costs [350]: net effect [- 600 + 350 = - 250].

This adjustment requires the recognition of the deferred tax effect, affecting the group's income. To be precise, income before taxes decreases by 250. Therefore, considering the tax rate, following the accrual principle, taxes have to be reduced by 125 (250 × 50%). This reduction in taxes has to be reported on the balance sheet recording a deferred tax asset.

Moreover, this adjustment requires reducing the value of the ending inventory by the full amount of the intercompany profit, since all inventories are still on hand in the buying company at the end of the year. Therefore, inventories are reduced by 250.

Adjustment # (6)

With this adjustment we eliminate the effects of the intra-group sale of the building, eliminating the gain recognised by ALPHA in its income statement for a value of 300 [800 (sales price) - 500 (Net book value)]. Moreover, this adjustment requires a decrease in the depreciation of buildings in order to bring it back to the pre-sale value. In fact, if we go back to the pre-sale situation, ALPHA was recognising depreciation for 90 [10% of his historical cost equal to 900] while BETA has recognised a cost of 160 [price paid = historical cost = 800 × 20%]. Therefore, depreciation needs to be adjusted and decreased by 70 [160 - 90].

This adjustment requires also the recognition of the deferred tax effect, affecting the group's income. To be precise, income before taxes decreases by 230 [300 - 70]. Therefore, taxes have to be reduced by 115 [230 × 50%]. This reduction in taxes has to be reported in the balance sheet as a deferred tax asset.

Adjustment # (7)

Finally, we record the share of profit belonging to non-controlling interests. We do that starting from the subsidiary's net income and adding only those adjustments that have an impact on the subsidiary's profit, which are in part attributable to the non-controlling interests. NC interests' net income is calculated as follows: (2,500 - 50 - 125) × 20% = 465

INCOME STATEMENT	ALPHA	BETA	Aggr.	(1)	(2)	(3)	(4)	(5)	(6)	(7)	(8)	Consol.
Operating revenues	150,000	130,000	280,000			-300		-600	-300			278,800
Operating expenses	141,000	121,000	262,000		100	-300		-350	-70			261,380
Operating income	9,000	9,000	18,000	0	-100	0		-250	-230			17,420
Financial income	2,000	6,500	8,500				-100					8,400
Financial expenses	4,000	10,000	14,000				-100					13,900
Income before taxes	7,000	5,500	12,500	0	-100	0	0	-250	-230			11,920
Income tax expense	1,200	3,000	4,200		-50			-125	-115			3,910
Net income	**5,800**	**2,500**	**8,300**	**0**	**-50**	**0**	**0**	**-125**	**-115**	**-465**		**7,545**
NC share of Income										**+465**		**465**

BALANCE SHEET	ALPHA	BETA	Aggr.	(1)	(2)	(3)	(4)	(5)	(6)	(7)	(8)	Consol.
Non-current assets												
Property, plant and equipment	29,000	6,000	35,000	1,000	-100				-230			35,670
Goodwill				280								280
Investments	5,000	1,000	6,000	-5,000								1,000
Financial receivables	10,000	2,800	12,800				-1,000					11,800
Deferred tax assets								+125	+115			240
Current assets												
Inventories	2,600	4,000	6,600					-250				6,350
Trade receivables	5,000	2,000	7,000			-300						6,700
Total assets	**51,600**	**15,800**	**67,400**	**-3,720**	**-100**	**-300**	**1,000**	**-125**	**-115**	**0**		**62,040**
Owners' equity												
Common stock	17,000	3,000	20,000	-3,000								17,000
Retained earnings	13,500	2,400	15,900	-2,400								13,500
Net income	5,800	2,500	8,300		-50			-125	-115	-465		7,545
NC Interests				1,180								
NC Common stock and reserves												1,180
NC Net income										+465		465
Non-current liabilities												
Financial payables	2,300	900	3,200				-1,000					2,200
Deferred tax liabilities				500	-50							450
Current liabilities	13,000	7,000	20,000			-300						19,700
Total liabilities and equity	**51,600**	**15,800**	**67,400**	**-3,720**	**-100**	**-300**	**-1,000**	**-125**	**-115**	**0**		**62,040**

EXERCISE 9 - COMPREHENSIVE EXERCISE

On 1 January X, company ALPHA acquired a 80% stake in company BETA paying a price of 11,000. The balance sheet of BETA at the date of acquisition showed equity of 10,000. The income statements and balance sheets of the two companies are reported at the end of the exercise.
At the same date (1 January X), the fair values of all assets and liabilities of BETA coincided with their book values, except for the following:

	Book Value	Fair Value
Property	7,000	9,000
Patents	1,000	3,000
TOTAL	**8,000**	**12,000**

The useful life of property is expected to be 20 years, while that of patents 10 years. The remaining positive consolidation difference is allocated to goodwill. Assume that at the date of consolidation the recoverable amount of goodwill exceeds its carrying amount.
In order to compute the deferred tax effects on surpluses, consider a tax rate of 50%. Assume that ALFHA opts for proportionate recognition of goodwill (NO full goodwill).
Moreover, during year X the following intercompany transactions took place:

A. BETA sold goods to ALPHA at a price of 4,000 making a profit of 2,000. At year end, 70% of the goods has been sold to third parties;
B. ALPHA purchased from third parties goods which are subsequently sold to the subsidiary BETA at a price of 5,000.

For the purchase of these goods ALPHA incurred a cost of 4,000. The entire purchase is still in the inventory of BETA at the end of the accounting period;

C. On 1 January BETA sold to ALPHA plant which was purchased at a price of 8,000 and depreciated for 2,000. The selling price was 7,000. BETA was depreciating the asset on a straight-line basis, recognising annual depreciation of 800; ALPHA, however, recognises annual depreciation (on a straight-line basis) of 500.

Make all the consolidation adjustments needed to build the consolidated financial statements of group ALPHA-BETA as of 31 December X.

INCOME STATEMENT	ALPHA	BETA	Aggregat	(1)	(2)	(3)	(4)	(5)	(6)	(7)	Consolidated
Operating revenues	10,000	6,000	16,000								
Operating expenses	5,000	3,000	8,000								
Operating income	**5,000**	**3,000**	**8,000**								
Financial income and expenses	-100	-80	-180								
Income before taxes	**4,900**	**2,920**	**7,820**								
Taxes	1,900	920	2,820								
Net income	**3,000**	**2,000**	**5,000**								
NC share of income											

BALANCE SHEET	ALPHA	BETA	Aggregat	(1)	(2)	(3)	(4)	(5)	(6)	(7)	Consolidated
Non-current assets											
Property, plant and equipment	10,000	10,000	20,000								
Goodwill											
Other intangible assets	1,000	1,000	2,000								
Investments	11,000		11,000								
Deferred tax assets											
Current assets											
Inventories	3,000	2,500	5,500								
Receivables	4,000	2,000	6,000								
Cash & other assets	3,000	1,500	4,500								
Total assets	**32,000**	**17,000**	**49,000**								
Owners' equity											
Common stock	20,000	9,600	29,600								
Retained earnings	1,000	400	1,400								
Net income	3,000	2,000	5,000								
NC share of equity											
Common stock and retained											
Net income											
Non-current liabilities											
Provisions	2,500	1,500	4,000								
Deferred tax liabilities	200		200								
Current liabilities											
Trade and financial liabilities	4,800	2,000	6,800								
Other liabilities	500	1,500	2,000								
Total liabilities and equity	**32,000**	**17,000**	**49,000**								

EXERCISE 9 - SOLUTION

In this exercise, the following adjustments are required:

Adjustment # (1)
Elimination of the investment in BETA [11,000] against the equity of the subsidiary at the date of acquisition [9,600 + 400 = 10,000] (excluding the net income of year X, realised after the acquisition).
Recognition of the surplus on property [2,000] and intangible assets (patents) [2,000].
Recognition of deferred tax assets on surplus value [4,000 × 50% = 2,000].
Recognition of goodwill = 1,400 → 11,000 (cost of investment) - 80%× [10,000 (BETA equity) + 4,000 (gross surplus on property and patents) - 2,000 (tax effect on surplus)].
Recognition of non-controlling interests 2,400 → 20% × [10,000 (BETA equity) + 4,000 (gross surplus on property and patents) - 2,000 (tax effect on surplus)].

Adjustment # (2)
Recognition of depreciation of surplus on property of 100 [5% × 2,000], since the expected remaining life is 20 years.
Recognition of depreciation of surplus on patents of 200 [10% × 2,000] since the expected life is 10 years.
This adjustment requires the recognition of the deferred tax effect, since it affects the group's income, which decreases by 300. Taxes have then to be reduced by 150 [300 × 50%] and deferred tax liabilities in the balance sheet are reduced by the same amount.

As far as goodwill is concerned, we need to compare its book value with the recoverable amount: since the recoverable amount is higher than the book value, there is no write-down (impairment) of goodwill.

Adjustment # (3)

Decreasing revenues [30% × 4,000 = 1,200]; decreasing costs [30% × 2,000 = 600]: net impact [-1,200 - (- 600) = - 600]. This adjustment requires the recognition of the deferred tax effect since it affects the group's income. Therefore, considering the tax rate, taxes have to be reduced by 300 [600 × 50%] and recognised in the balance sheet accordingly.

Moreover, this adjustment requires reducing the value of the ending inventory. Since 30% of goods are still in the acquiring company at the end of the year, inventories have to be decreased by 600.

Adjustment # (4)

Decreasing revenues [70% × 4,000 = 2,800]; decreasing costs [(70% × 2,000) + 70% (4,000 - 2,000) = 1,400 + 1,400 = 2,800]: net impact [-8,000 – (-6,400 – 1,600) = 0].

Adjustment # (5)

Decreasing revenues [100% × 5,000 = 5,000]; decreasing costs [100% × 4,000 = 4,000]: net impact [-5,000 - (-4,000) = -1,000]. This adjustment requires the recognition of the deferred tax effect, affecting the group's income. To be precise, income before taxes decreases by 1,000. Therefore, considering the tax rate, taxes have to be reduced by 500 [1,000 × 50%]. This reduction in taxes has to be reported on the balance sheet recording a deferred tax asset. Moreover, this adjustment requires reducing the value of the ending inventory by the intercompany profit. Since all the goods of this transaction are still in the buying company at the end of the year, inventories have to be reduced by 1,000.

<u>Adjustment # (6)</u>

This adjustment eliminates the gain recognised by BETA on the sale of the plant. The net book value of the asset, in fact, is 6,000. It has been sold at 7,000. We have to reduce the value of the asset on the balance sheet and eliminate the gain in the income statement; then we have to increase the depreciation charge of the year by 300 (the difference between the depreciation charges of ALPHA and BETA). The net impact is a decrease of income before taxes of 1,300, which entails lower taxes of 650 [1,300 × 50%] and deferred tax assets for the same amount.

<u>Adjustment # (7)</u>

This adjustment allocates part [20%] of the subsidiary's profit to non-controlling interests, both on the income statement (Non-controlling interests - NC interests - share of Income) and on the balance sheet (within the NC share of equity). Non-controlling interests, however, should be applied to the net income of BETA [2,000] <u>after</u> all the consolidation adjustments affecting it - (2), (3), and (6). The 20% of the non-controlling interests should be computed as 20% × 900 [= 20% × (2,000 - 150 - 300 - 650)] and equals 180. Down to this last adjustment, the group's profit is entirely attributed to the parent company; therefore, in order to allocate the non-controlling interests' share of income we deduct the amount of 180 from the parent company profit and show it in the NC share of income. The net income of the parent company goes from 3,400 to 3,220; the net income of the non-controlling interests from 0 to 180.

INCOME	ALPHA	BETA	Aggregate	(1)	(2)	(3)	(4)	(5)	(6)	(7)	Consolidated
Operating revenues	10,000	6,000	16,000			– 1,200	-2,800	-5,000	-1,000		6,000
Operating expenses	5,000	3,000	8,000		300	-600	-1,400 -1,400	-4,000	300		1,200
Operating income	**5,000**	**3,000**	**8,000**	0	**-300**	**-600**	0	**-1,000**	**-1,300**	0	**4,800**
Financial income and expenses	-100	-80	-180								-180
Income before taxes	**4,900**	**2,920**	**7,820**	0	**-300**	**-600**	0	**-1,000**	**-1,300**	0	**4,620**
Taxes	1,900	920	2,820		-150	-300		-500	-650		1,220
Net income	**3,000**	**2,000**	**5,000**	0	**-150**	**-300**	0	**-500**	**-650**	**-180**	**3,220**
NC share of income										**180**	**180**

BALANCE SHEET	ALPHA	BETA	Aggregate	(1)	(2)	(3)	(4)	(5)	(6)	(7)	Consolidated
Non-current assets											
Property, plant and	10,000	10,000	20,000	2,000	-100				-1,300		20,600
Goodwill				1,400							1,400
Other intangible assets	1,000	1,000	2,000	2,000	-200						3,800
Investments	11,000		11,000	-11,000							
Deferred tax assets						300		500	650		1,450
Current assets											
Inventories	3,000	2,500	5,500			-600		-1,000			3,900
Receivables	4,000	2,000	6,000								6,000
Cash & other assets	3,000	1,500	4,500								4,500
Total assets	**32,000**	**17,000**	**49,000**	**-5,600**	**-300**	**-300**	**0**	**-500**	**-650**	**0**	**41,650**
Owners' equity											
Common stock	20,000	9,600	29,600	-9,600							20,000
Retained earnings	1,000	400	1,400	-400							1,000
Net income	3,000	2,000	5,000		-150	-300		-500	-650	-180	3,220
NC share of equity											
NC Common stock and				2,400							2,400
NC Net income										180	180
Non-current liabilities											
Provisions	2,500	1,500	4,000								4,000
Deferred tax liabilities	200		200	2,000	-150						2,050
Current liabilities											
Trade and financial	4,800	2,000	6,800								6,800
Other liabilities	500	1,500	2,000								2,000
Total liabilities and	**32,000**	**17,000**	**49,000**	**-5,600**	**-300**	**-300**	**0**	**-500**	**-650**	**0**	**41,650**

EXERCISE 10 - CONSOLIDATION OF INVESTMENTS UNDER THE FULL GOODWILL METHOD

Company ALPHA holds a 50% investment in company BETA, which is owned by company THETA for the remaining 50%.

On the basis of a provision of its articles of association, ALPHA has the power to elect the majority of directors at the shareholders' meeting and, more generally, has the power to control the administrative and managerial decisions in order to obtain benefits from the economic activity of BETA. Therefore, BETA is considered a subsidiary of ALPHA that consolidates it under the "full goodwill" method. The income statements and balance sheets of the two companies are reported at the end of the exercise.

ALPHA purchased the 50% stake in BETA on 1.1.X at a price of 10,000. The equity of BETA at the acquisition date was 8,000. At the same date, the fair values of all assets and liabilities of BETA coincided with their book values, except for the following:

	Book Value	Fair Value
Property	10,000	11,000
Brand	0	6,000
Provisions	1,500	2,500
Total	**11,500**	**19,500**

Property and brands are depreciated and amortised at a rate of 10% and 5%, respectively.

Remember that on goodwill no deferred tax effect should be recognised.

Moreover, during year X the following transactions took place:

A. ALPHA sells goods to BETA at the price of 6,000 making a profit of 2,000. At year end only 20% of this profit has been realised with third parties, while the related receivable is entirely settled at year end;

B. The parent ALPHA grants funding to BETA for 3,000, which is to be entirely repaid (and indeed was) at year end together with interest recognised in financial expenses and income, respectively, for 200;
C. BETA sells ALPHA plant that is not yet fully depreciated and accounted for at a net carrying amount of 5,000. The selling price is 6,000. ALPHA depreciates the asset at a rate of 10% (the same that BETA would have used had it not sold the plant). The related invoice is paid at year end.

Any deferred tax assets and liabilities are accounted for on the basis of a tax rate of 50%. The fair value of the NCI at the acquisition date was 5,500.

Prepare the consolidated financial statements at 31 December X under the full goodwill method.

INCOME STATEMENT	ALPHA	BETA	Aggr.	(0)	(1)	(2)	(3)	(4)	(5)	(6)	(7)	Consol.
Operating revenues	16,000	8,000	24,000									
Other operating revenues		1,000	1,000									
Operating expenses	9,000	4,200	13,200									
Depreciation and write-offs	600		600									
Operating income	**6,400**	**4,800**	**11,200**									
Financial income and expenses	600	-1280	1320									
Income before taxes	**7,000**	**3,520**	**12,520**									
Taxes	2,800	1720	6,520									
Net income	**4,200**	**1,800**	**6,000**									
NC share of income												

BALANCE SHEET	ALPHA	BETA	Aggr.	(0)	(1)	(2)	(3)	(4)	(5)	(6)	(7)	Consol.
Non-current assets												
Property, plant and equipment	15,400	10,000	25,400									
Goodwill												
Other intangible assets	1,000	500	1,500									
Investments	10,000		10,000									
Deferred tax assets												
Current assets												
Inventories	3,000	6,800	9,800									
Receivables	6,000	1,000	7,000									
Cash & other assets	2,800	2,500	5,300									
Total assets	**38,200**	**20,800**	**59,000**									
Common stock	20,000	6,000	26,000									
Retained earnings	1,000	1,000	2,000									
Net income	4,200	1,800	6,000									
NC share of equity												
NC Common stock and RE												
NC Net income												
Non-current liabilities												
Provisions	2,500	1,500	4,000									
Deferred tax liabilities	200		200									
Current liabilities												
Trade and financial liabilities	8,800	7,000	15,800									
Other liabilities	1,500	3,500	5,000									
Total liabilities and equity	**38,200**	**20,800**	**59,000**									

EXERCISE 10 -SOLUTION

As in the previous exercises, to which we address readers for more detailed explanations of the initial steps, we start from the 'Aggregate' situation and assume that the financial statements are uniform so that we can proceed to eliminate the investment against BETA's equity (step #4a of Chater 6). We then perform the intra-group adjustments as usual and finally, after the allocation of the non-controlling interests' result, we build the consolidated financial statements.

When we start step #4a, we should however note that the equity value at the time of the acquisition (8,000) is different from what is indicated in the individual financial statement (6,000 + 1,000 = 7,000) and so we have to take this difference into consideration. Differences in the acquired entity's equity are likely to happen in practice, since each firm is a going concern. To prepare the consolidated financial statements correctly we then need to understand what happened to BETA's equity and see whether this had an intra-group effect which we should neutralise. Since nothing is specified in the exercise, we need to make a reasonable assumption. Since BETA reported profits both this year and in the years before this, we can see that the reduction was not due to accumulated losses. Then, given that there are no other items in BETA's equity, it is reasonable to assume that some dividends have been distributed. This is compatible with the financial income recognised by ALPHA in the income statement.

We then need to make the following:

- In computing BETA's goodwill we need to consider the value of BETA's equity at the acquisition date (i.e. 8,000) since the consideration paid referred to the situation in which BETA operated *at that time;*

- Among our consolidation adjustments, since part of the dividends distributed (i.e. ALPHA's part) did not exit the group, we need to write off 50% of the dividend distributed. We do this before proceeding with the other consolidation adjustments in order to rebuild the original structure of BETA's equity at the time of acquisition.

Adjustment # (0)

Dividends received by BETA: 1,000 × 50% = 500

Dividends received by BETA's non-controlling shareholders = 1,000 x (1 - 50%) = 500. As usual, we suppose there is no fiscal impact on dividends for simplicity.

	Debit	Credit
Financial revenues (-R, -SE)	500	
Retained earnings (+SE)		500
Non-controlling interests (-SE)	500	
Retained earnings (+SE)		500

Adjustment # (1)

Elimination of investment [10,000] against subsidiary's equity [8,000], excluding the net income of year X, realised after acquisition.

Recognition of surplus [1,000] on PPE.

Recognition of surplus [6,000] on other intangible assets (brand).

Recognition of higher value [1,000] on provisions.
Recognition of deferred tax assets on provisions [1,000 × 50% = 500].
Recognition of deferred tax liabilities on surpluses on assets [7,000 × 50% = 3,500].
Recognition of non-controlling interests for 5,500 (already given).
Recognition of goodwill = 4,500 → 10,000 (cost of investment) + 5,500 (non-controlling interests) - [8,000 (BETA's equity) + 7,000 (gross surplus on PPE and brand) – 3,500 (tax effect on surplus) – 1,000 (higher value of provisions) + 500 (lower tax effect)].

Adjustment # (2)

This correction ensures the recognition of the depreciation of surplus values previously not recognised, considering the (deferred) tax effect.
Recognition of depreciation of surplus on property of 100 [10% × 1,000], since the depreciation rate for the building is 10%.
Recognition of depreciation of surplus on brands of 300 [5% × 6,000] since the depreciation rate for the patent is 5%.
This adjustment requires the recognition of the deferred tax effect, affecting the group's income. To be precise, income before taxes decreases by 400. Therefore, taxes have to be reduced by 200 [400 × 50%] and deferred tax liabilities in the balance sheet are reduced by the same amount.
For goodwill, we need to compare its book value with the recoverable amount: because the recoverable amount is higher than the book value, there is no write-down (impairment) of goodwill.

Adjustment # (3)
This relates to the part of goods actually sold to third parties. We already know that they do not impact the consolidated net income but we need to deflate sales and COGS by 960 (i.e. 20% × 6,000).

Adjustment # (4)
Decreasing revenues [80% × 6,000 = 4,800]; decreasing costs [80% × 4,000 = 3,200]: net impact [-4,800 – (-3,200) = – 1,600].
This adjustment requires the recognition of the deferred tax effect, affecting the group's income. To be precise, income before taxes decreases by 1,600. Therefore, considering the tax rate, taxes have to be reduced by 800 [1,600 × 50%]. This reduction in taxes has to be reported on the balance sheet as a deferred tax asset.
Moreover, this adjustment requires reducing the value of the ending inventory. Since 80% of the goods are still in the buying company, inventories have to be decreased by 1,600 [i.e. 80% × (6,000 – 4,000)].

Adjustment # (5)
This adjustment eliminates financial income and expenses [200] related to the intercompany loan provided by ALPHA to BETA.

Adjustment # (6)
This adjustment eliminates the gain of 1,000 recognised by BETA on the sale of the plant. The net book value of the asset, in fact, is 5,000; it has been sold for 6,000. We have to reduce the value of the asset on the balance sheet and eliminate the gain in the income statement; then we have to decrease the depreciation charge of the year by 100 (the depreciation of the higher value recognised by BETA). The net

impact is a decrease of income before taxes of 900, which determine lower taxes (deferred taxes) of 450 [900 × 50%] and deferred tax assets for the same amount.

Adjustment # (7)

This adjustment allocates part [50%] of the subsidiary's profit to non-controlling interests, both on the income statement (Non-controlling interests - NC interests - share of Income) and on the balance sheet (within the NC share of equity). We only consider the net income of BETA [1,800] and all the consolidation adjustments affecting it: adjustment #(2), #(6). The 50% of the non-controlling interests should be computed as 50% × (1,800 - 200 - 450) and is 575.

INCOME STATEMENT	ALPHA	BETA	Aggr.	(0)	(1)	(2)	(3)	(4)	(5)	(6)	(7)	Consol.
Operating revenues	16,000	8,000	24,000				-960	-4,800				18,240
Other operating revenues		1,000	1,000							-1,000		0
Operating expenses	9,000	4,200	13,200			400	-960	-3,200		-100		9,340
Depreciation and write-offs	600		600									600
Operating income	**6,400**	**4,800**	**11,200**	**0**	**0**	**-400**	**0**	**-1,600**	**0**	**-900**	**0**	**8,300**
Financial income and expenses	600	-1280	1320	-500					+200 -200			820
Income before taxes	**7,000**	**3,520**	**12,520**	**-500**	**0**	**-400**	**0**	**-1,600**	**0**	**-900**	**0**	**9,120**
Taxes	2,800	1,720	6,520	0	0	-200	0	-800	0	-450	0	5,070
Net income	**4,200**	**1,800**	**6,000**	**-500**	**0**	**-200**	**0**	**-800**	**0**	**-450**	**-575**	**3,475**
NC share of income											**575**	**575**

BALANCE SHEET	ALPHA	BETA	Aggr.	(0)	(1)	(2)	(3)	(4)	(5)	(6)	(7)	Consol.
Non-current assets												
Property, plant and equipment	15,400	10,000	25,400		1,000	-100				-900		25,400
Goodwill					4,500							4,500
Other intangible assets	1,000	500	1,500		6,000	-300						7,200
Investments	10,000		10,000		-10,000							0
Deferred tax assets					500			800		450		1,750
Current assets												
Inventories	3,000	6,800	9,800					-1,600				8,200
Receivables	6,000	1,000	7,000									7,000
Cash & other assets	2,800	2,500	5,300									5,300
Total assets	**38,200**	**20,800**	**59,000**	**0**	**2,000**	**-400**	**0**	**-800**	**0**	**-450**	**0**	**59,350**
Common stock	20,000	6,000	26,000		-6,000							20,000
Retained earnings	1,000	1,000	2,000	+500	-2,000							0
Net income	4,200	1,800	6,000	-500		-200	0	-800	0	-450	-575	3,475
NC share of equity												
NC Common stock and retained				-500	5,500							5,000
NC Net income											575	575
Non-current liabilities												
Provisions	2,500	1,500	4,000		1,000							5,000
Deferred tax liabilities	200		200		3,500	-200						3,500
Current liabilities												
Trade and financial liabilities	8,800	7,000	15,800									15,800
Other liabilities	1,500	3,500	5,000									5,000
Total liabilities and equity	**38,200**	**20,800**	**59,000**	**0**	**2,000**	**-400**	**0**	**-800**	**0**	**-450**	**0**	**59,350**

EXERCISE 11 - CONSOLIDATION ACCOUNTING USING THE EQUITY METHOD

On 1 January X INVESTOR acquires 20% of the share of INVESTEE paying 60 million in cash. At acquisition, the book value of INVESTEE's owners' equity is 180 million. The difference between the acquisition cost and the net book value is due to unrecognised brands whose gross fair value is estimated as 20 million, and to property whose carrying amount is undervalued by 30 million. The remaining difference is allocated to goodwill.
The brands and goodwill have indefinite useful life. The property has a remaining useful life of 10 years.
The companies apply a tax rate of 50%.
During period X, INVESTEE distributes dividends for 15 million. At the end of the period, INVESTEE reports a net profit of 20 million.

a) Show what are the accounting entries made by INVESTOR in relation to the different events that occurred during period X.
b) Calculate the value of the investment in INVESTEE as of 31 December X using the equity method.

EXERCISE 11 - SOLUTION

In order properly to apply the equity method, we need first to allocate the acquisition cost to its different components.

ALLOCATION OF THE ACQUISITION COST

Net book value of INVESTEE's equity	20% × 180	36
Unrecorded brands	20% × 20 × (1 – 0.5)	2
Undervalued property	20% × 30 × (1 – 0.5)	3
Goodwill		19
TOTAL COST		60

INVESTOR will make the following accounting entry upon acquisition:

	Debit	Credit
Investment in INVESTEE (+A)	60	
Cash(-A)		60

When dividends are collected, INVESTOR will make the following entry:

	Debit	Credit
Cash (+A)	3	
Investment in INVESTEE (-A)		3

At the end of the period, INVESTOR will calculate the adjusted income from the investment.

ADJUSTED INCOME

Net income	20% × 20	4
Depreciation on property	3 /10	(0.3)
Adjusted income		3.7

To record the adjusted income, INVESTOR will make the following entry:

	Debit	Credit
Investment in INVESTEE (+A)	3.7	
Income from investment-equity method (+R)		3.7

At the end of the period, the carrying amount of the investment in INVESTEE will be 60.7 million (=60-3+3.7)

EXERCISE 12 – CONSOLIDATION ACCOUNTING USING THE EQUITY METHOD

On 1 January X MOTHER acquires 40% of the share of DAUGHTER paying 420 million in cash. At acquisition, the book value of DAUGHTER's owners' equity is 900 million. The difference between the acquisition cost and the net book value is due to the following:

- PPE undervalued by 50 million (remaining useful life 5 years);
- provisions undervalued by 20 million;
- goodwill;

The companies apply a tax rate of 50%.

During period X, the following events occur:

1. DAUGHTER sells inventory to MOTHER, selling price 80 million, cost of sales 60 million. At the end of the period, 90% of this inventory is still unsold;
2. DAUGHTER applies the revaluation model to its buildings and records a revaluation surplus of 10 million;
3. DAUGHTER realises a net profit of 50 million.

Required:

a) Show what are the accounting entries made by MOTHER in relation to the different events occurring during period X.
b) Calculate the value of the investment in DAUGHTER as of 31 December X using the equity method.

EXERCISE 12 - SOLUTION

In order properly to apply the equity method, we need first to allocate the acquisition cost to its different components.

ALLOCATION OF THE ACQUISITION COST

Net book value of DAUGHTER's equity	40% × 900	360
Undervalued PPE	40% × 50 × (1 - 0.5)	10
Undervalued provisions	40% × 20 × (1 - 0.5)	(4)
Goodwill		54
TOTAL COST		420

MOTHER will make the following accounting entry upon acquisition:

	Debit	Credit
Investment in DAUGHTER (+A)	420	
Cash(-A)		420

When DAUGHTER records the revaluation surplus, MOTHER will adjust its investment as follows:

	Debit	Credit
Investment in DAUGHTER (+A)	4	
Revaluation surplus-equity method (+OE)		4

At the end of the period, MOTHER will calculate the adjusted income from its investment in DAUGHTER.

ADJUSTED INCOME

Net income	40% × 50	20
Depreciation on property	10 / 5	(2)
Unrealised gain		(3.6)
Adjusted income		14.4

The unrealised gain was calculated as follows:

Total gross unrealised gain	90% x (80 – 60)	18
Net of tax unrealised gain	18 × (1 – 0.5)	9
Share of net of tax unrealised gain	40% × 9	3.6

To record the adjusted income, MOTHER will make the following entry:

	Debit	Credit
Investment in DAUGHTER (+A)	14.4	
Income from investment–equity method (+R)		14.4

At the end of the period, the carrying amount of the investment in DAUGHTER will be 438.4 million (=420+4+14.4).

EXERCISE 13 - CONSOLIDATION ACCOUNTING USING THE EQUITY METHOD

On 1 January X company SKY acquires 25% of the shares of MOON, a joint venture, paying 180 million in cash. At acquisition, the book value of MOON's owners' equity is 600 million. The difference between the acquisition cost and the net book value is due to the following:

- patent undervalued by 100 million (remaining useful life 10 years);
- inventory undervalued by 16 million;
- goodwill.

The companies apply a tax rate of 50%.

During period X, the following events occur:

1. SKY sells a building to MOON, selling price 10 million, net book value 6 million. The building was depreciated by SKY at 5% on its historical cost (12 million), while MOON depreciates it at 10%;
2. MOON sells to third parties all the inventory that was on hand as of 1 January;
3. MOON distributes dividends for 30 million;
4. MOON realises a profit of 32 million.

Required:

a) Show what are the accounting entries made by SKY in relation to the different events that occurred during period X.
b) Calculate the value of the investment in MOON as of 31 December X using the equity method.

EXERCISE 13 – SOLUTION

As usual, to apply the equity method, we first need to allocate the acquisition cost to its different components.

ALLOCATION OF THE ACQUISITION COST

Net book value of MOON's equity	25% × 600	150
Undervalued patent	25% × 100 × (1 – 0.5)	12.5
Undervalued inventory	25% × 16 × (1 – 0.5)	2
Goodwill		15.5
TOTAL COST		180

SKY will make the following accounting entry upon acquisition:

	Debit	Credit
Investment in MOON (+A)	180	
Cash(-A)		180

When MOON distributes dividends, SKY will adjust its investment as follows:

	Debit	Credit
Cash (+A)	7.5	
Investment in MOON (-A)		7.5

At the end of the period, SKY will calculate the adjusted income from its investment in MOON.

ADJUSTED INCOME

Net income	25% × 32	8
Depreciation on patent	12.5 / 10	(1.25)
Reversal of inventory		(2)
Unrealised gain on building		(0.45)
Adjusted income		4.3

The unrealised gain on building is calculated as follows:

Total gross gain from the sale	(10 – 6)	4
Higher depreciation calculated by MOON	(10 × 10%) – (12 × 5%)	0.4
Total net profit	(4 – 0.4)	3.6
Total net of tax profit	3.6 × (1 – 0.5)	1.8
Share of unrealised profit	25% × 1.8	0.45

The surplus on inventory is reversed once the inventory is sold. The reason for this adjustment is that - whatever profit MOON has realised on that inventory - the real profit from the point of view of SKY will be 2 million lower, as the cost of that inventory borne by SKY was originally 2 million higher than what recorded by MOON in its books.

To record the adjusted income, SKY will make the following entry:

	Debit	Credit
Investment in MOON (+A)	4.3	
Income from investment - equity method (+R)		4.3

At the end of the period, the carrying amount of the investment in MOON will be 176.8 million (=180-7.5+4.3).

Appendix A

INTERNATIONAL FINANCIAL REPORTING STANDARDS: A BRIEFING

This Appendix summarizes, in a concise and non-technical fashion, the main principles of International Financial Reporting issued at 1 January 2012. A brief description of each standard is provided.

IFRS 1 - First-time Adoption of International Financial Reporting Standards

The Standard applies when an organization first adopts IFRSs in its annual financial statements or to interim financial reports for any part of the period covered by the entity first IFRS financial statements. It is aimed to guarantee the information transparency of an organization's first IFRS financial statements. The first IFRS financial statements have to contain an unambiguous and unreserved statement of compliance with IFRSs. A first-time adopter identifies and measures all assets and liabilities as if it had always applied IFRSs (retrospective application). The date of transition to IFRSs is the beginning of the earliest period for which full comparative information in accordance with IFRSs is presented. Moreover, the financial statements have to explain how the transition from previous GAAP to IFRSs affected the organization's reported financial position, financial performance and cash flows.

IFRS 2 - Share-based Payment

The Standard requires an organization to report share-based payment transactions in its financial statements. Equity-settled share-based payment transactions are generally those in which shares, share options or other equity instruments are granted to employees or other parties in return for goods or services. These transactions are measured at the fair value of the goods or services received.

Cash-settled share-based payment transactions are generally those that are to be settled in cash or other assets. They are share-based because the payment amount is based on the price of the organization's shares. Cash-settled share-based payments are measured at the fair value of the liability.

IFRS 3 - Business Combinations

The purpose of the Standard is to increase the relevance, reliability and comparability of the information about business combinations and their effects. It applies to all transactions or events in which a reporting organization obtains control of one or more businesses. In a business combination, the acquirer recognizes the assets acquired and the liabilities assumed at their fair values, including, in some circumstances, those that may not previously have been recognized by the acquiree (e.g. intangibles). IFRS 3 does not apply to:

- The formation of a joint venture;
- The acquisition of an asset or a group of assets that does not constitute a business;
- A combination of entities or businesses under common control.

Goodwill is measured as the difference between the considerations transferred in the transaction and the fair value of the acquiree's identifiable assets liabilities.

IFRS 4 - Insurance Contracts

The Standard postulates financial reporting regulations for insurance contracts issued by any organization. Moreover it specifies accounting for reinsurance contracts issued or held by an insurer. It applies to these contracts regardless of whether the organization is regulated as an insurer and whether the contract is regarded as an insurance contract for legal purposes. The IFRS restricts accounting policy changes. Any changes in accounting for insurance contracts have to result in information that is more relevant and no less reliable, or more reliable and no less relevant, than previous accounting.

IFRS 5 - Non-current Assets Held for Sale and Discontinued Operations

The Standards specifies the accounting for non-recurrent assets and groups of assets and liabilities whose carrying amount will be recovered principally through a sale transaction, and the presentation and disclosure of discontinued operations. To be classified as a non-current asset held for sale:

- The asset have to be available for immediate sale in its present condition;
- The sale has to be highly probable.

Non-current assets held for sale are measured at the lower of fair value less costs to sell and carrying amount, and, for this reason, are not depreciated.

A discontinued operation is a component of an organization that either has been disposed of or is classified as held for sale and:

- Represents a separate major line of business or geographical area of operation;
- Is part of a single coordinated plan to dispose of a separate major line of business or geographical area of operations;
- Is a subsidiary acquired with the exclusive aim of reselling it.

Discontinued operations are presented separately within profit or loss in the statement of comprehensive income.

IFRS 6 - Exploration for and Evaluation of Mineral Resources

The Standard specifies the financial reporting for the expenditure in exploration for, and evaluation of, mineral resources before the technical and commercial feasibility of extraction is demonstrable. IFRS 6 has limited scope and has been issued as an interim measure to fill a gap in IFRSs.

IFRS 7 - Financial Instruments: Disclosures

The Standard specifies disclosure for financial instruments. It applies to financial risks arising from all financial instruments of all organizations. The extent of the disclosure required depends on the extent to which the organization uses financial instruments and its exposure the related risk. The Standard requires disclosure of:

- The significance of financial instruments for an organization's financial position and performance;

- Qualitative information about exposure to risk;
- Quantitative information about exposure to risks arising from financial instruments, including minimum information about credit risk, liquidity risk and market risk.

IFRS 8 - Operating Segments

The Standard requires the disclosure of information about an organization's operating segments, its products and services, its main geographical markets, and its major clients. The aim is to enable users to evaluate its business activities and the environment in which it operates. An organization has to report a measure of operating segment profit or loss and a measure of operating segment liabilities, operating segment assets and particular income and expense items if such measures are regularly provided to the chief operating decision maker. Moreover an organization has to report information about the revenues derived from its products or services, the geographical areas in which it earns revenues, and about major customers.

IFRS 9 - Financial Instruments

The Standards specifies how an organization should classify and measure financial assets and financial liabilities. The aim is to provide relevant and useful information for an organization's existing and potential investors, lenders and creditors to assess the amounts, timing and uncertainty of an organization's cash flows arising from such financial items.

Initially, financial assets are measured at fair value plus transaction costs. After, a financial asset is measured at amortized cost if:

- The asset is held within a business model whose objective is to hold asset to collect contractual cash flows;
- The contractual terms of the financial asset give rise on specified dates to cash flows that are solely payments of principal and interest on the principal amount outstanding.

All other financial assets have to be measured at fair value.

IFRS 10 - Consolidated Financial Statements

The Standard provides a single consolidation model that identifies control as the basis for consolidation of all types of organizations. Organizations with one or more subsidiaries have to present consolidated financial statements. When a parent owns less than 100 per cent of a subsidiary, it recognizes non-controlling interest. A parent does not need to present consolidated financial statements if it is itself a wholly-owned subsidiary. Moreover, a subsidiary is not excluded from consolidation because its business activities are different from those of the other organizations within the group.

IFRS 11 – Joint Arrangements

The Standard provides principles for financial reporting by parties that have an interest in arrangements that are controlled jointly. A joint arrangement is an arrangement of which two or more parties have joint control; they are either joint operations or joint venture. The disclosure requirements for joint arrangements are specified in IFRS 12.

IFRS 12 – Disclosure of Interests in Other Entities

The Standard requires an organization to disclose information that enables existing and potential investors, lenders and other creditors to evaluate the nature of, and risks associated with its interests in other organizations. It includes disclosure standard for:

- Subsidiaries;
- Joint arrangements;
- Associates;
- Unconsolidated structured organizations.

IFRS 13 – Fair Value Measurement

The Standard defines the concept of fair value, sets out a framework for measuring it, and requires disclosures relating to fair value measurements. It applies to all IFRSs requiring or permitting fair value measurements or disclosures. The standard has to be applied for annual periods beginning on or after 1 January 2013. The aim is to provide users with information to assess the valuation techniques and inputs used to develop the fair value measurements and the effect of the measurements on profit or loss or other comprehensive income for the period.

IAS 1 - Presentation of Financial Statements

The Standard sets the requirements for the presentation of financial statements, guidelines for their structure and minimum requirements for their content. It specifies minimum line items to be presented in the statement of financial position, statement of comprehensive income and statement of change in equity. Financial statements have to provide a fair presentation of the financial position, financial performance and cash flows of an organization, by compliance with IFRSs.

IAS 2 - Inventories

The Standard specifies the requirements for the recognition of inventory as an asset and an expense, the measurement of inventories and disclosures relating to inventories. It applies to all inventories except work in progress on construction contracts, financial instruments, biological assets and agricultural produce at the point of harvest. Inventories are measured at the lower of cost and net realisable value.

IAS 7 - Statement of Cash Flow

The Standard requires disclosures about the historical changes in cash and cash equivalents of an organization. The aim is to assist existing and potential investors, lenders and other creditors to assess the ability of the organization to generate cash equivalents and to utilize those cash flows. With limited exceptions, cash flows are reported as gross flows and are classified by activities (investing, financing and operating). Cash flows from operating activities can be reported using:

1. Direct method: major classes of gross cash receipts and gross cash payments are shown;
2. Indirect method: profit or loss is adjusted to determine operating cash flow.

Cash flows from investing and financing activities are reported in the same manner, regardless of the method adopted for the reporting of operating activities. Transactions that do not require cash or cash equivalents do not have to be reported in the statement of cash flow.

IAS 8 - Accounting Policies, Changes in Accounting Estimates and Errors

The Standard specifies the criteria for selecting and changing accounting policies and specifies the accounting and disclosure requirements when an accounting policy is changed. Moreover it sets the accounting and disclosure requirements for changes in accounting estimates and corrections of prior period errors. The purpose is to increase the relevance and reliability of an organization's financial statements and the comparability of those statements over time and with those of other organizations. Accounting policies have to comply with IFRSs and have to be applied consistently over time.

IAS 10 - Events after a Reporting Period

The Standard specifies that when an organization should adjust its financial statements for events after the reporting period (i.e. events that occur between the end of the reporting period and the date the financial statements are authorized). Financial statements are adjusted for those events that after the reporting period provide evidence of conditions that existed at the end of the reporting period. Non-adjusting events reflect conditions that arise after the reporting period. Moreover the Standard requires disclosures about the date when the financial statements were authorized for issue and about events after the reporting period.

IAS 11 - Construction Contracts

The Standard specifies the accounting treatment of revenues and costs associated with construction contracts. It applies to contractors, including those providing services directly related to a construction project, such as project managers and architects. If the outcome of a construction contract can be estimated reliably, contract revenue is reported as the work is performed and is matched with contract costs. If the outcome cannot be estimated reliably, all contract costs are reported as expenses when incurred and revenues are reported to the extent that costs incurred are recoverable.

IAS 12 - Income Taxes

The Standard sets the accounting treatment for income taxes, including how to account for the current and future tax consequences of:

1. Transactions and events of current period reported in the financial statements;
2. Future recovery of the carrying amount of assets in the statement of financial position;
3. Future settlement of the carrying amount of liabilities in the statements of financial position.

IAS 16 - Property, Plant and Equipment

The Standard sets the accounting treatment for property, plant and equipment to be used for more than one accounting period, for the production or supply of goods and services or for administration. They have to be initially recorded at cost, including all expenditure to get the item ready for use. After, an organization may choose to measure property either at cost less accumulated depreciation and accumulated impairment, or at a revalued amount less any subsequent accumulated depreciation and accumulated impairment.

IAS 17 - Leases

The Standard categorizes leases (i.e. an agreement that conveys to the lessee a right to use an asset for a specified period of time) based on the extent to which risks and rewards incidental to ownership of a leased asset lie with the lessor or the lessee. Abolished the different classification between financial and operating leases, they are now accounted for as executory contracts and the asset and liabilities arising from the lease agreement are not reported by the lessee. Moreover, the standard specifies the accounting treatment for leases.

IAS 18 - Revenue

The Standard specifies the accounting treatment for revenues from:

1. The sales of goods;
2. The rendering of services;
3. The use by others of organization's assets yielding interest, royalties and dividends.

In the first case, revenue is reported when significant risks and rewards of ownership have been transferred to the buyer, and when the organization has neither continuing managerial involvement in, nor effective control over the goods. The second kind of revenue is reported as the work is performed, with reference to the "stage of completion method". Interest is reported over time and computed on the effective yield on the asset. Royalties are reported as earned in accordance with the substance of the transaction. Dividends are reported when the shareholder has the right to receive payment.

IAS 19 - Employee Benefits

The Standard specifies the accounting for, and disclosure of, employee benefits by employers. Employee benefits are all forms of payback given by an organization in exchange for services rendered by its employees and include:

1. Short-term benefits such as wages, salaries, paid annual leave and sick leave, profit-sharing and bonuses and non-monetary benefit;
2. Post-employment benefits such as pensions, life insurance, and medical care;
3. Other long-term benefits such as long-service leave, and bonuses and other benefits not payable within 12 months;
4. Termination benefits such as early retirement and redundancy pay.

When an employee has provided service in return for benefits to be paid in the future, a liability has to be reported. An expense is reported as the employees provide the service to the organization.

IAS 20 - Accounting for Governments Grants and Disclosure of Government Assistance

The Standard specifies the accounting for, and disclosure of, government grants and the disclosure of government assistance from which the organization has directly benefited. Government grants have not to be reported until there is reasonable assurance that the organization will comply with any specified conditions and that the grants will be received. A government grant that relates to assets can be initially reported in the statement of financial position as deferred income. Alternatively, the grant can be reported in profit or loss over the life of a depreciable asset as a reduced depreciation expense.

IAS 21 - The Effects of Changes in Foreign Exchange Rates

The Standard postulates how to include foreign currency transactions and foreign operations in the financial statements of an organization and how to translate financial statements into a presentation currency that is different to the functional currency[1]. Transactions in a currency other than the functional currency are translated at the exchange rate at the date of the transaction.

IAS 23 - Borrowing Costs

The Standard specifies the accounting treatment for borrowing costs (i.e. interest and other cost incurred with the borrowing of funds). It requires the capitalization of borrowing costs that are directly attributable to the acquisition, construction or production of an asset that necessarily takes a substantial time to get ready for its intended use or sale.

---

[1] The functional currency is the currency of the primary economic environment in which it operates.

IAS 24 - Related Party Disclosures

The Standard is aimed to guarantee that the financial statements disclose enough information about the chance that the financial position and profit or loss may have been affected by the existence of related parties and by transactions and outstanding balances with such parties. A related party may be a person or an organization. A person is related to a reporting organization when:

1. He/she has control, joint control or significant influence over the reporting organization;
2. He/she is a member of the key management personnel of the reporting organization.

An organization is related to a reporting organization when:

1. They are both members of the same group;
2. One organization is an associate or joint venture of the other organization;
3. Both organizations are joint ventures of the same third party, or of different third parties;
4. The organization is a post-employment benefit plan for the benefit of employees of the reporting organization or any of its related parties;
5. The organization is controlled or jointly controlled by any person identified as a related party above;
6. A person whose control or joint control over the reporting organization, or a close member of that person's family, has significant influence over the organization or is a member of the key management team of the organization.

IAS 26 - Accounting and Reporting by Retirement Benefit Plans

The Standard applies to the financial statements of retirement benefit plans (i.e. formal or informal arrangements providing benefits for employees on or after termination of their employment). The Standard requires the recognition and measurement of the present value of future expected payments based on a reasonable assumption. The purpose is to provide users of financial statements with useful information about the potential future cash flow of the plan.

IAS 27 - Separate Financial Statements

The Standard specifies accounting and disclosure requirements for investments in subsidiaries, joint ventures and associates when an organization presents separate financial statements. Consolidated financial statements present the group's financial position and financial performance as a single economic organization.

However, in some jurisdictions an entity must present or has the possibility to prepare separate financial statements. The standard requires investments in subsidiaries, joint ventures and associates to be accounted for either at cost or in accordance with IFRS 9.

IAS 28 - Investments in Associates and Joint Venture

The Standard specifies accounting and disclosure requirements for investments in associates and joint venture. These investments have to be accounted for using the equity method (i.e. recognising the investment initially at cost and then adjusting the investment for the post-acquisition change in the investor's share of the associate's or joint venture's net assets). When the investor is a wholly-owned subsidiary, its securities are not publicly traded or in the process or becoming publicly traded, and its parents publish IFRS-compliant financial statement available to the public, the investor does not have to use the equity method. In the same way, there is an exemption from the requirement, if an investment in an associate or joint venture is held by, or is indirectly held through, venture capital organizations, mutual funds, unit trusts and similar organizations including investment-linked insurance funds.

IAS 29 - Financial Reporting in Hyperinflationary Economies

The Standard sets requirements for the restatement of the financial statements of any organization whose functional currency is the currency of a hyperinflationary economy.[2] The aim is providing financial information more meaningfully. An organization whose functional currency is that of a hyperinflationary economy has to disclose:

1. The fact that the financial statements have been restated;
2. The price index used for the restatement;
3. Whether the financial statements are prepared on the basis of historical or current costs.

IAS 32 - Financial Instruments: Presentation

The Standard specifies the principles for presenting financial instruments as liabilities or equity and for offsetting financial assets and financial liabilities. A financial instrument is classified as liabilities or equity depending on whether there is an obligation to deliver cash. Instruments that embody an obligation to deliver cash are defined liabilities.

IAS 33 - Earnings per Share

The Standard deals with the calculation and presentation of earnings per share. It applies to organizations whose ordinary shares or potential ordinary shares are publicly traded. The aim is to improve performance comparisons between different organizations in the same reporting period and between different reporting periods for the same organization. The Standard specifies how to determine the numerator and denominator of both basic and diluted EPS calculations. When an organization presents consolidated financial statements, EPS measure is based on the consolidated profit or loss attributable to ordinary equity holders of the parent. When an organization discloses profit or loss from continuing operations separately, basic and diluted EPS have to be reported in respect of continuing operations. Moreover, an organization that reports a discontinued operation has to present basic and diluted amounts per

---

[2] The standard does not define hyperinflation, but it is indicated by factors such as dramatically increased prices, interest and wages linked to a price index and when cumulative inflation over a three-year period is approaching, or is in excess of, 100 %.

share for the discontinued operation, either in the statement of comprehensive income or in the notes.

IAS 34 - Interim Financial Reporting

The Standard specifies the minimum content of an interim financial report (i.e. a complete or condensed set of financial statements for a period shorter than a full financial year) and prescribes the principles for recognition and measurement in complete or condensed financial statements for an interim period.

IAS 36 - Impairment of Assets

The Standard specifies the method required to ensure that an asset is not carried at more than the highest amount expected to be recovered through its use or sale. If the carrying amount of an asset exceeds its recoverable amount, the asset is defined impaired. The organization has to reduce the carrying amount of the asset to its recoverable amount and reports an impairment loss. The aim is to provide useful information to existing and potential investors, lenders and other creditors, since those assets are expected to contribute, directly through their sale or indirectly through their use, to future cash flows. At the end of each reporting period, managers have to consider potential signals that an asset or cash-generating unit[3] may be impaired (e.g. a decline in an asset's market value; adverse changes in the technological, market, economic or legal environment; an increase in market interest rates; obsolescence of or damage to an asset; etc).

IAS 37 - Provisions, Contingent Liabilities and Contingent Assets

The Standard differentiates between provisions and contingent liabilities and sets out recognition criteria, measurement bases and disclosures for provisions, contingent liabilities and contingent assets. The aim is to

---

[3] A cash-generating unit is the smallest identifiable group of assets that generates cash inflows that are largely independent of the cash inflows from other assets or groups of assets.

provide users with information about the nature, timing and amount of uncertain future cash flows.

A provision is a liability of uncertain timing or amount and is measured at the best estimate of the expenditure required to settle the liability at the end of the reporting period.

Contingent liabilities include possible obligations whose existence will be confirmed by the occurrence or non-occurrence of uncertain future events, and obligations that are not reported because their amount cannot be measured reliably. A contingent liability is not reported as a liability in the financial statements.

Contingent assets are potential assets whose existence will be confirmed by the occurrence or non-occurrence of uncertain future events. Contingent assets are not reported in the statement of financial position, and disclosure is provided in the notes to the financial statements if it is likely that an inflow of benefits will occur.

IAS 38 - Intangible Assets

The Standard specifies norms for the recognition, measurement and disclosure of intangible assets (i.e. an identifiable non-monetary asset without physical substance) excluding those within the scope of other Standards. Expenditure relating to intangible items is reported as a cost, unless the item meets the definition of an intangible asset, and:

1. It is probable that there will be future economic benefits from the asset;
2. The cost of the asset can be measured reliably.

After initial recognition, an organization commonly measures intangible assets at cost less accumulated amortization and accumulated impairment.

IAS 39 - Financial Instruments: Recognition and Measurement

The Standard contains principles for the impairment of financial assets measured at amortized cost and for hedge accounting. An organization has to assess if there is sign of impairment for a financial assets measured at amortized cost. The loss is reported in profit or loss with either a direct reduction in the asset or an allowance account.

Hedge accounting reports the offsetting effects of changes in the fair values of the hedging instrument and the hedged item. Before hedge accounting is possible:

1. There has to be formal designation and documentation of a hedge;
2. The hedging instrument has to be expected to be highly effective in achieving offsetting changes in fair value or cash flows of the hedge item;
3. For cash flow hedges a forecast transaction being hedged has to be highly probable;
4. Hedge effectiveness has to be reliably measurable;
5. The hedge has to be assessed on a continuous basis.

IAS 40 - Investment Property

The Standard specifies that an investment property (i.e. a land or a building held to earn rentals or for capital appreciation or both) is initially measured at cost (including transaction cost). On subsequent measurements, an organization can adopt either the fair value model or the cost model for all investments properties. If the cost model is chosen, the fair value has to be disclosed. An organization can change the accounting policy selected only if the change will result in more relevant information for potential investors, lenders and other creditors.

IAS 41 - Agriculture

The Standard prescribes the accounting for, and reporting of, biological assets related to agriculture activities (i.e. the management of the biological conversion of living animals or plans and the harvest of biological assets). Biological assets are measured at fair value less costs to sell, unless this value cannot be measured reliably. In such a case the asset is measured at cost less accumulated depreciation. Agricultural produce at the point of harvest has to be measured at fair value less cost to sell. Variations in the fair value of biological assets are reported in profit or loss in the period in which they occur. Biological assets attached to land are measured, and accounted for, disjointedly from the land.

Appendix B

CURRENT SITUATION FOR THE LARGEST EUROPEAN ECONOMIES

Here we summarize the current situation among most the European Union Country and try to address to following questions: Is IFRS required or permitted for listed companies? And what are the requirements for Subsidiaries of foreign companies and foreign companies listed on local exchanges?

Country	Is IFRS required or permitted for listed companies?	Subsidiaries of foreign companies and foreign companies listed on local exchanges
Austria	Required for consolidated financial statements*	Same rules
Belgium	Required for consolidated financial statements of companies listed on NYSE Euronext. Also required for consolidated financial statements of all banks and other credit institutions, real estate investment trust companies and insurance companies (since 2012), whether listed or not.	Same rules
Denmark	IFRS is required for consolidated financial statements and standalone financial statements if consolidated financial statements are not prepared. For companies preparing consolidated financial statements, presentation of separate financial statements under IFRS is permitted. For financial services entities, the requirement to prepare IFRS financial statements applies only to consolidated financial statements.	Foreign companies listed in the local stock exchange follow requirements for the country of domicile. Subsidiaries of foreign companies are not subject to different rules.
Finland	Required for consolidated financial statements. Permitted for standalone/separate financial statements. If listed companies do not prepare consolidated financial statements, their stand alone financial statements are required to be prepared in accordance with IFRS.	Foreign companies listed in the local stock exchange follow requirements for the country of domicile. Subsidiaries of foreign companies are not subject to different rules.
France	Required for consolidated financial statements.	Non-EU companies can apply Japanese, US or Canadian GAAP.

Germany	Required for consolidated financial statements	The European Union has granted equivalence in relation to certain third country GAAPs under the Prospectus and Transparency Directives, granting issuers using US, Japanese, Chinese, Canadian, SS. Korean and Indian GAAP a permanent (US, Japan) or temporary (China, Canada, S. Korea, India) exemption from having to file IFRS financial statements, as long as the overseas parent whose subsidiary is listed on an EU exchange uses and publishes financial statements under one of the GAAPs mentioned above.
Greece	Required for consolidated and standalone/separate financial statements. This requirement also applies to the subsidiary companies of these listed entities.	Same rules
Greenland	IFRS is required for consolidated financial statements and standalone financial statements if consolidated financial statements are not prepared. For companies preparing consolidated financial statements, presentation of separate financial statements under IFRS is permitted. For financial services entities, the requirement to prepare IFRS financial statements applies only to consolidated financial statements.	Foreign companies listed in the local stock exchange follow requirements for the country of domicile. Subsidiaries of foreign companies are not subject to different rules.
Ireland	Required for consolidated financial statements; Permitted for standalone/separate financial statements.	Foreign companies need not use IFRS for their consolidated accounts
Italy	Required for consolidated and standalone/separate financial statements.	No. All companies (i.e. local and foreign companies) listed on Italian stock exchange are required to file IFRS financial statements.
Luxembourg	Required for consolidated financial statements. Permitted for statutory financial statements.	No, except if reporting framework is deemed equivalent by the EU.

Netherlands	Required for consolidated financial statements. Permitted for standalone/separate financial statements.	There are certain consolidation exemptions subject to the 7th EU directive. In general, foreign companies listed on the stock exchange are required to file IFRS financial statements. Companies outside the EU who are listed on the local exchange may qualify for certain exemptions.
Norway	Required for consolidated financial statements and for some companies in the financial industry. From 2011 required for entities which don't have any subsidiaries. Permitted for separate financial statements.	Foreign listed companies registered within EU/EEA are required to use IFRS. Third country issuer may use US-GAAP or Japanese-GAAP as they are deemed equivalent with IFRS. Accounting standards from China, Canada, South Korea and India have granted temporary equivalence for accounting periods beginning on or after January 1, 2012. Third country issuer listed on Oslo Stock Exchange normally have to adopt the same regulations as Norwegian companies listed at Oslo Stock Exchange, as long as there are no similar requirements in the country where the company is registered.
Poland	Required for consolidated financial statements and for banks. Permitted for standalone/separate financial statements.	A listed company with a seat in a country from the EU prepares financial statements according to local GAAP or IFRS and consolidated financial statements in accordance with IFRS. Listed companies with a seat in foreign countries other than the EU must prepare its financial statements in accordance with local GAAP, IFRS or other accepted GAAP; and consolidated financial statements in accordance with IFRS or other accepted GAAP.
Portugal	Required for consolidated and standalone financial statements. Permitted for separate financial statements if they file a statutory audit report.	Same rules
Spain	IFRS is required for consolidated financial statements for listed companies (issuers of debt or equity securities).	Same rules

Sweden	Required for consolidated financial statements on regulated markets	Same rules
United Kingdom	Required for consolidated financial statements. Permitted for standalone/separate financial statements	Same rules

Appendix C

ELIMINATING UNREALISED GAINS AND LOSSES WHEN APPLYING THE EQUITY METHOD IN PRACTICE

ALTERNATIVE APPROACH

When dealing with unrealised profits/losses arising from upstream or downstream transactions, rather than adjusting the investment and the related income, some companies prefer to follow a different approach. This alternative approach requires some adjustments to be made directly to the financial statements of the investor, in particular to those items that were affected by the transaction between the investor and the investee.

Here below we use two examples better to explain this alternative approach.

Example C1 – Downstream transaction with unrealised gain

On 1 January X company ITALY acquires a share of 40% of company EUROPE, a newly established joint venture. EUROPE is accounted for in accordance with the equity method. The acquisition cost is 300 million, paid cash. During period X, ITALY sells to EUROPE inventory realising revenue of 50 million. The cost of the inventory sold is 40 million. At the end of the period, all the goods are still unsold in EUROPE's inventory. At the end of period X, EUROPE reports a profit of 35 million.

For sake of simplicity, let us ignore the fiscal effect.

***

Upon acquisition, ITALY will record its investment in EUROPE at cost as follows:

	Debit	Credit
Investment in EUROPE (+A)	300	
Cash(-A)		300

EUROPE being a newly established company, the acquisition cost is equal to the acquired share of the net book value of the joint venture and so we do not need to adjust its income accordingly.

At the end of the period, ITALY will make the following journal entries:

	Debit	Credit
Investment in EUROPE (+A)	14	
Income from investment - equity method (+R, +OE)		14

This first accounting entry increases the value of the investment for the share of net income realised by EUROPE and attributable to ITALY (= 40% × 35).

In order to take into consideration the unrealised gain from the downstream transaction, ITALY will make an additional journal entry:

	Debit	Credit
Sales revenue (-R, -OE)	20	
Cost of goods sold (-E, +OE)		16
Investment in EUROPE (-A)		4

All the amounts in the journal entry above are calculated as 40% of the original amount of revenues, cost of goods sold and - as a consequence - unrealised profit.

Differently from the standard approach (under which ITALY would have adjusted the income from the investment by reducing it by 4 million), under this approach the unrealised profit is not taken from the investment income, instead it is removed indirectly by eliminating the unrealised revenue and unrealised cost of goods sold from the investor's accounts.

The 4 million that reduces the value of the investment is related to the unrealised profit incorporated in the value of the inventory of EUROPE.

Example C2 – Upstream transaction with unrealised gain

Let us use the previous example assuming that EUROPE is the selling company and ITALY is the buyer. All data are the same.

At the acquisition date, ITALY will still record its investment in EUROPE at cost as follows:

	Debit	Credit
Investment in EUROPE (+A)	300	
Cash(-A)		300

At the end of the period, ITALY will make the following journal entries:

	Debit	Credit
Investment in EUROPE (+A)	14	
Income from investment-equity method (+R,OE)		14

Similarly to what we have seen before, this first accounting entry increases the value of the investment for the share of net income realised by EUROPE and attributable to ITALY (=40%*35). No adjustment is made at this stage.

In order to take into consideration the unrealised gain from the upstream transaction, ITALY will make an additional journal entry:

	Debit	Credit
Income from investment - equity method (- R, -OE)	4	
Inventory (-A)		4

Differently from the downstream transaction, in this case the unrealised gain is removed from the investment income, because it was included originally in EUROPE's income. ITALY, on the other hand, adjusts the value of its inventory in order to remove the unrealised intra-group gain. The value of the investment is not affected by this adjustment.